BY THE SAME AUTHOR

Novels and Romances

SINISTER STREET
SYLVIA SCARLETT
GUY AND PAULINE

CARNIVAL
FIGURE OF EIGHT
CORAL
THE VANITY GIRL
ROGUES AND VAGABONDS

THE ALTAR STEPS
THE PARSON'S PROGRESS
THE HEAVENLY LADDER

THE MONARCH OF THE GLEN
THE RED TAPEWORM
POOR RELATIONS
APRIL FOOLS
RICH RELATIVES
BUTTERCUPS AND DAISIES
WATER ON THE BRAIN

VESTAL FIRE
EXTRAORDINARY WOMEN

EXTREMES MEET
THE THREE COURIERS

OUR STREET
THE DARKENING GREEN

THE PASSIONATE ELOPEMENT
FAIRY GOLD
THE SEVEN AGES OF WOMAN
THE OLD MEN OF THE SEA

THE FOUR WINDS OF LOVE:
    THE EAST WIND
    THE SOUTH WIND
    THE WEST WIND
    WEST TO NORTH

In Preparation

    THE NORTH WIND

History and Biography

GALLIPOLI MEMORIES
ATHENIAN MEMORIES
GREEK MEMORIES
AEGEAN MEMORIES

PRINCE CHARLIE
PRINCE CHARLIE AND HIS LADIES
CATHOLICISM AND SCOTLAND
MARATHON AND SALAMIS
PERICLES
THE WINDSOR TAPESTRY

Essays and Criticism

A MUSICAL CHAIR
UNCONSIDERED TRIFLES
REAPED AND BOUND
LITERATURE IN MY TIME

Plays

THE LOST CAUSE

Children's Stories

SANTA CLAUS IN SUMMER
TOLD
MABEL IN QUEER STREET
THE UNPLEASANT VISITORS
THE CONCEITED DOLL
THE ENCHANTED BLANKET
THE DINING-ROOM BATTLE
THE ADVENTURES OF TWO CHAIRS
THE ENCHANTED ISLAND
THE NAUGHTYMOBILE
THE FAIRY IN THE WINDOW BOX
THE STAIRS THAT KEPT ON
    GOING DOWN

Verse

POEMS 1907
KENSINGTON RHYMES

'Wind of Freedom' is produced in complete conformity with the Authorized Economy Standards

Aera! Aera! Wind! Wind!

The battle-cry of the Evzones

Compton Mackenzie

WIND OF FREEDOM

THE HISTORY OF THE INVASION
OF GREECE BY THE AXIS POWERS
1940-1941

CHATTO & WINDUS
LONDON

PUBLISHED BY
Chatto & Windus
LONDON
*
The Macmillan Company
of Canada, Limited
TORONTO

1943
Printed in Great Britain

CONTENTS

ILLUSTRATIONS

AUTHOR'S NOTE

THE full story of the sublime struggle of the Hellenic people against the new Barbarians cannot be told now because the material is wanting. With all the help that various members of the Greek Government have kindly given me there are many gaps in my book which should be regarded purely as a provisional attempt to present an outline of the story. Information available about the military operations may be inadequate, but it is a rich mine compared with the information about the struggle still going on. We get occasional lantern-gleams from the darkness; but a continuous narrative of events since the Germans, Italians, and Bulgarians have been battening on Hellas is out of the question yet, and it seemed wiser not to make the slightest attempt to anticipate the immortal tale of courage, endurance, self-sacrifice, and ardent faith. A few cold statistics of what the Hellenic forces in the field, in the air, and on the sea are contributing to the war effort of the United Nations have been given in an appendix: but that is only part of the contribution being made by the Hellenes to win freedom for the world from the most monstrous aggregation of evil that has yet threatened the future of humanity. The mountains of Rhodope, the mighty range of the Pindus, the sacred heights of Parnassus, Olympus, and Taygetus give sanctuary to dauntless bands who prey upon the enemy from their fastnesses. There are at least 25,000 of those warriors, free as the very oreads themselves. And with them are many happy warriors of the British and Imperial Forces. The whole population of Crete surges as restlessly as the sea against its own rock-bound coast, and there are some 13,000 guerrillas fighting from the mountains, they too the hosts of many British and Imperial soldiers who fight beside them.

In February 1941 a letter from two citizens of Crete called upon me to continue to present the claims of Hellas to be the permanent Ally of Great Britain. The letter was addressed to the Channel Islands, and by the time it reached me in the Outer Hebrides both the Channel Islands and Crete had been overrun by the enemy.

If even a single one of my fellow-countrymen who reads this book does not feel bound to Hellas by an infrangible tie of gratitude, I have failed those two citizens of Crete through my own failure as a chronicler. The memory of England, unlike that of her sisters of Scotland, Ireland, and Wales, is short; but surely she will not forget what Hellas did on October 28th in that year of fate 1940 or what Hellas has continued to do ever since. Mr Stelios Dimitrakakis, formerly Minister for War and now Minister for Justice in the Greek Government, recalls a moment during the Battle of Crete when he was watching from the terrace of the Government building a platoon of The York and Lancaster Regiment moving forward under heavy fire to attack at the point of the bayonet the Germans landing from gliders. One of those white-and-red rose soldiers caught sight of a rose in the garden below, stopped to pick it, put it in his buttonhole, and charged on. May the roses of Crete blossoming in peace year after year be able to keep ever for Cretan hearts the fragrance of England as fresh as it was to that English soldier in the heat of battle round Herakleion!

I do not hesitate to claim that I speak for an overwhelming majority of the people of Britain when I declare that the country would abominate the slightest encouragement to Bulgar hopes of holding on to Hellenic territory by a well-timed desertion of the Axis. The country would abominate equally the idea of any secret bargains between the British Government and other powers at the expense of just Hellenic aspirations to reunite to Hellas nearly 400,000 of her children in Cyprus, 130,000 in the Dodecanese, and 120,000 in Northern Epirus. To fulfil such aspirations will not be an extravagant recompense for a little nation which has saved Europe at the cost of blood, of famine, and of hope deferred through months of agony. 430,000 died from starvation alone.

Let there be no doubt about it: if Greece had accepted the Italian ultimatum in October 1940 there might have been no Battle of El Alamein to fight in October 1942, and what is more, Moscow would probably have fallen in October 1941. It was meet that the most powerful foe democracy has had to face should find his doom in the land where democracy was born.

It is in consonance with the age-long democratic history of Hellas that the present Greek Government has declared that as soon as Hellas is free it will resign to make way for a Government elected by the Hellenic people.

x

And now a word about the title of the book. It was originally intended to call it *The Rape of Hellas*, but on consideration it seemed that such a title paid an excessive compliment to the virility of the Italian assault. The battle-cry of the Evzones came to the mind: Aera! Aera! Wind! Wind! When before that battle-cry the Iulia Alpini Division of the Italians broke and fled on the night of November 9th-10th, 1940, another Marathon had been fought for freedom.

Wind of Freedom is dedicated to the Army of the Enchained Victors. This is a secret organization in which dwells the indomitable soul of Hellas.

All the translations from the Greek in the text are my own, both in verse and prose; but I wish to thank most warmly the authors and publishers who have given me leave to quote from invaluable books written out of a first-hand experience of the great events in Greece which, alas, I was not privileged to win for myself. I am particularly grateful to that anonymous Gunner whose vivid letters were so kindly put at my disposal.

Finally, I wish to make it clear that all the opinions expressed in these pages are my own. The Greek Government, true to its tradition of a pure democracy, has not attempted to curb or prompt the expression of those opinions.

ΣΤΟ ΣΤΡΑΤΟ ΤΩΝ ΣΚΛΑΒΩΜΕΝΩΝ
ΝΙΚΗΤΩΝ ΜΕ ΒΑΘΥΤΑΤΟ ΘΑΥΜΑΣΜΟ
ΚΑΙ ΖΩΗΡΗ ΕΥΓΝΩΜΟΣΥΝΗ

To the Army of the Enchained Victors with
the profoundest admiration and the liveliest
gratitude

CHAPTER ONE

WHEN on March 25th (O.S.)—April 6th (N.S.)—1821 Archbishop Germanos raised at Kalavryta the blue-and-white banner that proclaimed the revolt of Hellas against Turkish domination, only a fortnight earlier Austrian troops had marched into Naples to reimpose the Bourbon despotism, and two days later, on April 8th, at Novara the insurrection in Piedmont would be crushed. Those who were able to escape went, some to fight for constitutionalism in Spain, others to fight for the independence of Greece. The noblest of them all, Santorre di Santarosa, fell like a hero at Sphacteria in 1825. During the next thirty years many insurgent Italians found a refuge in Greece, and in 1859 the proposal of King Otto to allow Austrian merchant ships the protection of the Greek flag against the passionate desire of the Hellenes for the victory of united Italy precipitated that decline of his people's respect which was to end in driving him from the throne.

By the close of the nineteenth century the slow and painful struggle of the two nations in Europe with the longest history to emerge as national unities from the various disruptions, invasions, and foreign occupations which had been their lot for so many hundreds of years had made Italy the least of the six Great Powers, and left Greece one of about a dozen other States. On that July day in 1900 when Humbert I was assassinated by an anarchist at Monza, the idea that Italy would in the course of his successor's reign become the mortal foe of Greece was unimaginable.

It is true that, if it were accepted as even a plausible interpretation of history, the Fascist attempt to present modern Italy as the heir immediately of Venice and ultimately of Imperial Rome could revive an agelong tale of enmity. It is true that as far back as 281 B.C. Pyrrhus, King of Epirus, invaded Italy to support the city of Tarentum in its quarrel with Rome. He took with him some elephants, the equivalent of tanks in those days, and defeated the Romans on the field of Heraclea, but at such a cost to himself that from that day onward the world has called such a result of battle a Pyrrhic victory. It will seem absurd to be writing of 281 B.C. in connection with the

Greece and Italy of to-day, and yet this Pyrrhic victory was used by Italian propaganda in A.D. 1940 to belittle the Greek victories in Epirus.   Such an exploitation of the past is dangerous for Italy.   It may backfire.   It might create a fresh irredentist problem because it might lead at a Peace Conference of the future to a Greek claim on Magna Graecia and Sicily if the Greeks were as easily inflated by their own wind as the Italians.   That would be just as logical as the claim of contemporary Italy to dominate the Eastern Mediterranean because the Venetians had been its masters until they were dispossessed by the Turks.   Fantastic though it may appear, such really is the Italian contention.   This neo-Venetian nonsense took definite shape on April 22nd, 1912, when Italian naval and military forces occupied Astypalaea (Stampalia) and with a view to impressing the Italian public extended their operations to the rest of the Dodecanese.   On May 4th, 1912, an army corps under General Ameglio, supported by a strong fleet under Admiral Amero d'Aste Stella, disembarked at dawn in the Bay of Callithea on the east coast of Rhodes, quickly reached the outskirts of the capital, and demanded its surrender.   The Turkish garrison withdrew to a strong position in the interior, but surrendered almost at once to the Italian forces, thanks to the help of the Greek inhabitants who welcomed the Italians as liberators.   As at Rhodes so it was in the other islands which fell into Italian hands with hardly any bloodshed.   There was reason for the islanders' faith after reading the proclamation issued by General Ameglio when he landed at Rhodes:

> *Inhabitants of the Island of Rhodes,*
> *Italy, linked with you by glorious memories and a kindred civilization, has been compelled by the course of the war to occupy your island.   By order of His Majesty, the King of Italy, Victor Emmanuel III, my august Sovereign, I enter into my civil and military functions among you, and I declare that although Italy is at war with the Government and the Army of Turkey, she recognizes the peaceful population of Rhodes as friends, and intends to give to it the greatest possible proof of good-will and at the same time to show henceforth the profoundest respect for your adherence to the Greek Orthodox Church, for your customs, and for your traditions.*

Alas, all too soon it became evident that Italy, intoxicated by her occupation of the Dodecanese, had no intention of liberating the islanders.   When peace was made with Turkey she retained the

Dodecanese provisionally as a guarantee that the complete evacuation of all Turkish troops from Tripoli would be carried out; but the real reason for this occupation was to prevent these islands, like the rest of the islands under Turkish sway, from falling into the hands of Greece whose fleet in the Balkan War was baulked by the 'provisional' Italian occupation from naval action in the Dodecanese. On one pretext or another Italy contrived to maintain her hold until the First World War broke out. By the secret Treaty of London with the Entente Powers signed on April 26th, 1915, Italy was granted a zone of influence in Southern Asia Minor and as a corollary full possession of the Dodecanese. Instead of contributing in any way whatever to the vigorous conduct of the war in the Eastern Mediterranean, Italy impeded the British and French naval and air forces in every possible way and so far as the Dodecanese was concerned devoted all her energy to what amounted to a persecution of the Greek population.

The masterly handling of the Greek case at the Peace Conference by Venizelos and Mr Lloyd George's belief, rational or instinctive, in the vital importance of a strong Greece to British interests in the Mediterranean, coupled with the accession to power in Italy of the Liberal statesman Nitti, finally secured the Venizelos-Tittoni agreement of July 1919. By the terms of this eleven islands of the Dodecanese were to be transferred immediately to Greece, a liberal measure of autonomy was to be granted to Rhodes within two months, and if after fifteen years Great Britain should have restored Cyprus to Greece, Italy was to grant a plebiscite for the population of Rhodes to decide whether it wished to be Greek or Italian. There was a stipulation, however, that if Italy did not obtain satisfaction for all her claims in Asia Minor she was not bound by the terms of the Agreement. The Nitti Government fell soon after this, and the Giolitti Government which followed had the crafty and long-sighted Count Sforza as Foreign Minister. As Italian High Commissioner in Constantinople he had launched Mustafa Kemal upon his enterprise, for he had realized that Italian hopes of Smyrna would be baffled and he counted on Turkish gratitude to give his country commercial advantages in the future and allow Italian immigration on a large scale. At his urgent demand the Venizelos-Tittoni Agreement was denounced in July 1920. By this time the long-drawn-out Treaty of Sèvres was ready for signature, and Venizelos

countered Sforza's action by refusing to sign.   In this protest he was
supported by the British Government, which put pressure on the
Italian Government by threatening to withhold the signature for
the Tripartite Agreement that defined the economic spheres of influence in Anatolia for Great Britain, France and Italy.   Italy
yielded and a fresh agreement about the Dodecanese was drawn up
and signed on August 10th, 1920.   The execution of it, however,
was now made dependent on the ratification of the Treaty of Sèvres,
which both the Italians and the French were sure would be never.
Both of them worked hard to make Mustafa Kemal's task easy.
The French left him all the munitions amassed in Cilicia.   The
Italians poured in arms and munitions through Adalia.   For the first
time since Napoleon III laid hands on Nice the two nations worked
together in complete accord.   So matters went on through 1921
and into 1922.

Venizelos was in voluntary exile.   Lloyd George was beginning
to totter as the Conservatives dug away the ground faster and faster
beneath his feet.   Mustafa Kemal struck.   The Greek Army, deprived of most of the excellent officers who had supported Venizelos,
was defeated at Afium Karahissar.   Into the flames of Smyrna Italy
flung the fragments of the Venizelos-Tittoni Agreement.   Lord
Curzon tried to save it by making the cession of Jubaland depend on
the evacuation of the Dodecanese; but he had no support from his
Government, and in 1924 Ramsay MacDonald handed over Jubaland unconditionally.

Two months after the Venizelos-Tittoni Agreement was disowned the Fascists achieved power, and Mussolini's notions of Italian
aggrandisement did not coincide with Mustafa Kemal's plan for a
Turkish future.   The evident intention to construct a great naval
base at Leros was not at all reassuring.   No more was heard of
Count Sforza's Italian immigration into Asia Minor and the consequent development of the Levant.   Indeed, no more was heard of
Count Sforza himself whose disgust at the triumph of Fascism sent
him into exile.

With the orientation that Mussolini's obsession with the past gave
to Fascist dreams about the future, Italy gazing from the bastions of
Rhodes no longer turned her eyes toward Adalia, but with a question
at the back of them toward Egypt and Syria and Palestine.   Year
after year the armament went in.   Year after year the native Greeks

went out. It was in May 1912 that Italian forces landed in Rhodes. In May 1941 Italian forces from Rhodes landed in Crete.

It may be asked why first place is given to the Dodecanese as an inspiring motive of Italian hatred of Greece rather than to Corfu or the Epirus, particularly as Greece did not persist in her claim to the Dodecanese. The answer is that the possession of the Dodecanese begat in the Italian mind the idea that Greece stood between her and this outpost of the Levant which was not only a real token of Venice preserved, but was also an omen of Imperial Rome's rebirth. The idea thus begotten grew into an idea that Italy might again be as much master of Greece as once was Rome. Greece where she stood, with Britain behind her (much more solidly behind her in Italian belief than she ever really was), barred the way. Moreover, nowhere as in the Dodecanese had Italy betrayed so basely the spirit of her own Risorgimento, and she had to ease her conscience by applying the counter-irritant of hate.

The purest democracy left, the nearest to the old city states of the Hellenes, was that in the islands of the Dodecanese. Even the Turks until the Young Turks got into power had respected that democracy through four centuries. The Italians set out to destroy it ten years before ever Fascism was spawned, and at the same time directed against the Orthodox Church the worst kind of ecclesiastical imperialism. The outrage in the early dawn of October 28th, 1940, was perpetrated by a man who, striving to outdo the original Colossus, had planted one foot in Rhodes and the other in Durazzo; but if General Ameglio had not set his foot in Rhodes that May dawn in 1912 there might not have been a second Colossus.

If the directors of British policy during the years after the First World War could bring themselves to ignore the significance of the intensive fortification of the Dodecanese for no other purpose than ultimate offensive action, they were not likely to regard what seemed Italy's natural anxiety to secure herself in the Adriatic as evidence of her ambition to dominate the Mediterranean. Moreover, throughout these years British foreign policy in that part of the world was affected by four irrational beliefs. The first was that no concatenation of untoward circumstances could eliminate the French fleet as an ally. The second was that Italy could never afford to go to war against Britain on account of her geographical situation. The third was that a defensive alliance with Turkey would restore the balance of power in the Mediterranean to the condition in which it had remained until Germany had corrupted Turkey. The fourth was that the failure of Greece to take advantage of the opportunity given to her in 1919 proved that the military opinion which had always deprecated the Lloyd George philhellene policy had been right and that the creation of a strong Greece as a vital bastion against a tremendous assault upon the British Empire was an impossibility. And to these four irrational beliefs may perhaps be added a fifth, that because Napoleon was as dead as Queen Anne an imaginatively grandiose assault upon the British Empire would never be delivered.

Italy's influence in Albania had been sedulously diffused for years before the First World War; but when Austria incorporated Bosnia and Herzegovina in 1908 and thus made the First World War a certainty within a few years she had not the courage to declare a protectorate over Albania, although that was the obvious moment to do it. At that date Albania included the whole of Epirus, and Corfu on the map looked almost as near to Italy as to Greece. During the Balkan wars after Greece had captured Jannina, one of the sacred places of Hellenism, and occupied Southern Epirus the Italian Government began to grow restive under what looked like becoming a successful occupation of Northern Epirus. Venizelos thereupon agreed privately with the Italian Government that Greek forces should not enter either Valona or Berat, in return for which the Italians promised not to offer any opposition to the definite annexation by Greece of Southern Epirus. There was no signed treaty, but in order to show his good faith Venizelos arranged for the evacuation of the minute island of Sasseno which commands the entrance to the Gulf of Valona. This dot on the map some sixty miles north of Corfu had passed to Greece when Great Britain ceded the Ionian Islands in 1863. It is worth noting at this point that, when Venizelos was in London in December 1912 for the Balkan peace negotiations, the possibility of arranging for a permanent lease of Argostoli in the island of Cephalonia in exchange for the cession of Cyprus to Greece was discussed unofficially with Mr Lloyd George (the Chancellor of the Exchequer), Mr Churchill (the First Lord of the Admiralty), and the First Sea Lord, Prince Louis of Battenberg. What brimming bushels of precious fruit might have been garnered if the blossom of that conversation had set!

CHAPTER ONE

When the Balkan Wars were finished the Great Powers decided to create an independent Kingdom of Albania, and the first Mpret (a corruption of *imperator*) was to be a German princeling, William of Wied. At the international circus which was still performing at Scutari on the eve of the First World War Austria and Italy pressed for the evacuation of Northern Epirus by Greece. That Italy should take this line was a clear enough indication of her secret hopes. If she had supposed that Austrian influence would last in Albania there would have been no point in showing such interest in the mainland so near to Corfu. That the Triple Alliance wanted Northern Epirus disposed the Powers of the Entente to support Greek claims; but Austria and Italy would not give way, and finally a Commissioner, a Dutchman, was appointed to find a solution on the language basis. The simple method of taking a plebiscite to ascertain whether the inhabitants wanted to be in Albania or Greece was neglected. As a result of the Commissioner's activities it was decided that Northern Epirus should be a part of Albania. The Greek Government yielded; but the population rebelled, and a minor war began between the Epirots and the Albanian Moslems who were led by Italian officers. Finally Northern Epirus was reconstituted as a self-governing province of Albania.

At the time of the outbreak of the First World War the new Kingdom of Albania was in a complete confusion of internecine strife. William of Wied went back to Prussia. The Italians occupied Valona. Greek troops re-occupied Northern Epirus. The future of Albania and Epirus was postponed for decision after the war. Even if Italy had already declared war on Austria by then it is doubtful if by more extensive action in Albania she would have dared face the risk of an attack by her old enemy on the other side of the Adriatic.

During the unhappy division of opinion about Greece's entry into the war Italian policy played a Machiavellian part, never failing to take advantage of every turn of events to further its own aims and much helped by a perfectly clear notion of what those aims were. It was the surrender of Fort Rupel to the Bulgars in May 1916 which gave Italy the excuse to oust the Greek troops from the Northern Epirus. The argument used was that these troops were just as likely to accede to an Austrian advance from Berat as they had been willing to accede to a Bulgarian advance in Eastern Macedonia. The argument was strengthened by the comparative loyalty of the troops in Epirus to King Constantine, which was an established fact. Commanders of the Allied forces in Salonika welcomed the prospect of an Italian front across Albania as a safeguard to their left flank. So Northern Epirus was occupied by Italian troops, and their line ran from Valona to make contact with the French left at Koritza. The next opportunity came when the French with the British acquiescing decided to demand the abdication of King Constantine. On June 3rd, 1917, a week before the demand was to be presented by the French High Commissioner, the independence of Albania as an Italian protectorate was declared, and this was immediately followed by an Italian advance into Southern Epirus, the occupation of Jannina and the expulsion of the Greek authorities. The excuse was the alleged hostility of Epirot Greeks to the Entente. The return of Venizelos and the absorption of the Provisional Government of National Defence in the Royal Hellenic Government made it impossible for the Italians to remain in Greek Epirus; but by arguing about it at the Allied Conference of July 1917 in Paris they managed to retain their position in Northern Epirus, and one of the sins held up against Venizelos by his opponents was that in his zest for Greek expansion in Asia Minor he did not put up a good enough fight at the Peace Conference for Northern Epirus, which Italy secured for Albania.

The delimitation of the Greco-Albanian frontier by an International Commission was still going on in August 1923, and on August 27th the Italian President of the International Commission, General Tellini, was murdered with four members of his staff while motoring on Greek territory. This gave Mussolini, not yet in power for a year, a chance to display to the world Fascism's capacity for dynamic action, and at the same time impress on the people of Italy that his right to lead them to a glorious future was not based merely on rhetorical assertions and that if his lungs were of brass the chest that contained them was of tempered steel.

An ultimatum was sent to Greece demanding full and official apologies, the rendering of military honours to the Italian flag by the Greek fleet, the holding of an enquiry by an Italian officer on the scene of the murder, capital punishment for all found guilty, and an indemnity of 50,000,000 (£500,000) Italian liras to be paid within five days. Greece in her reply accepted the first two demands, but rejected the last three on the ground that they were incompatible with her sovereignty and honour. Mussolini's reply to this was an action that has set the standard of truculent barbarism in international relations to which Fascism in its various guises has conformed ever since. On August 31st he ordered out the Italian fleet to bombard Corfu as a preliminary to its occupation by Italian troops. Sixteen Greek and Armenian refugees were killed and a number of people wounded.

The Greek Government appealed to the Council of the League of Nations which was then in session at Geneva, requesting it to appoint one or more neutral representatives to superintend in Greece the judicial enquiries already begun by the Greek Authorities, and also the trial of those who might be accused of the murder, and secondly to instruct a Commission composed of three high judicial authorities, a Greek, an Italian, and a neutral, to settle the amount of indemnities which Greece should pay to the families of the victims, while the Greek Government in its turn would deposit in a bank in Switzerland 50,000,000 liras as guarantee of the immediate payment of whatever indemnities should be decided upon. Mussolini's reply was a flat refusal to accept the arbitration of the League of Nations with a threat that Italy would quit it if pressed, and, to show he meant what he said, the occupation of four more Greek islands.

Mussolini had chosen the moment well for his defiance of European opinion. Great Britain and France were at a moment of extreme tension over German reparations. The long protracted negotiations with Turkey had only just been concluded by the Treaty of Lausanne, and public opinion was weary of 'questions'. In Great Britain itself the first Baldwin Government was just three months old, but already the enervating influence of Safety First and anything for a quiet life was making itself felt. There was an inclination to regard Mussolini as a tonic, and ignore the fact that many other poisons have tonic qualities in small doses.

Liberal opinion throughout Europe was disgusted by this first demonstration of Fascist action outside its own borders; but like so much Liberal opinion it did not express itself beyond academic disgust, and the League of Nations allowed its authority to pass to the Conference of Ambassadors in Paris, that coprolite of war-time diplomacy, which on September 8th offered the results of its mediation as follows:

1. Apologies to be offered by the highest Greek military authorities to the diplomatic representatives at Athens of Great Britain, France, and Italy whose delegates formed part of the Delimitation Commission.

2. A funeral service to be celebrated at Athens in honour of the victims and in the presence of the members of the Greek Government.

3. Naval honours to be rendered by the Greek fleet to warships of the three Allied Powers at Phaleron.

4. Military honours to be rendered by a Greek unit to the bodies of the victims.

5. The Greek Government to ensure the necessary conditions for the search and exemplary punishment of the culprits.

6. A Commission consisting of representatives of Great Britain, Italy, and France under the presidency of a Japanese (!) delegate to supervise the enquiry, which had to be concluded by September 27th.

7. The Greek Government to undertake to pay an indemnity the amount of which should be determined in summary procedure by the Permanent Court of International Justice at the Hague, the Greek Government for this purpose depositing in the Swiss National Bank a sum of 50,000,000 Italian lire.

These terms were accepted by both parties, and the ceremonial portion of the penalties was performed on September 19th, the people of Athens remaining indoors throughout. By September 25th the International Commission of Enquiry had failed to discover any of the culprits and the Conference of Ambassadors in a Note to the Greek Government decided to close the incident, but ordered Greece, as a penalty for failing to capture and punish the culprits, to pay the Italian Government the whole deposit in the Swiss National Bank. On September 27th the Italian troops evacuated Corfu. Mussolini offered a small part of the indemnity paid by Greece for the relief of the refugees in Corfu. They declined to accept a penny of it.

With all the evidence available in their favour, the Greek Press had incriminated Albania in the murder of General Tellini, and the Albanian Government of Ahmed Zogu (who was to become King Zog five years later under Italian patronage) published a Red Book with documents purporting to pin the assassination upon the Greeks. In Italy it was whispered at the time that Mussolini himself had arranged the murder, to stage an exhibition of his strong foreign policy and at the same time rid himself of an honourable officer he distrusted. The mystery has never been solved. It is strange that the International Commission of Enquiry was willing within a bare fortnight to accept as a fact the impossibility of discovering the culprits, and equally strange that Mussolini should have agreed to accept half a million pounds as the price of allowing the Greek Government deliberately to conceal the culprits, if they *were* Greeks.

The Corfu outrage has been related in much detail because it is directly linked with the Italian ultimatum of October 28th, 1940, and because acquiescence in it by Europe without demanding Mussolini's surrender to international justice as the murderer of those fifteen refugees brought Europe before the bar of Divine justice, and by Divine justice Europe has been sentenced to suffer for the impious crime. Nor is it without significance in the human tragedy not yet played to its unpredictable end that America which had disowned the League of Nations was in this very year of 1923 turning with ever-increasing enthusiasm to the belief that responsibility can be avoided like a midge by blinking an impatient eyelid.

In Greece itself the bitterness between the two political factions was not sweetened by the humiliation, and Republican feeling grew rapidly. People were saying more and more emphatically that if Venizelos returned from his voluntary exile the State might recover from the ills which beset it. The consciousness of this stirred the Monarchists led by General Metaxas to attempt a *coup d'état*, and a military rebellion with its centre at Corinth broke out. It collapsed within a few days, and on October 28th, 1923, General Metaxas escaped to Italy. Note the date.

Venizelos returned to Greece; but before the Republic was proclaimed on March 25th, 1924, he had found the internal strife too much for him and resigned the Premiership. King George II had already gone into exile. Out of the confusion of the politicomania which something in the air of Greece seems to feed and which must not be derided, because it is the preservative of liberty, General Pangalos achieved his brief dictatorship. His Foreign Minister was Mr Rouphos, a member of the Royalist Party, and Greece having achieved a dictatorship it was felt that Mussolini might be willing to contemplate an improvement in Greco-Italian relations. In March 1926 conversations in Rome between Mr Rouphos and the Duce resulted in a new Commercial Treaty which was signed in November. Those who believe that Mussolini did not turn against

Great Britain until the Abyssinian business should note that in the course of these conversations he objected to the British Naval Mission in Greece because its existence was likely to contribute toward British naval supremacy in the Mediterranean. The Pangalos régime accepted the validity of this objection and it was announced that both the British Naval Mission and the French Military Mission would be terminated. The Dictator, however, soon faded from the political scene, and the two Missions remained.

Venizelos came back into power as Prime Minister in July 1928 and devoted his consummate skill as an exponent of foreign policy to improving the relations between Greece and her neighbours. With his domestic policy we are not concerned.

The Pact of Friendship, Conciliation, and Judicial Settlement with Italy which was signed in Rome by Venizelos and Mussolini on September 23rd, 1928, was a diplomatic achievement because it was carried through at a time when Italian relations with Yugoslavia were strained and when France was growing nervous of Italian intentions. The outstanding clauses of the Treaty were those which provided for the neutrality of either of the contracting Parties should the other be the victim of an unprovoked act of aggression, for the mutual rendering of political and diplomatic help in the event of either Party's being threatened by invasion, and an agreement to consult about any measures to be taken in the event of international complications. There was another clause which bound both Parties to submit to a special conciliatory procedure, set out at length in the Treaty, any questions which might divide them and could not be settled by ordinary diplomatic procedure. And there was a clause which expressly stated that the Treaty was not invalidated by the exercise of any rights or obligations in virtue of the Covenant of the League of Nations to which the present Treaty was to be communicated for registration. The Treaty, which was to be ratified as soon as possible and come into force immediately afterwards, was for a period of five years and unless denounced by either Party six months before the expiration of that period it was to remain in force for a further period of five years.

A favourable atmosphere for these conversations in Rome had been brought about by the promptitude with which on September 4th Greece had recognized the conversion of Albania into a kingdom by the proclamation of Ahmed Bey Zogu as King Zog I of the

Albanians, who was under Italian patronage. This recognition was followed in November 1928 by a Commercial Treaty and Neutrality Convention between Greece and Albania.

The Treaty with Italy achieved, Venizelos visited Belgrade within a week or two of its ratification in order to allay any apprehensions that might exist in Yugoslavia. Here the question of Salonika was discussed in a friendly spirit and a period of negotiation set on foot; and an agreement was followed by the signature of a Pact of Friendship, Conciliation, and Judicial Settlement.

There was a good deal of discontent both in Greece and Yugoslavia about the efforts to bring about a better understanding with Italy. The Croats and Slovenes accused the Serbs of selling them to Italy for their own protection, when the Yugoslav Government recognized the new Kingdom of Albania, and in Epirus there was much dissatisfaction over the Italian *rapprochement*. However, Venizelos was undeterred, and in 1930 he achieved the supreme triumph of settling all outstanding questions between Greece and Turkey, so that at a banquet given in his honour at Ankara he was able to declare that the conflict between Greece and Turkey which had lasted for a thousand years was finished. The auspicious year 1930 saw also the first meeting of the Balkan Conference, the credit for promoting which belonged to Mr Papanastasiou. Representatives of Greece, Turkey, Yugoslavia, Rumania, Bulgaria, and Albania attended and in the atmosphere of general good-will many pacific projects for the future seemed attainable. Indeed, there is no doubt that something like a Federation of the Balkan States might soon have been well on the way to being achieved if the Great Powers could have acquired a comparable spirit of mutual conciliation. In the following year the agitation in Cyprus for reunion with Greece flamed up; but Venizelos discouraged irredentist hopes and insisted that if the Powers in occupation of islands with Greek populations were resolved to maintain such an occupation it must be accepted. It was evident from the attitude of the Greek statesman that he recognized Great Britain's vital interest in Cyprus so long as the Dodecanese remained under the Italian flag.

As things were, the increasing tension in Europe made the signature of the Balkan Pact in February 1934 more of an expression of peaceful hopes than of a solid guarantee. The refusal of Bulgaria to sign was of bad omen, and the anxiety of the other signatories to exclude aggression by a non-Balkan power as an obligation to render mutual help reflected Balkan uneasiness about the future. Fascist Italy looked coldly at the Balkan Pact, not because it discovered in it a threat but because anything that might contribute were it never so little toward European tranquillity seemed undesirable to a régime which required war not merely for growth but even for the nourishment that would keep it alive.

In the summer of 1935 Greece, like the other small States of Europe except Austria, Hungary and Albania, followed Great Britain's lead in applying economic sanctions to Italy under Article 16 of the Covenant of the League of Nations. In spite of a natural feeling of relief in Greece that Italian expansionism seemed to be moving in the direction of Africa, indignation at the Italian method of expansion was acute. In notifying the Italian Government of this action Greece reminded it of the clause in the 1928 Treaty of Friendship and Conciliation which provided for obligations incurred under the Covenant of the League. On December 6th, 1935, Great Britain enquired if the smaller States would support her should Italy go to war with her over the sanctions. This was a more serious business than applying economic sanctions, and several small States refused the promise of military aid. In the Balkans, Greece, Yugoslavia, and Turkey gave the understanding asked from the British Government.

It was perhaps unfortunate that these three States should be those which had most to fear from Fascist Imperialism, and it was certainly unfortunate that Great Britain, after giving her small supporters the impression that she was at last going to take a firm stand against Mussolini, should have feebly surrendered to the policy of appeasement almost as soon as they were committed to a pledge of forceful action.

When the Treaty of Friendship, Conciliation, and Judicial Settlement signed on September 23rd, 1928, came to an end on September 23rd, 1938, no attempt was made to renew it or to discuss the terms of a fresh one.

CHAPTER TWO

IT was 1939. The Ides of March had come and gone. Hitler had swallowed what was left of Czechoslovakia. The haggard shape of Rumour swept across Europe and darkened every country with her shadow. On March 17th an official communiqué was issued from Rome in which Rumour's whisper of an imminent Italian intervention in Albania was stigmatized as a malicious lie spread abroad with the object of disturbing the peace of the Adriatic. One medium used by the troublesome goddess was the Moscow radio, and the Greek Minister in Belgrade paid a visit to the Ministry of Foreign Affairs to find out if any information there warranted nervousness about the immediate future. Officials at the Yugoslav Ministry of Foreign Affairs were unperturbed. Such a project was at odds with formal assurances lately given by the Italian Government of a determination to maintain the status quo in the Adriatic. Indeed, that very day the Italian Minister in Belgrade had called upon the President of the Council to renew the assurances.

Mr Rosettis was not convinced. One of the Secretaries of the Greek Legation had been told by a member of the German Legation that nobody *au courant* paid any attention to the Italian *démenti* because in present circumstances the occupation of Albania was a necessity. However, a week later he telegraphed again to Athens that the speech from the Crown to the new Italian Chamber in which the assurances of the Italian Government about Albania were solemnly and royally reiterated had quietened any lingering doubt left in Belgrade. Nearly a fortnight later diplomatic opinion in Rome was convinced that Italy cherished no plans against Albania, and on April 4th, the Tuesday of Holy Week, Count Ciano gave a formal assurance to the British Ambassador that the Italian Government had no intention of intervening in Albania, stressing its unwillingness to be involved in fresh complications at such a time. On Maundy Thursday Mr Simopoulos, the Greek Minister in London, was summoned to the Foreign Office to be informed of this interview, the details of which had already been telgraphed to Athens by the Greek Chargé d'Affaires in Rome on the day it had taken place.

15

On Good Friday the Greek Minister in Tirana telegraphed to Athens that at 6 A.M. five Italian warships accompanied by two transports had started to bombard Durazzo, and that Italian planes had been dropping leaflets over Tirana, inviting the population to offer no resistance to the Italian military forces which would remain in the country only long enough to establish peace, order and justice. On Holy Saturday Count Ciano, who after all had no reason as an Italian nobleman to feel ashamed of copying the deplorable example set by his own King, assured the British and American Ambassadors that Italy had no intention of destroying the independence of Albania and that the Italian troops would withdraw as soon as order had been established and a Government friendly towards Italy installed. The officer commanding the first Italian battalion that entered Tirana had other ideas. He declared that the Italians had come to Albania for the purpose of enlarging it. Mr Skeferis, the Greek Minister, reflecting that any such enlargement would have to be at the expense of his own country's frontiers, telegraphed this ominous remark to General Metaxas.

Appeasement was still the fashionable mood. Like the old man in Edward Lear's poem the Governments outside the Axis were saying:

How
Shall we flee from that horrible cow?
We will sit on this stile,
And continue to smile,
Which may soften the heart of that cow.

In view of the meek way in which the British Government had accepted the lies and cynical promises of the Italian Government it was not to be expected that the Greek Government would feel in a position to take a stronger line. Therefore we are not surprised to find General Metaxas appeasing Italy by instructing the Greek Legation in Rome to assure Count Ciano that King Zog's inopportune arrival at Florina did not mean that any countenance would be given to his political activity while an unwelcome guest of Greece. King Zog's offence in Mussolini's eyes was that having been established on the throne of Albania as a puppet he had come to life like the mischievous Pinocchio and would not obey his own artificer.

On Easter Sunday Mussolini telegraphed to the Italian Legation in Athens :

16

"See Metaxas personally and tell him I desire to express my satisfaction over the attitude observed by Greece in regard to Zog and I thank him for all the measures taken to prevent any manifestations on the part of Zog that might cast a shadow, however light, upon the so cordial relations which unite our two countries the maintenance of which will be the basis of my policy now and in the future."

In case General Metaxas should have failed to note the immensity of such condescension the Permanent Under-Secretary of the Rome Foreign Office emphasized to the Greek Legation that this was no ordinary communication but a message from the Head of the Italian Government.

On that Easter Sunday the Greek Minister in London telegraphed to Athens that Count Ciano had informed Lord Perth in confidence that some time ago King Zog had asked for Italian help to attack Yugoslavia. They hesitated to believe this in London, Mr Simopoulos commented; and the hurried return of the British Prime Minister from Scotland suggested that Italian assurances were not regarded as quite satisfactory. The telegram concluded with the disquieting postscript that according to information from a German source Italy intended to occupy Corfu. No doubt it was only a coincidence that the Italian Chargé d'Affaires in London visited the Foreign Office on Easter Eve to suggest to Lord Halifax that the rumoured British occupation of Corfu would provoke complications. Lord Halifax told the Italian that such behaviour was not an English habit, and availed himself of the opportunity to warn his visitor that the British Government would take a grave view of an Italian occupation of Corfu. The Chargé d'Affaires assured Lord Halifax that he had never heard of such a project and that it could not possibly be true because it would be quite at variance with Mr Mussolini's instructions to himself. Oddly enough, Lord Halifax seemed less impressed by this than he was evidently expected to be and he insisted again that any action like the occupation of Corfu would be a matter of the gravest concern to the British Government. There must be no misunderstanding about this and he asked the Chargé d'Affaires to take particular care that his actual words were correctly reported to Rome. He suggested, too, that the assurance of the Italian Government about Corfu to the British Government should be repeated to the Greek Government.

So on Easter Monday (April 10th) the Italian Chargé d'Affaires in Athens called on General Metaxas and read him this communication from the Duce:

"Every rumour which has been spread or may be spread in the future about imaginary Italian action against Greece is false. Such rumours can only be spread by agents provocateurs. Fascist Italy confirms her intention to respect absolutely the integrity of both the mainland and the islands of Greece. Fascist Italy desires to maintain and to develop still further the cordial relations of friendship which unite the two countries. She is disposed to give concrete proof of this desire."

Mussolini protested the innocence of Fascist Italy's intentions in the accents of a bawd guaranteeing virginity in a brothel.

Whatever his inward distrust may have been, General Metaxas asked Mr Fornari to thank Mr Mussolini for his communication. Public opinion in Greece certainly had been rendered rather nervous and uneasy by rumours spread over the radio, among others by several Italian stations. To-day's communication would lift the shadow which had tended to cool slightly the cordiality of the relations between the two countries.

Meanwhile, Count Ciano was making speeches to Albanian notables about the realization of Albanian aspirations, which coincided ominously with Italian aspirations; and officers of the invading forces were talking openly about forthcoming action against Kossovo (in Yugoslavia) and Tsamouria which was on the other side of the Greek frontier. It looked as if the good intentions of Fascist Italy would hardly pave a square inch of the road to hell.

Even Mr Chamberlain was affected with doubts and on April 13th the House of Commons was informed by him, the House of Lords by Lord Halifax, that in the event of any threat to the independence of Greece or Rumania which the Greek or Rumanian Governments found it necessary to resist the British Government would hold itself obliged to give to Greece and Rumania any help in its power. Mr Daladier speaking for the French Government repeated this declaration in a communication to the Press. Next day General Metaxas instructed the Greek Ministers in London and Paris to convey the appreciation of the people of Greece for the noble and spontaneous gestures by Great Britain and France. In a conversation between Mr Simopoulos and the German Chargé d'Affaires in London the former stressed the fact that the Greek Government had not asked for the Anglo-French guarantee and the German expressed his delight that Greece now had guarantees from both sides. So far as the Italian guarantee went it was like congratulating a child on having been tipped a bad half-crown by the neighbour opposite.

On April 16th the King of Italy accepted the Crown of Albania offered to him by a lavishly-bribed Constituent Assembly, that pauper Crown which had been hawked round Europe for the last thirty years. To the deputation which came to Rome with the offer of this piece of pinchbeck the Duce promised the aggrandizement of their country, and with the continuous strengthening of the Italian forces in Albania General Metaxas felt bound to warn Greek consular representatives against the faintest sign of unfriendliness. Mr Churchill had asked in the House of Commons why the British Fleet had not been concentrated in the Adriatic before the Italian assault was made. He thought such evidence of British determination might have discouraged Italy from even attempting it. The British Government preferred to declare its intention to lock the door of the stable if any more horses should be stolen and continued to treat a horse thief and a liar as a gentleman.

We have a vivid picture of that gentleman in a despatch of May 12th from the Greek Minister in Rome. The occasion was a dinner given at the Quirinal in honour of their Royal Highnesses Prince Paul and Princess Olga of Yugoslavia, and in the course of the evening Mr P. Metaxas, the Greek Minister, had the privilege of a short conversation with the Duce who, appearing preoccupied and rather disagreeable, began by reminding Mr Metaxas of the guarantee he had recently given to Greece on account of ill-founded rumours that were circulating.

"A guarantee," observed Mr Metaxas, "which was duly appreciated in Greece and welcomed with great satisfaction by public opinion, as the reply of General Metaxas testified."

"Then what need was there for him to accept another guarantee from M. Daladier?"

The Greek Minister asked if the Duce was alluding to the Anglo-French guarantee given a few weeks before not only to Greece but also to Rumania.

At this point Count Ciano, who had been listening to the conversation so far without joining in, explained that this was the guarantee to which the Duce referred.

Then followed a repetition of assurances that in accepting such a guarantee Greece had not intended to suggest any attitude more particularly hostile toward Italy than Rumania had suggested by sharing in the guarantee, to all of which the Duce himself listened without the slightest sign of being convinced. When the time came for the interview to finish, the Duce, with the air of a man resolved to have the last word, observed darkly that it was good policy for a country to know how to measure its friendliness by the proximity of its friends. In plain language the horse thief and the liar was inviting honesty to pay blackmail for its own protection. To call the "bloodthirsty guttersnipes" of the Axis gangsters is trite enough by now, but it is useful to be reminded from time to time how exactly their methods do correspond with those of their prototypes.

Toward the end of that fatal August, when Europe was sliding faster than ever down the slope that led to the abyss of war, General Metaxas took advantage of a call paid him by the Italian Minister on his return to Athens from Rome to make an attempt to clarify the prospect on which their two countries gazed. The Greek Prime Minister insisted that there was no reason for Italy to mistrust Greek friendship. If Greece had joined in the imposition of sanctions so had Rumania and Bulgaria. So indeed had most of Europe. Count Grazzi declared that the question of sanctions was over and done with.

"It certainly is," General Metaxas agreed. "But it comes to life all the time in the Italian Press."

And then he went on to remind his visitor that notwithstanding the Italian treatment of the Greek inhabitants of the Dodecanese, Greece had abandoned any intention to mix herself up in the politics of the islands. To be sure, an improvement in the treatment would go far to influence public opinion in Greece, which could not fail to be disturbed by the presence of 10,000 Dodecanesian refugees at the Piraeus who had found life in their own islands too intolerable, but like sanctions the question of the Dodecanese was, politically speaking, over and done with. Other points at issue between the two countries were then mentioned until at last General Metaxas reached the crucial point, which was the Anglo-French guarantee offered to Greece after the invasion of Albania. Why should the Duce take such exception to that when he took no exception to the guarantee offered simultaneously to the Rumanian Government for whose representative in Rome he always reserved a particularly cordial welcome?

Here Count Grazzi interjected, with that ingenuousness which is a more constant attribute of Italian diplomacy than the subtlety with which it is usually credited, that the guarantee to Greece must be directed against Italy because Italy was the only Power that could attack Greece. General Metaxas, whom one fancies resisting a sardonic smile, replied that Count Grazzi was mistaken. Bulgaria might attack Greece, in which case England and France would have the same obligation to intervene.

"But," General Metaxas added, "how can we persuade the people of Greece that they are in no danger from Italy when your soldiers on the way to the Dodecanese sing a special song, 'Sbarcheremo al Pireo e conquisteremo tutto l' Egeo' (We'll disembark at the Piraeus and conquer the whole of the Aegean); when your officers and soldiers in Albania talk every day of invading Greece; when Marshal Badoglio has spoken publicly in Albania of the extension of the Albanian frontier; when for the reception of Count Ciano at Koritza placards had been prepared bearing in black letters the names of Kossovo and Tsamouria? As for Kossovo, that belongs to Yugoslavia with whom you are in particularly friendly relations, but Tsamouria belongs to Greece."

Poor Count Grazzi was obviously disconcerted by these questions, and countered with one of his own by asking how the Anglo-Turkish alliance affected the Greek situation, seeing that Greece was also an ally of Turkey. If Turkey started an offensive war against Italy what would be the Greek attitude?

General Metaxas pointed out that the Anglo-Turkish alliance was purely defensive, and that in the unimaginable event of Turkey's starting a war against Italy, Greece was not bound by the Balkan Pact to follow suit.

And now came the question up to which all this had been leading.

"If England should put pressure on you to hand over your ports, what would you do?"

General Metaxas replied that England had never mentioned the question of the Greek ports and would never put pressure on Greece to make use of them.

"If we should ever hand over our ports," he went on, "that would signify the abandonment of our neutrality, and therefore war against you. But we do not contemplate any such eventuality and we have no reason to contemplate it."

"Do you authorize me to telegraph that to Rome?"

General Metaxas replied that Count Grazzi could telegraph to his Government that Greece was not inclined to move against Italy or go to war with her, unless Italy should attack her vital interests and above all her territorial integrity.

"Will you telegraph that in such an event Greece will defend her honour and that territorial integrity?"

Count Grazzi protested that Italy had never contemplated such an act of aggression and would never commit it.

"Then why all this hostility towards us?" General Metaxas asked. "I hear from Rome of the accusations M. Ciano makes against us, accusations devoid of the least foundation that one can only presume in him an inherent ill will. As for M. Mussolini, I still remember the rage which seized him when it was reported that our Military Attaché in Belgrade had criticized the Italian army to one of his foreign colleagues. I hastened to give satisfaction to M. Mussolini by eulogizing the Italian army myself and, although the baselessness of the accusation against our officer was proved and confirmed even by the Italian Military Attaché in Belgrade, nevertheless, in my anxiety not to leave M. Mussolini in the least doubt about our intentions, I at once removed our officer from his post and, in spite of his innocence, refused to allow him to serve on the General Staff. This is how I behave when I want to keep on good terms with the Head of another Government. I cannot say as much for M. Mussolini in respect of us. As you see, you treat us badly, and that gives us the right to suppose that you are not amicably disposed towards us."

Once more Count Grazzi protested his country's good-will and declared it would be enough for Italy to feel certain that Greece had no hostile intentions against Italy to put an end to everything of which General Metaxas complained.

"Allow me to doubt that," General Metaxas concluded, "although it is my great desire. I hope that you will do all you can to remove this unjust prejudice against Greece. But, I repeat, if our territorial integrity or our vital interests are attacked it is absolutely certain that we shall fight to defend them."

"You would be perfectly right," Count Grazzi replied. "But such an eventuality is never likely to occur."

The irony of this conversation was never surpassed on the tragic stage of ancient Hellas.

A week passed. Stalin and Ribbentrop had clinked glasses over the Russo-German Pact. Hitler was couched to spring at the throat of Poland. The jackal of Italy whined nervously. He was not ready yet for major war. On August 29th General Papagos, the Chief of the Greek General Staff, reported to General Metaxas that the Italian Military Attaché just back from Rome had been enquiring anxiously about the concentration of Greek troops along the Albanian frontier, and said he had been charged by Mr Pariani, the Minister of War, to reaffirm the guarantee given last April that Greek soil would not be violated. General Papagos had replied that he was delighted to receive the assurances of Mr Pariani and that Greece desired nothing better than the friendliest relations with Italy.

"But," the General had continued, "the ostentatious concentration along our frontier of almost the whole of the Italian forces in Albania and the constant violations of Greek territory by Italian planes which often penetrate deep inside it do not contribute, unfortunately, to create the atmosphere which we aim at and which, as you assure me, your Minister of War also aims at."

The Military Attaché had evaded the first point and suggested that the behaviour of the Italian planes was due to youthful enthusiasm and inexperience, perhaps even to a little lack of discipline. General Papagos had observed that if a formal order were given by the Italian Command he could not believe they would continue to display such lack of discipline, which after all was the one indispensable virtue for every armed force.

The Military Attaché had promised to bring the matter to the notice of his Government, and then after receiving the assurance of respect for territorial integrity he had come to the real point of this conversation. They were afraid in Italy that Greece would concede naval bases to England.

General Papagos had replied that Greece wished to remain outside any conflict between the Great Powers, and that in his opinion the concession to England of Greek naval bases would certainly constitute an act directly hostile to Italy and therefore liable to involve

Greece in the war she desired to avoid.

This interview between the Chief of the Greek General Staff and the Italian Military Attaché sharply illuminated Fascist hopes and fears on the eve of war. For nine months the black foetus of Mussolini's ambition would swell within the womb of opportunity to emerge in June and claw at the breast of dying France. Meanwhile, the task set him by Hitler was before all to keep the Eastern Mediterranean quiet until it could be exploited to the top of their mutual advantage.

Immediately after the outbreak of war Count Grazzi called on General Metaxas to suggest in the friendliest way that inasmuch as the Italian Government had declared its intention to abstain from any kind of military operation, the concentration of Greek troops on the Albanian frontier should be relaxed. General Metaxas expressed his willingness to respond at once to any withdrawal of Italian troops from the frontier. On September 9th Count Grazzi called again to say he had been summoned to Rome, and by the air of importance he cast over this journey conveyed the impression that he hoped to return with a practical plan for the improvement of Greek and Italian relations.

This took the shape of a communication signed by Mussolini himself in Rome on September 12th, 1939:

1. Italy has already declared on September 1st that she does not intend to initiate any military guarantees.
2. This decision by the Council of Ministers, which applied generally, applies particularly to Greece.
3. In the event of Italy's position as a Great Power compelling her to intervene in the war, she will not initiate any operations in regard to Greece.
4. To show in a concrete manner the sentiments by which the Italian Government and particularly the Duce himself are animated in regard to Greece, the withdrawal of Italian troops to a distance of 20 kilometres from the Greco-Albanian frontier will be ordered.
5. The Duce does not exclude the possibility, notwithstanding actual circumstances, of taking up again and stabilizing the policy of an entente between Italy and Greece 'qui eut sa consécration dans les accords ad hoc de caractère diplomatique'.

This last sentence has been left in the Duce's own language of pompous obscurity. It is not surprising that a society called Mystico Fascismo exists at Milan the object of which is to provide a synthesis and an interpretation of all the Duce has written and said since the Fascio was invented.

The immediate result of Count Grazzi's interview was a communiqué issued to the Press by the Ministry of Foreign Affairs at noon of September 20th, 1939:

"The Royal Hellenic Government and the Royal Italian Government having decided it would be useful, in the present situation of Europe, to turn their attention to the actual condition of the relations between the two countries, have been happy to ascertain that these relations continue to be sincerely friendly and to be inspired by a spirit of complete mutual confidence.

"A tangible proof of these sentiments has been furnished by the decision of the Royal Italian Government to withdraw its military forces from the Greco-Albanian frontier, and similar measures are being taken by the Royal Hellenic Government."

Over in Rome Count Ciano was so delighted by the apparent success of the plan to lull Greece into security that he was extremely cordial to the Greek Minister and begged him to repeat once more to General Metaxas how much Italy desired the strengthening of the relations of trustful friendship between the two countries.

On September 30th General Metaxas handed the Italian Minister a memorandum in reply to the Duce's communication of September 12th and ten days later Count Grazzi had a conversation with Mr Mavroudis, the Permanent Under-Secretary for Foreign Affairs. He told Mr Mavroudis what satisfaction the memorandum had given in Rome, and asked on behalf of his Government that it might be accorded the dignity of a Note formally signed to which he would reply with another, after he had obtained his Government's approval of the text. Then in strict confidence Count Grazzi went on to reveal that the Italian Government had decided to make soon a solemn declaration of its intention to remain indefinitely neutral so that if the Balkan States would adopt a similar attitude the horrors of war might be avoided in the Eastern Mediterranean. He let it be understood that what had led Italy to take that decision was the recent intervention of Rumania in Eastern Europe. Although the two Notes were dated September 30th, they were not published until November 3rd.   Here is the text in full:

THE LETTER OF THE PRESIDENT OF THE COUNCIL AND MINISTER OF FOREIGN AFFAIRS TO THE ITALIAN MINISTER

Athens, September 30th, 1939

Monsieur le Ministre,

I have the honour to inform Your Excellency that the Hellenic Government has taken note of the Communication which on the instructions of the Duce you were good enough to make known to me on the Twelfth of this month, and highly appreciates the spirit of it.

The fresh assurances contained in this communication, which testify to the friendly disposition of Italy toward Greece, have been welcomed with the liveliest satisfaction.   This friendly disposition, which corresponds exactly with the sentiments of Greece towards Italy, has created an atmosphere of cordiality between our two countries by which the Hellenic Government is delighted.

The spontaneous gesture of the Head of the Italian Government in withdrawing the Italian troops from the Albano-Greek frontier has profoundly touched the Greek People, which has followed with the liveliest sympathy the Duce's efforts toward maintaining Peace.

In warm response to the sentiments which have inspired this gesture the Hellenic Government hastened to order similar military steps to be taken.

The Hellenic Government is happy to seize the occasion to reaffirm its intention to pursue its policy of peace, to which it remains deeply attached, as well as its sincere desire to see the inauguration between Italy and Greece of a new era of friendship and understanding stamped with the greatest national confidence.

In the inspiration of this policy and the conviction that it is wholly shared by the Italian Government the Hellenic Government firmly hopes that the development of the international situation will provide the two governments in the near future with the opportunity to give their relations a more solid shape, directed toward a confident and fruitful collaboration in every sphere.

Meanwhile, the Hellenic Government is resolved to find inspiration in the principles of friendship and collaboration enunciated in the Pact of Friendship, Conciliation and Judicial Settlement signed in Rome on September 23rd, 1928, between Italy and Greece.

Veuillez agréer, Monsieur le Ministre, les assurances de ma haute considération.

Metaxas.

CHAPTER TWO

Athens, September 30th, 1939

Monsieur le Président du Conseil,

In your Note of to-day's date, Your Excellency has been good enough to make known to me that the Hellenic Government is happy to seize the occasion offered by the atmosphere of cordiality existing between the two countries, etc. etc. . . .

On the instructions of the Government I have the honour to inform Your Excellency that Italy, being inspired by the same sentiments as Greece, shares her intention to pursue a policy of peace, to which she remains deeply attached, and reaffirms her sincere desire to see the inauguration of a new era of friendship and understanding stamped with the greatest mutual confidence.

The Royal Italian Government also firmly hopes that the development of the international situation, etc. etc.

Meanwhile, the Royal Italian Government is resolved to find inspiration in the principles of friendship and collaboration enunciated in the Pact of Friendship, Conciliation, and Judicial Settlement signed in Rome on September 23rd, 1928, between Greece and Italy.

Veuillez agréer, Monsieur le Président du Conseil, les assurances de ma plus haute considération.

Emanuele Grazzi.

These two letters repeat word for word the memorandum of General Metaxas except in the last sentence. The Greek Prime Minister originally wrote the '*principles enunciated in the Pact*'. It was a direct suggestion of the Italian Government that the words '*of friendship and collaboration*' were inserted after '*principles*'. Presumably this was done in order to claim that Greece was committed to collaboration with Italy but at the same time to avoid the formal renewal of the Pact which had expired just a year ago.

It can be argued that during the six months after the exchange of the Notes the British and French Governments were justified in continuing their efforts to appease Mussolini and that, given the earnest wish of the great majority of the Italian people to keep out of the war, they had grounds for believing in the possibility of achieving such abstention. Yet the anxiety of Italy to adjust matters with Greece might have indicated to the directors of Anglo-French foreign policy the advantage of taking a firmer line. A demand in October 1939 for the immediate evacuation of the Dodecanese, with war as the alternative, would have changed the course of history. Destiny had ruled that at this hour there should not be one man in Britain, France, Yugoslavia, Turkey or Greece in a position to initiate the policy of constructive energy required to throw the Axis out of alignment.

On February 16th, 1940, the world was startled by an aggressive action on the part of Great Britain, when the British prisoners made by German raiders were removed from the *Altmark* in the territorial waters of Norway.

The fury of the German wireless revealed the dread that this was the preliminary to a British occupation. For a day or two Italy flirted with the idea of selling war material to the Allies, and France actually placed an order there for training-planes. Dr Clodius, the German Economic Adviser in Rome, had to notify the Italian Government that if such negotiations continued Italian ships would be sunk. On March 1st Great Britain notified Italy that German exports of coal by sea would no longer be tolerated. The argument lasted for eleven days, when as a gesture of good-will that curiously resembled a feeble shrug of the shoulders Italian coal-ships taken into British ports for search were released. On that March 11th Ribbentrop arrived in Rome with an arrangement to supply Italy overland with the coal she required. No doubt at the same time he brought Mussolini Hitler's invitation to meet on the Brenner and hear from the fountainhead what springs of future action were welling.

It can be presumed that in that monstrous railway train the German plans for 1940 were fully disclosed for the first time. The British had failed to follow up the *Altmark* incident. Now, when they did, Germany's counter-action was ready. Denmark, Norway, Holland, Belgium, France, England, Victory, Peace, and then at the right moment Russia. There must be no precipitate action in the Eastern Mediterranean. Now that Finland was done with, Russia might move toward the Balkans. All in good time. All in good time. Fascist Italy should have what it wanted, and moreover without any undue expenditure of blood or treasure.

On March 20th Mr Jean Politis, who had replaced Mr P. Metaxas as Greek Minister in Rome, asked Count Ciano how far the future of the Balkans had been discussed on the Brenner. The Italian declared at first that the Balkans had not been mentioned; but when the Greek Minister armed with information from a sure source pressed him, Count Ciano admitted that the question of the Balkans had been touched upon and that the policy of maintaining peace there would be continued. Count Ciano begged the Greek Minister not to see anything extraordinary in the Brenner meeting. It was a routine affair provided for to discuss from time to time the internal affairs of the Axis. Once again before they parted the Italian statesman assured his visitor that there was nothing to worry about in the Balkans. "Rebus sic stantibus," he added, breaking into Latin like his father-in-law or any other Caesar.

By April 11th reports from all over Europe were coming to the Ministry of Foreign Affairs in Athens that the Italians were planning to occupy Corfu. Two days later General Metaxas invited Count Grazzi to suggest an explanation of them. The Italian Minister avowed that they must have been circulated by the English who mistrusted the friendly relations between Greece and Italy. Certainly they could not have come from any Italian source at a time when these relations were so particularly cordial. It was hardly necessary to declare that they were entirely devoid of any foundation. The baselessness of the rumour General Metaxas accepted as a matter of course; but he pointed out that it could scarcely have emanated from British sources because the British Government had continuously advised an improvement in Greco-Italian relations and both England and France had expressed the greatest satisfaction over the exchange of Notes last October. Count Grazzi insisted upon the British Government's lack of sincerity; and when General Metaxas pointed out that Greece was too small a country to provoke so much rivalry he argued that the geographical position of Greece was a matter of fundamental importance as much for England as for Italy.

The rumour, which died away almost immediately after this conversation, was probably a *ballon d'essai* to test British reactions. If the British, thwarted in Norway by the rapidity and thoroughness with which the Germans had forestalled them, were planning similar action in Greece this tale about a proposed Italian occupation of Corfu might flurry them into a premature disclosure of their project. It is difficult for the quick malicious Latin mind to believe that British policy is not inspired by a profound cunning because it has so often seemed to outwit the more obvious villains. The Latin cannot believe that this success is usually due to a masterly inactivity inspired by an odd combination of laziness and decency. The German is equally at a loss to grasp the British character. He understands and despises the laziness, but the decency he cannot even despise because it is beyond his comprehension; and therefore he too attributes British success to cunning.   Probably the fundamental explanation of the sympathy between Britain and Greece which has survived one or two difficult moments since 1821 is the ability of the Greeks to appreciate British motives.   General Metaxas, who was not conspicuous for his love of England, was never under the slightest apprehension about British intentions in the matter of naval bases.

On May 11th the Greek Permanent Under-Secretary for Foreign Affairs telegraphed to Mr Politis that the Italian Minister on his return from Rome had stressed the unlikelihood of his country's entering the war, but had added that, if her position as a Great Power should make it necessary to do so in order to obtain the satisfaction of outstanding claims, such claims had nothing to ask from Greece or indeed from the Balkans generally.   Even if Italy should go to war with England she would not attack Greece unless Greece became a British base.   The truly laconic reply of Mr Politis to this communication suggests that in the Greek Legation in Rome General Metaxas and Mr Mavroudis were thought to be indulging in the opium of wishful thinking which too long had been the refuge of European statesmen from the New Barbarism:

Rome, May 15th, 1940

The assurances given by the Italian Minister contain reservations which destroy their value.   Besides, I am convinced that if Italy goes to war she will apply strictly, despite any declaration to the contrary, the method of the surprise attack.

With that unerring shaft Mr Politis transfixed the black heart of Fascism.   The records of diplomacy exhibit few such notable examples of prescience.   And for the rest of that May and early June, when the vultures were gathering in that Italian sky, once beloved of Liberty, Mr Politis marked how they dipped and rose, dipped and rose, waiting for the victim's dying agony before they would swoop to their feast.

His telegrams at that time despatched from Rome to Athens have a classic quality which forbids paraphrase, as the following exerpts will show:

May 26th, 1940

Public opinion is being actively worked up.   It is now presented as demanding war and hardly to be restrained.   The speeches of the leaders to mass meetings and the resolutions voted by them at their instigation compete with one another in bellicose ardour and in pompous warnings that the explosion is imminent.

The parts have been distributed to the various instruments of the Fascist orchestra. Posters sneer at England. Bands yell slogans like 'Corsica Italiana'. M. Balbo's paper has been entrusted with the attack on Egypt. M. Gayda occupies himself with the Balkans and after having stressed the military significance of their coasts from Dalmatia to Crete, winds up by denouncing them as bases already of the British blockade. Count Ciano has taken it upon himself to squeeze out of the Albanians irredentist claims on Tsamouria and Kossovo. In resolutions voted by Fascist clubs drafts are drawn on Tunis, Gibraltar, and Corfu. In a word, the storm is proclaimed to be on the verge of bursting and that all is ready to meet it.

This is the façade. As for what is going on behind it, one can do no more than give an approximate estimate. Public opinion, fearful and fatalistic, waits resigned for the Duce to give the signal as if it were waiting for its own death-sentence. The Duce perfectly aware of this state of mind, follows hour by hour the gigantic struggle in Flanders, spying out the moment for an easy victory. When will he give the signal? All depends on the success of the German arms. In what direction will Italy march? That is a completely open matter. No declaration, no assurance, no threat offers the slightest indication.

Every doubt and every apprehension is justified. Italian policy is being played out upon the battlefield of Flanders.

May 29th, 1940

The Giornale d' Italia *publishes to-day an article from its correspondent in Athens under the title 'Greek youth and the present political situation'.*

Having attended a march-past of groups of the National Organization of Youth (the Neolaia), *the writer pretends to have observed that the young people were entirely without juvenile* élan *and indeed did not appear to belong to the phalanx of youth at all. In default of a revolution capable of creating new moral values, not only the Organization of Youth but every other activity of the régime of the Fourth of August (i.e. the* Metaxas *régime) find themselves without any ideological fire lacking which this national movement seems built on sand. The reason for this state of affairs is that, in spite of the Fourth of August, the whole country continues to live in the nightmare of Freemasonry which the Fourth of August Revolution has not ventured to touch because most of its chiefs are Freemasons themselves. Freemasonry in Greece means English and French capital. But already the brilliant German victories are opening to Greek Youth new horizons where it can find its own place.*

June 1st, 1940

The Popolo di Roma *and the* Stampa *of Turin publish to-day from their special correspondent in Athens:*

"*Among the islands and in the bays of Greek waters British war-ships cruise as sovereigns, for the ships are supported by the pound sterling. Here in two words is the policy of Greece, a poor country entirely dependent on the sea. From the day when another flag re-places the British flag in the Eastern Mediterranean the existence of Greece will depend upon this new flag as it depended on the Crescent in bygone centuries. Having established the fact that Greece relies now more upon the military help of Turkey than on that of the Demo-cratic Powers, are we really going to assist the realization of this Turkish protectorate? A protectorate which would confer on Mo-hammedan Asia power over the Christian Cross, even though it be only a Greek Cross? The Greeks applaud: they are probably un-conscious of what they are doing.*"

June 2nd, 1940

I must let you know how uneasy I am at the way that Greece has recently been presented by Italian news and comment as a country at the mercy of foreign influence and in danger of losing her sovereignty. It is significant that this happens at the moment when Italy is pre-paring to enter the war. I must lay equal stress on the way Greece has taken the place of Yugoslavia which for some time has ceased to be the target of similar calumnies.

In Italian eyes Greece apparently offers an open field for their plan of campaign and an attempt is being made through the Italian Press to create beforehand a justification for a case in which the violation of Hellenic sovereignty might be considered opportune or necessary.

June 3rd, 1940

The Nationalist Organization 'Opera Azurra' has just been pla-carding Rome and other Italian cities with a characteristic example of the state of mind they wish to induce here. This manifesto takes the form of slogans like the following: 'The only way to make Peace in Europe durable is for the great to absorb the small'. In virtue of incontestable historic might as well as of the right of supremacy, the whole of central and southern France, the bases of the Mediterranean, the Adriatic, Croatia, Dalmatia, Greece, Cyprus, Albania, and Jeru-salem belong to Italy.

June 10th, 1940

The Minister of Foreign Affairs has confirmed to me that the decision to enter the war has been taken and he left me to understand that it would be acted upon immediately. I asked him if I could count *on the recent assurances given by Italy to my Government, so that we might feel sure that the Balkans and in particular Greece had nothing to fear from any repercussions. He replied that I could feel sure that all his assurances held good and that Italy was firmly resolved to preserve peace in the Balkans. He added that he had given assurances of a similar kind to Yugoslavia and Turkey.*

At six o'clock on that June evening Mussolini bellowed from the balcony of the Palazzo Venezia:

"Now that the die is cast and our will has blown up the bridges behind us, I solemnly declare that Italy does not propose to drag into the conflict her neighbours by land or sea. Let Switzerland, Yugoslavia, Greece, Turkey, and Egypt take note of my words. The fulfilment of them depends on them, and on them only."

Once upon a time Cleon the Tanner bawled as loud as this from the Bema, and Athens followed his voice along the road to ruin. Juliet the wags of Rome called Mussolini, because he was for ever appearing on balconies. One day, will true Italians fling that greasy bag of wind to the Roman mob surging below and make of their Juliet a Jezebel?

CHAPTER THREE

T HE effect of Fascism on the human mind has an affinity with the mental condition we call arrested development, and the historian whose task it is to record Italian behaviour toward Greece during the period between June 10th and October 28th, 1940, finds himself embarrassed by what he knows will be the contemptuous astonishment of posterity. He feels that he is being invited to chronicle the mischief and lies of snivelling schoolboys who should be birched and sent to bed in eternal oblivion but who by a monstrous accident of human history have to be treated like Alexanders and Napoleons. It is a humiliation of the Muse of History, but truth must be served and the sorry tale must be unfolded.

It begins on June 18th when the Italian Minister in Athens called on General Metaxas to inform him that the Italian Government had ascertained that a British aircraft-carrier with several cruisers and destroyers had stayed in a Cretan port above the twenty-four hours allowed by international law. Toleration of such action was a breach of the neutrality Greece had promised to observe.

This accusation was immediately rebutted. Not a single British warship of any kind had anchored in a Cretan port or had even been signalled in the offing.

The day before this *démenti* Mr Anfuso, who represented Count Ciano on the days when the latter was being an airman by his father-in-law's orders, had sent for the Greek Minister in Rome to complain of the use being made by British warships of Suda Bay and Candia (Herakleion). Mr Politis at once asked if Mr Anfuso could tell him when these ships were observed and how their presence in the ports beyond twenty-four hours had been established. Mr Anfuso recognized that this was a counter-attack and hastily assured his assailant that the Italian Navy was able to verify the presence of these ships without infringing Greek neutrality.

Next day, armed with the *démenti* from Athens, Mr Politis visited Mr Anfuso, who anticipated what he had to say by expressing his pleasure at hearing from Count Grazzi that it had all been a mistake and that there was nothing to be discussed. Mr Politis, however,

34

was disinclined to let him off too easily, and went on to express his astonishment that the Italian Admiralty should have been able to establish not merely the presence of a whole fleet in two Greek ports but even the length of its stay.

"I know," Mr Politis added, with exquisite sarcasm, "that the military authorities always grow nervous in war-time, and so I should not have been astonished if having seen two ships they should have spoken of ten, or if instead of reckoning ten hours of anchorage they should have counted thirty; but it turns out there was not even one ship or one hour of which to make a story."

Mr Anfuso agreed that it was all most surprising and suggested it must be the result of inaccurate reconnaissance by planes. Thereupon he called to the telephone the Admiral who acted as liaison and begged him to insist in future on accurate reports because he had just bothered the Greek Minister with one which had no shadow of foundation.

A week later Mr Anfuso had a new complaint. The Greek Minister in Ankara was working against the Axis. He hinted that his recall would help to clear up any misunderstanding. Mr Politis observed that the accusation against one of Greece's most experienced diplomats was too vague for disciplinary action, and in this he was supported by the Greek Ministry of Foreign Affairs.

Four days later Count Ciano, taking advantage of his alternate week on earth, graciously allowed Mr Politis to hear that the information laid against the Greek Minister in Ankara had been laid by his colleague the Italian Ambassador. Mr Politis pointed out that the Ambassador's information was not first-hand and suggested that the whole business savoured of an intrigue set on foot by interested parties.

"Well, I can't start a police enquiry to convince you," snapped Count Ciano, whose manners reveal the parvenu to diplomacy. "Besides, I am not making a *démarche* about this matter. I am simply passing on to you my information and leaving you to draw what conclusions from it you like."

"Apropos of police enquiries," said Mr Politis, who obviously enjoyed baiting this fretful puppy, "I'm sorry to find in you such an absolutely unjustified spirit of mistrust. It must exist or otherwise it would be difficult to explain why the Greek Legation is spied upon by secret agents who follow all our movements, take note of all our visitors and even come prying into the courtyard. That is hardly a normal way of treating the representative of a friendly Power."

Count Ciano replied with obvious insincerity that those were measures taken in every country to look after the safety of diplomats, but added that if they annoyed Mr Politis he would have them stopped.

"Oh, if the Italian authorities consider the Greek Legation suspect, I have no objection to their keeping an eye on it," Mr Politis assured him blandly. "Such surveillance might end in convincing them of the contrary."

Count Ciano brought the interview to a hasty close with a display of expansive courtesies; but, three days later, he summoned the Greek Minister again to the Ministry where in rude and angry tones he said he had to raise an extremely grave question which might have terrible consequences. He had proof that British warships were using the ports and territorial waters of Greece for their attacks upon Italian naval forces. Such a state of affairs was intolerable, and if it were not at once stopped Italy would take action. Count Ciano proceeded to read from a document of the Italian General Staff:

> On *June 13th* an Italian submarine was attacked by British planes forty miles off Leucas (Santa Maura).
> On *June 28th* another submarine was attacked by planes and destroyers not far from Zante.
> On *June 29th* a submarine was attacked and probably sunk by planes and destroyers coming from the direction of Zante.
> On *June 30th* and *July 1st* four British destroyers were at Melos.

"From a technical point of view," Mr Politis asked, "does the presence of British planes forty miles west of Leucas prove automatically that they came from Greece?"

"This is not the moment for a war of words," the Count muttered like a sulky boy. "Italy has given Greece every proof of her good intentions and has scrupulously kept her promises. But now she knows how far she can trust Greek promises; in any case, the French documents seized by the Germans have already enlightened her in that direction."

"It is unfair to make insinuations without producing any evidence to support them," the Greek Minister observed.

To this Count Ciano made, with the epithet of Mr Politis, the 'bizarre' reply that the documents he alluded to referred to the past and that he would rather leave them out of it.

"The more recent proof, constituted by the help Greece has given to the British Fleet, is enough for us," he asserted. "That means war with Italy and Germany. It is time Greece took account of the fact that the Axis has already won the war, and gave up Utopias."

The Greek Minister in analysing for his Government what lay behind the Italian *démarche* gave it as his own opinion that it was not so much a simple complaint of violating the obligations of neutrality, justified or not, as a political threat designed to secure for Italy the geographical advantages of Greece.

In his reply General Metaxas expressed his pained surprise at the obstinate lack of confidence evinced by the Italian Foreign Minister. He insisted that the attacks by British planes and destroyers came from Egyptian bases remote from Greece, and as for the four destroyers in Melos they were four Greek destroyers which had been stationed there since June 10th. Then at some length he repeated yet again the reasons which lay behind Greece's earnest and anxious desire to keep out of the war and maintain a strict neutrality.

Count Ciano's naval intelligence having been proved inaccurate, he fell back on the political intelligence revealed by the French documents which at the previous interview he had relegated to the past. He much hoped that it would not be necessary to make use of them. Mr Politis suggested that it was impossible for him to refute mysteries and wished nothing better than to see these documents brought to light.

"You know I am quite *au courant* with the things they say against Italy in Athenian salons and clubs," said the protean and ebullient Count, assuming the shape of Sherlock Holmes.

"Naturally, every shade of opinion finds expression in private conversations," Mr Politis replied. "But I'm afraid your zealous informers send you every bit of tittle-tattle without estimating the importance it deserves."

"I attach no importance to such indications," declared the Count, reassuming haughtily the shape of a Minister for Foreign Affairs. "It was not to them I was alluding when I spoke of our intelligence about Greek intentions."

Between the *démarche* on July 3rd and this second interview on July 6th Count Ciano had visited Berlin, and thus deepened the suspicion of Mr Politis that these *démarches* were soundings preliminary to diplomatic action on a vaster and more substantial scale.

He had heard in several well-informed quarters that the ambiguous attitude of Russia was making a reconsideration of Axis policy in the Balkans imperative. He fancied Greece might be on the verge of being subjected to a diplomatic offensive. He felt that throughout his interviews with Count Ciano the question, "What use to you henceforth is the British guarantee?" was always on the tip of his tongue. And then after a further amplification of his analysis of Italian motives he was asking himself in the last short paragraph of a long despatch whether one ought not to see in these *démarches* the preliminaries to military action.

On July 12th General Metaxas was having to protest to the Italian Legation because that morning three Italian planes, after bombing and machine-gunning the Greek lighthouse-tender *Orion*, had attacked the destroyer *Hydra* which had gone to the help of the *Orion*. Three days later the Italian Legation was asking General Metaxas to thank the Greek Authorities who had helped to save the lives of the crew of an Italian seaplane which had been forced down in the waters of Cephalonia.

The mysterious documents discovered by the Germans in the archives of the French High Command were published in Berlin on July 23rd. There were only three which concerned Greece.

No. 33 was a reply by General Gamelin to General Weygand's request for the despatch of war material for the eventual landing of an army corps in Macedonia.

No. 34 was a confidential order of May 15th arranging to use the names of American States for Greece, Turkey, Crete, Salamis, Salonika, etc., in correspondence between the French Commander-in-Chief and General Weygand.

No. 35 was a refusal by General Gamelin to send General Weygand the military reinforcements he asked for.

As the Permanent Under-Secretary observed to the Greek Minister in Berlin, "The new documents of the French General Staff just published speak for themselves and offer convincing evidence that Greece was completely ignorant of any such plan."

So this was the damp squib with the explosion of which Count Ciano had been threatening Mr Politis. No wonder he kept it in his pocket when the Greek Minister dared him to light it.

The catastrophe that overwhelmed Greece in April 1941 has left the contemporary chronicler without any documentary evidence by which he can hope to establish with unimpeachable exactitude what were the diplomatic relations between Greece and Germany during that summer and autumn of 1940, and when to such a gap is added his ignorance of how far Italian plans coincided with German and how far they differed the gap widens into a chasm to span which he is dependent upon the frail bridge of speculation.

We may take it as certain that Italy's resentment at being jockeyed out of her place in the Mediterranean by her partners in the First World War was predominant in the mind of Mussolini and that he was first and foremost determined this should not happen again. The swiftness of the French collapse had to some extent caught him unawares. He had an unquiet feeling that the feminine wiles of France were more accomplished than those of the unsexed Italy of whom he had tried to make an Amazon; and perhaps he meditated on the disastrous spell Hitler could cast over old men—Hindenburg, Chamberlain, and now Marshal Pétain. If the projected invasion of Britain by the Germans should succeed he might find himself left in the lurch at the Peace Conference. The time was not ripe for the grand invasion of Egypt. Moreover, there was the British fleet: that inglorious flight of his naval forces from a squadron of it on July 9th and ten days later the sinking of the *Bartolomeo Colleoni* off Crete by a cruiser of lighter armament. British air strength, too, was growing. In spite of the menace to their own shores their aircraft were able to make themselves felt in North Africa.

All through the first nine months of the war a *pax Romana* had been proclaimed over the Balkans, and in the general craving for peace Mussolini had been able to persuade many people that he was, after all, a statesman; but after June 10th the Balkan nations turned away from him and looked anxiously toward Germany for their hope of preserving peace. An appearance was made, when Ciano paid his visit to Germany at the beginning of July, of bringing him into the discussion of the territorial adjustments between Hungary and Rumania, but it was plain enough that the Transylvania settlement was entirely a German conception. So, too, was the restoration of the Dobrudja to Bulgaria: and for that matter the advice given to Rumania to hand over Bessarabia to the Soviets. Yugoslavia under the guidance of the Prince Regent Paul and the Cvetkovitch Government was being drawn within the German ambit, and there was no inclination at Berchtesgaden to encourage Italian aggression in that direction. Finally, it was clear that, if Turkey had not entered the war beside Great Britain when the Italian die was cast, it was from fear of Germany and doubt of Russia, not out of the slightest awe of Italy. Nothing was likely to bring Turkey into the war unless she were deliberately attacked. There remained Greece.

The overrunning of Greece by a sudden attack, so sudden, so swift, and so ruthless that complete surrender followed by occupation must be a matter of no more than a few days, would present his partner with a *fait accompli*. Apart from the immediate strategic advantages of Greece's geography for an attack on Egypt or Palestine, such an occupation would cover the right flank of any German move in the future through Turkey and place Mussolini in a much stronger position to upset the *rapprochement* between France and Germany which was threatened. Moreover, if Britain should be brought to her knees by September before Mussolini had had time to set his African armies in effective motion he might fare even worse at a Peace Conference than Orlando once upon a time. As far as can be judged the aggression planned against Greece in that August of 1940 was planned in recognition of the proverb which notes that a bird in the hand is worth two in the bush, unless it was merely a device to test Greek and British reactions.

As a preliminary to the coup in mind the campaign of provocation was intensified. Italian planes violated Greek neutrality almost every day.

The Greek destroyers *King George* and *Queen Olga* were bombed in the Gulf of Corinth, as also were two submarines lying in the port of Lepanto. The immediate recall of Mr Scarpas, the Greek consul at Trieste, was insolently demanded by Count Ciano because he was reported to have laughed at the Italian army. That jackanapes even accused British warships of flying Greek colours when they were in Greek waters.

The record of a conversation at the Palazzo Chigi between Mr Politis and Mr Benini, the Under-Secretary of State for Albanian Affairs, gives a picture of the Italian state of mind at the beginning of that August. They had been discussing some petty provocation at Tirana, and that done with, Mr Benini said suddenly:

"I hear with great regret that relations between our two countries have become delicate."

Mr Politis was struck by this phrase. Only three or four days earlier the Permanent Under-Secretary had telegraphed from Athens that the Rumanian Foreign Minister had told Mr Collas, the Greek Ambassador in Bucharest, that the Duce had led him to understand that Greco-Italian relations had become 'delicate'.

"What makes you say that?" Mr Politis asked.

"I heard so from Count Ciano. I should add that the Minister was in a very bad humour over Greece."

Mr Benini paused to give Mr Politis an opportunity to shake his head in doleful agreement, and seemed surprised when his visitor gave no sign of being aware of this bad humour.

"Haven't you seen Count Ciano for some time?" he asked.

"Yes, I saw him quite recently; but I didn't get the impression of anything new, for the simple reason that during the last few weeks every time I've had the pleasure of meeting the Foreign Minister he has always been in a bad humour and never for any good cause. But perhaps you know what's responsible for this bad mood?" Mr Politis pressed.

"I've been told that you are flirting with the English," the Under-Secretary replied. "It's a pity. Our relations were on the right track and now you are stepping off it."

"I think that when you impute to us a certain attitude you have an elementary duty to produce the data on which you base your deductions. Some weeks ago Count Ciano summoned me to the Ministry in order to level accusations in the spirit of those you've been repeating to-day. When I persisted in asking for proofs of our favouring the English arms, I found we were being reproached because some British planes which had attacked your submarines in the Ionian Sea had come from our islands and because four British warships had been lying for several days in the roadstead of Melos. Two days later I was able to inform him that the four warships were Greek destroyers which had been stationed at Melos for months and that no aerodrome existed in the islands mentioned by Count Ciano."

"That was decisive," the Under-Secretary admitted.

"Nevertheless, because of these two groundless suppositions Count Ciano threatened me with war, and those explanations furnished by my Government which you characterize as 'decisive' were far from producing the effect on which one had a right to count. In fact, only a few days ago General Butti, speaking in Count Ciano's name, went over the whole indictment again from the beginning. And now here are you yourself resuming it to-day, and in the same vague mysterious manner. I shall have to be frank and confess that I bring away with me from every visit to the Ministry an impression that Italy has no good intentions toward Greece. I'll take advantage of this opportunity to cite some other curious symptoms.

"Latterly your air force has been indulging in an almost systematic bombing of our ships in our territorial waters. I fancy that the Italian air force has not quite appreciated, indeed I suspect it may have misconstrued, the discretion of the Hellenic Government over the first incident, for a short while afterwards this was followed by a second and then a third and our protests to you remain unanswered.

"In return for this solid proof of the friendly spirit which animates us, I must point out that any *démarches* you intend to make to us are known the day before not merely in diplomatic circles but are the common talk of Roman salons. This gives me the right to suppose that there are elements interested in prejudicing public opinion against us.

"But allow me to add a few more observations still more material. Among the proofs of Italian policy's good intentions Count Ciano cited with some emphasis the considerable diminution of Italian troops in Albania. Yet, my own information is that ever since my arrival in Rome your forces in Albania have been slowly but steadily augmented. Certainly the whole force has not yet reached disquieting proportions, but I am bound to take note of this steady increase when the Minister of Foreign Affairs believes in the contrary.

"Nor can you suppose that I ought to recognize as an excellent augury of our future relations the proclamation of territorial claims by Albanian irredentists, particularly when such proclamations coincide with the visits of Count Ciano to Albania."

"Oh, merely student activities," the Under-Secretary interposed deprecatingly. "Besides, that was officially contradicted," he added, trying vainly to remember where and how.

"I never saw such a *démenti*," Mr Politis remarked. "And as for your theory that they were merely the activities of students, I'm afraid that is not so. My information is that agents of the Italian administration were involved in them. Anyhow, in view of the perfect organization and discipline of the Fascist Empire one might expect that such demonstrations would be prevented, at least while the Minister of Foreign Affairs was staying in Albania. And another point. You surely do not suppose I have failed to notice the resolutions passed by Fascist organizations and given publicity in the Press in which various Greek islands are mentioned among Italian claims?

"In these circumstances I should be justified in asking *you* what was at the back of *your* intentions. You can imagine my astonishment, then, when I hear from you that our relations have become delicate through *our* fault. I've been turning matters over in my mind for the last few days and so far I've been able to discover only two possible explanations: either your Naval General Staff is too deeply prejudiced against us to accept the assurances of the Ministry of Foreign Affairs, or you yourselves have changed your policy towards us, for reasons unknown to us and which you are perhaps anxious we should not find out."

The Under-Secretary was a very courteous man, and this Mr Politis found remarkable enough to record, so rarely was any Fascist official at ease with good manners lest he should be suspected by men of the older world of having been a waiter or a shop-assistant. He listened to the Greek Minister's exposition with attention and he seemed genuinely astonished by the other side of the picture thus presented.

"If you like," he offered, "I will tell Count Ciano what you have just told me. I can see no reason why he should have any hostile prejudices against you. If some misunderstanding has crept in, it should not be difficult to clear it up. I take it that you like myself recognize the value of sincere collaboration between our two countries. At this moment particularly, when it seems quite certain that England has lost the war once and for all, a vast field of possibilities opens before us."

"By all means convey the tale of my mystification to Count Ciano," Mr Politis assented, "although he has heard most of the details already from my own lips. Count Ciano knows well that the prime thought of the Hellenic Government is to preserve the country from the calamity of war, which so far as we are concerned can only be achieved by the strictest neutrality. Therefore it would be inconsistent for us to run counter to our own objective by flirting with the English. Our policy is clear and loyal, our conscience is perfectly calm. We want to hope to the last moment that this will be properly appreciated."

In commenting on this conversation Mr Politis pointed out that before it took place Mr Benini and Count Ciano had been summoned to the Palazzo Venezia to hear their instructions from the Duce himself. Therefore, he concluded, he no longer had the slightest doubt that all the direct attacks and all the indirect menaces had been psychological preparation for the discussion of some kind of collaboration which would involve the repudiation of the British guarantee and still further concessions of every sort. *"The method is certainly a bad one and deprived of all psychological sense, but it is essentially Fascist,"* his despatch concluded.

Only three days before this conversation there had been another example of Fascist inability to grasp the working of a more mature mind, when on the anniversary of the Metaxas régime of the Fourth of August the Stefani Agency published a fulsome tribute to it. On the same day the Rome Radio broadcast a talk in Greek about the great results achieved by the National Government and the political virtues of General Metaxas, thanks to whom Greece would find herself in the 'clime' of the Axis and of the New Europe. Presumably these ingenuous cocks crowing on the Fascist dunghill expected an immediate response of humble gratitude from the Hellenes. When it was not forthcoming another trick was played.

On August 11th the Stefani Agency announced:

"The Albanian population under Greece is much upset by a horrible political crime committed on the Albanian frontier. Hoggia, the great Albanian patriot born in the *irredenta* of Tsamouria, was savagely murdered on Albanian territory. His corpse was found without its head. It was established that the murderers were Greek emissaries, that they carried with them to Greece the decapitated head, and handed it over to the Greek authorities who for a long time had put a price on the head of our compatriot. It was established further that the head had been carried round from village to village by order of the Greek authorities and publicly exposed to intimidate our brothers of the *irredenta*. Hoggia had been obliged, some time ago, to flee from Tsamouria to escape the persecution of the Greek authorities, who did not forgive his untiring propaganda to reunite Tsamouria to the motherland."

This sensational opening was supplemented by false figures about the relative strength of the Greek and Albanian populations in that district, where out of a total of 60,000 it was alleged that 50,000 were persecuted Albanians who hoped that the hour of their deliverance was at hand. This was the technique of Hitler in Czechoslovakia and Poland. The correct figures showed a total of 65,074 inhabitants of whom only 18,109 could claim Albanian extraction.

The facts about the patriot Hoggia were not more accurate. He had been murdered in his sleep two months earlier by a pair of fellow Albanian shepherds who had fled across the frontier and whose extradition the Italian Government had notified the Greek Government they would formally request. This request had never been made. Hoggia himself, or more correctly Daout Hodza, had been in point of fact a fugitive from justice for twenty years. His bloody record was noteworthy even in a country like Albania where life is cheap. In October 1919 he had been sentenced by default to imprisonment for life for the premeditated murder of two Albanian Musulmans with the help of two Christian accomplices and a fellow Musulman. In November 1919 he had been sentenced by default to twenty years' imprisonment for the murder of two more Musulmans. In June 1921 he had been sentenced by default to seventeen years' imprisonment for acts of brigandage, cattle-robbing, attempt at murder, and carrying prohibited arms. In December 1921 he had been sentenced by default to four years' imprisonment for attempted blackmail. In 1923 he had been sentenced by default to eighteen years' imprisonment for attempted murder. In May 1925 he had been sentenced to death by default for rape and blackmail, and finally in October 1925 he had been once more sentenced to death by default for brigandage.

The lies of the Stefani Agency were contradicted from Athens; but these contradictions were not published in the Italian Press, which gave itself over to a debauch of hysterical comment. The peak of this was reached on August 14th. Farinacci in the *Regime Fascista* wrote that the carrying round of Hoggia's head from village to village which had excited so much horror all over Europe was an 'ordinary phenomenon' in Greece where the Albanian massacres had taken the colour out of the worst Armenian massacres. The picture of a Europe which had survived the horror of what the Germans had done in Poland being shaken by the thought of the treatment accorded to this piece of carrion which Mussolini was nuzzling so voluptuously is a typical expression of the New Inhumanism.

Gayda discovered in the murder of Hoggia the latest chapter of the policy of terrorization directed by Athens against Albania at English instigation in order to create a military diversion. Hieromancy led the *Popolo di Roma* to extract from Hoggia's headless corpse evidence of how necessary Venetian sovereignty had been for Corfu and added that in the plan for the reconstruction of Europe such a sovereignty would include the whole section between the Adriatic and the Black Sea. The Italian advance into British Somaliland had gone to Mussolini's head. The Doge had been content to wed the Adriatic. The Duce demanded for himself a harem of the Adriatic, the Ionian, the Aegean and the Marmora seas. He was dreaming of Constantinople to which by a Fascist reading of history he was entitled through the Venetian aggression of Dandolo in the Fourth Crusade.

In Rome Mr Politis tried to make up his mind what all this bellowing portended. Was an attack on Greece imminent or were the Italians merely going to raise the question of Tsamouria? Positive data on which to hazard an opinion were at present lacking. In diplomatic circles it was taken for granted that Germany did not want the peace of the Balkans disturbed at present and that Italy would not be able to act alone. The general opinion was that Mussolini intended to raise the question of Tsamouria and try to drag Greece along the road of concessions as had been done so successfully by his partner with the Rumanians.

Mr Politis, however, thought it would be a mistake to rely too much on these conclusions, however plausible they appeared. He had positive information that the invasion of England had been postponed for the present. It was impossible to know what modifications this change of military plans might entail for the policy of the Axis in general, and more particularly as it affected the Balkans. It was difficult to estimate how far German policy fitted in with Italian ideas about the future. It was difficult for the lucid mind of Mr Politis then, and the subsequent events of two years have not made the solution of the riddle any easier.

Probably the best answer was given by the Roman cynic who said, 'If the English win we shall lose, if the Germans win we shall be lost.'

On the Feast of the Assumption, the day after Mr Politis sent that perplexed telegram to Athens, the Greek light cruiser *Helle* was torpedoed by an Italian submarine in the harbour of the island of Tenos.

46

CHAPTER FOUR

IN the first year of the war of Greek Independence the Blessed Virgin appeared in a dream to a nun on Tenos and revealed to her the spot where an eikon of the Annunciation was buried. The eikon was found, and ever since it has been the medium of innumerable miraculous cures. The two great Feasts on which the eikon is exposed to the veneration of the faithful are the Annunciation of Our Lady on March 25th and the Assumption of Our Lady on August 15th. The former Feast has had for a hundred and twenty years a political as well as a religious significance, for it celebrates, besides the Angelic Message on the fulfilment of which Christendom has been built, the raising of the standard by Archbishop Germanos and the proclamation of Greek Independence on that heartening day in the year of grace and glory 1821. The pilgrims who thronged to the island every year on that Spring Feast found there a perpetual refreshment of Panhellenic aspirations in the long decades of deferred hope that dragged on during the nineteenth century. From Crete and Rhodes and Cyprus, from the mountains of the Epirus and Macedonia, from Anatolia and the vales of Thessaly, from the Ionian isles, from Constantinople and Alexandria, and even from the far Crimea, Hellenes met at Tenos; and with the passage of the years some of these ancient Greek places came back to Greece. Once upon a time the little island of Delos a few miles away from Tenos was the centre of a Pan-hellenic festival, and between the pilgrims who sailed to Delos from the Piraeus nearly two and a half millenniums ago and the pilgrims who sail from the Piraeus to Tenos to-day the difference is slight enough.

The other great Feast kept on the Assumption is entirely religious and devoid of any political significance, and this was the one Mussolini chose to desecrate. Presumably he selected Tenos for the outrage because it had once been a Venetian stronghold, and because to this day half the population is Roman Catholic. Yet the end of the Venetian rule was ignoble enough. It provides indeed a perfect illustration of the reasons why Venice failed, and why the more virile Greeks who rescued from the Turks the land of their ancestors

47

abandoned to them by the Venetians are right to resent the claims of modern Italy to be the posthumous child of the wedding between the Doge and the Adriatic.

The ruined fortress of Exoburgo, its very name half Greek half Latin, stands on the highest peak of Tenos, surrounded by the crumbling remains of the Venetian settlement. In 1714 the Proveditore Balbi decided to give it up to the Turks. He and his garrison of fourteen badly-dressed soldiers, half of whom were French deserters, marched out with full military honours and left behind them two hundred Catholic families to be sold as slaves in Africa. Even degenerate Venice found the behaviour of their Proveditore beyond the limit and he was sentenced to lifelong imprisonment when he returned home. Two hundred and twenty-six years later a plebeian of the Romagna would challenge the record for cynical cowardice established in Tenos by a patrician of Venice.

Until after the First World War the Greek and Latin calendars maintained the difference of thirteen days; but when Mussolini decided to profane the Feast of the Assumption in the year 1940 it was profaned equally for Latins and for Greeks. The Ursuline Nuns up at Loutria were as much affronted as their Orthodox sisters of the Idiorrhythmic Rule, which with typical Greek individualism changes the superior periodically and gives every nun a house to herself. This nunnery claims a life of twelve hundred years; and the tresses of hair cut from novices centuries back hang like dusty cobwebs in the charnel-house where the skulls stand in rows, the oldest of them eyeless before the first stone was hewn for Exoburgo.

At half-past eight on the morning of August 15th the light cruiser *Helle*, dressed with bunting from peak to stern in honour of the Feast, was moored in the roadstead 800 metres off the pier of the little harbour of St. Nicolas, successor he in the lordship of the Aegean to Poseidon who once had a temple here. The quays and the greenish pier were black with people. The diminutive market-place, the balconies, windows and roofs overlooking the harbour, the street winding up toward the white marble church, all were black with people.

Suddenly a torpedo struck the *Helle* amidships under the boiler. Two other torpedoes narrowly missed the cruiser and travelled across the peacock-coloured water to explode against the pier, where an Armenian woman died of heart-failure and several other people were

Gunners aboard a Greek Torpedo Boat

Evzones guarding the Greek flag on the Acropolis

slightly injured. The boiler of the *Helle* burst. The fuel catching fire poured through the ship and kept her unable to move. The crew tried with the help of steamers in the port to tow her into shallow water, but the hawsers parted and the fire raging below forced the crew to abandon ship. The officers and the captain were the last to leave the *Helle*, which sank at a quarter to ten. Only one of the crew was killed, but twenty-nine were injured.

It will need much more gallantry than the Italian Navy has so far shown to wash from its red, white and green ensign the stain of that foul deed. Perhaps already one of the crew of that submarine has gasped in death an agonized appeal to some black Byzantine Virgin in the church of his home high in the limestone above the Salernian Gulf or by the long Parthenopean shore. Let Hellenes of their charity remember that the crimes committed against their bodies were committed by Fascism against the souls of simple folk in Italy.

At twenty-past six on the evening of that same August 15th the old Brindisi packet-boat *Frinton* was machine-gunned by two Italian planes when two miles off the coast of Crete.

In the official communiqué issued from Athens about the sinking of the *Helle* the submarine was stated to be 'of unknown nationality'. This was strictly true at the time; but a naval enquiry held on board the *Averoff* on August 21st established conclusively from the fragments of the two torpedoes which missed the *Helle* that they were Italian. So anxious were the Government not to allow the result of the enquiry to be known in Greece that an order was issued forbidding the Press to publish any news about the nationality of the submarine or even general speculations about the sinking of the *Helle*. The mood of the Greek Government at this moment was expressed by Mr George Vlachos in his open letter to Adolf Hitler which was published in the *Kathimerini* of March 8th, 1941, the relevant extract from which is given now:

"When, after the sinking of the *Helle* by an Italian submarine in the port of Tenos, she found the remains of torpedoes and with them the proof that those torpedoes were Italian, Hellas was silent. Why? Because if she had divulged the truth she would have been compelled either to declare war or to have war declared against her. Hellas never wanted war with Italy, neither by herself nor with allies, whether those allies were British or Balkan. She wanted only to live as tranquilly as possible in her own little bit of the world because she was worn out, because she had fought too many wars, and because her geographical position exposed her unfavourably alike to the enmity of Germany by land or to the enmity of Britain by sea.

"At the time when the *Helle* was sunk, Hellas, besides her own yearning for peace, had a guarantee bearing two signatures: the signature of Italy, which guaranteed her against all aggression by Italy and the signature of Britain which was a spontaneous guarantee of Hellenic integrity. Nevertheless, when, a little while after the sinking of the *Helle* Italy was displaying clearer signs than before of future aggression, Hellas, now convinced that the first signature was worthless, did not turn as she ought to have turned toward the country which had given her that second signature. She turned—do you remember, Excellency?—toward yourself, and she asked for your protection. What was the answer we were given then? Exactly what was said I do not claim to know, but this I do know, because I heard it from the lips of our late President himself, that Germany replied to our request by advising us not to offer any pretexts—that is to say, not to mobilize—and to remain peaceful."

The exact date of that appeal to Hitler, which would have been unimaginable from the lips of a Venizelos, does not transpire; but there seems no doubt that the sinking of the *Helle* was regarded in Berlin at the time not as a crime against humanity, but as a crime against expediency, which was much more serious.

On August 16th Mr Politis notified Athens that the conference of foreign correspondents in Rome had been informed that the sinking of the *Helle* was an English manœuvre to upset the Balkans and embitter still further Greco-Italian relations. The proof of this was that the English before they had had time to verify the facts had rushed to announce by radio that no British submarine was in these waters. By contrast Italy, faithful to her well-known tradition of honesty, had required three days in order to make the necessary verifications which enabled her to declare to-day that no sinking had been signalled to the Naval General Staff and that no Italian submarine was in the neighbourhood. When asked, no doubt with a suggestion of astonishment, what was the date of the sinking, the Director replied that it was either August 13th or August 14th.

It is to be noted that the Italian Press campaign against Greece reached its apogee on August 14th, so that for the aggression then contemplated it may have been planned to sink a Greek warship on that very date and as usual with the incompetent Italian Navy the plan had gone wrong. On the other hand the warning from Berlin which Mussolini had certainly received by August 15th may have inspired this evasiveness about the exact date. The Italian Press was ordered on the 16th to reduce the fervour of its polemics against Greece.

No evening papers were published in Italy on the 15th on account of the holiday, and the morning papers of the 16th gave no news of the *Helle*; they published instead a personal attack on the King of the Hellenes whom they presented as more English than Greek, and having secured beatification for Hoggia, the Albanian martyr, they now started the process of canonization.

The news of the *Helle* was first published in the evening papers of the 16th, and on the following morning the trend of the comment was to insist that this British attempt to divert attention from the horrors and atrocities being committed against Albanians must be guarded against. Farinacci, one of the major ruffians of Fascism, squirting ink from his organ, the *Regime Fascista*, pretended that the damage caused by the English sinking of the *Helle* would be shared because the English shipbuilders had not yet been paid for her by the Greeks. It was stressed that in Germany the sinking of the *Helle* was attributed to Churchill with the object of extending the war to the Balkans. The presentation of the British Prime Minister as a peripatetic Guy Fawkes is a permanent feature of the German Press. It was a comic strip started the day after war broke out when the *Athenia* was sunk.

By August 18th Italian comment on the *Helle* outrage was mute. It had been made clear to Mussolini that this was not the moment to set the Balkans ablaze, and thereby imperil Germany's work in Rumania, Bulgaria, and Yugoslavia, not to mention Turkey. Italy's right to the Mediterranean as her sphere of action was recognized by Germany, but not if her action there might upset Axis plans for the war as a whole. If Mussolini was insisting that the occupation of Corfu and the Epirus was vital to his security, he was probably told that this must be achieved by diplomacy not by force, or, to write in terms of Axis morality, by blackmail not by thuggery. Perhaps he was reminded at the same time that the offensive against Egypt would provide him with plenty of the action he desired in the Mediterranean; the evacuation of Fort Capuzzo after a British naval bombardment did not suggest that this offensive was proceeding as it should. No doubt Hitler himself, who lost 180 planes on August 15th, was in no mood to be amenable.

Diplomatic persuasion over the Epirus was resumed with fresh ardour. The Press was filled with insults to the Hellenic nation. The Greeks were vain, good at commerce because of their cunning, not at all warlike, strangers to the proud and upright virtues which distinguished a martial people, experts of deceit and brutality. This paved the way for the assertion next day that eight Albanian notables of Tsamouria had been burnt alive in a church by the Greek authorities, which was clear evidence according to Virginio Gayda, the mouthpiece of Mussolini smeared with his master's spittle, that there was an arrangement between Greece and Great Britain to invade Albania.

Italy must thwart this plot by the firmness of her policy which, though it would not embark upon any adventures (a promise to the big shot in Berlin to abstain from hi-jacking), was ready to defend the national rights of Albania and establish law and order in the Balkan peninsula. It was time that Greece paid attention to the advice yapped by the now muzzled Yugoslav Press that she should follow the example of Rumania and repudiate the British guarantee. enlisted by the Italian Press to bring Greece to her senses. The correspondent of the *Giornale d' Italia* in San Sebastian telegraphed that for the last forty-eight hours British propaganda had been busy spreading disquieting rumours about Greco-Italian relations obviously in order to find a pretext for implementing the British guarantee. But what could England do for Greece at this moment when she could not even find the troops necessary to defend Somaliland? The guarantee was nothing but a trap to secure Greek naval bases. And then, as abruptly as all this hubbub in the Press had started on August 11th, on August 27th it subsided.

No doubt Hitler had insisted once again that for the present the Balkans must not be disturbed. He had to settle the Transylvanian dispute between Hungary and Rumania at the end of the month. Moreover, the failure of his own offensive against Britain meant that the grand strategy of the war would have to be re-examined.

While the Press campaign was raging in Italy, intelligence was reaching the Greek General Staff of the steady reinforcement of. Italian troops in Albania and of an intention to concentrate them not only in the direction of the Epirus but also of Macedonia.

On August 23rd General Metaxas informed the Greek Ministers in Berlin and Rome that these concentrations on the Albanian frontier had made it imperative for reasons of elementary prudence to call up certain categories, not classes, of reservists from this region to reinforce the troops covering the frontier. There was no question of mobilization but simply of reinforcing the frontier garrisons. This notification to Berlin suggests that General Metaxas' appeal to Hitler had already been made.

That same August 23rd Mr Politis telegraphed to Athens that Count Ciano, when asked by the representative of a Great Power (Russia or the U.S.A.?) if it was true that an ultimatum to Greece was imminent, had replied that the rumour was absolutely false and only due to the recent activity of the Press. The Italian Foreign Minister added that he was hopeful of a pacific solution. In sending this information Mr Politis begged General Metaxas to use every vigilance that could not be construed as provocative. He said he mistrusted these Italian assurances on principle. They were too much like those given about Albania a few hours before its invasion in 1939.

Mr Politis took the opportunity to remind General Metaxas that recent German intervention had nothing of the character of a stable guarantee. Germany's moderating influence depended on a given military situation and would follow the course of circumstances. Although Italy occupied only an inferior position in the Axis as a dynamic force, she was nevertheless necessary to it, and the consciousness of this afforded Italy the possibility to exploit her position. Italy had gotten herself into a longer war than she expected, and she urgently required a substantial success. Moreover, it was to be remembered that the rulers of Italy regarded Greece as a disagreeable obstacle in the way of their ambitious plans and that from the very beginning of Fascism it had been thus. Italy was fearful of missing an opportunity perhaps unique. Rightly or wrongly Italy believed that Turko-Russian relations were far from good and that this would neutralize Turkey. She might have decided that a sudden occupation in overwhelming force of those parts of Greece in which she was interested would present the world with a *fait accompli*. It was not known what importance the Italians attached to the eventual danger of a simultaneous occupation by the British of other parts of

Greece the moment the latter found the Italians would not face them at sea. Although for the moment an attack seemed unlikely it was more than ever indicated that Greece should never lose sight of the fact that such an attack was possible at any moment. What would do most to mitigate the aggressive ardour of the Italians would be their appreciation that the enterprise would not be so easy.

Anybody who has watched blackshirts gathered in mass will have perceived the impression they give of swarming cockroaches, and it is like cockroaches that one hears them crack and split under the polished boots of the Greek Minister in Rome. His analysis is masterly, and his far-sighted estimate of what Germany would do is remarkable.

And here for a moment before the curtain rises on the sublime tragedy itself it is worth while to pause and savour the tragic irony of an article by the mouthpiece of Mussolini, Virginio Gayda, once a journalist of international renown whose soul was converted by Fascism into cash:

"The problem of the relations between Italy, Albania, and Greece has now taken shape and the loud protests in the Italian Press caused by recent events in Tsamouria show signs of dying down, but the fulminating excitement of the Greek Press continues. This now frequently takes a literary turn, and assumes the elocution of declamatory heroics, although in the presence of hard facts, of the grave political situation, and of the problem set for solution these papers should have been careful to express themselves less ridiculously.

"Here is the academician Spyro Melas brandishing in the columns of the *Hestia* not only his own sword but the spear of Pallas Athene fetched down from the Parthenon to defend the alleged rights of the Hellenes. 'Greece,' Mr Melas claims, 'has held aloft for three thousand years the torch of clarity and calm, of poise and moderation.'

"The *Kathimerini* declares that all Greeks are at one with the opinion of their Chief—an opinion, by the way, which to us is still unknown, and 'will not hesitate to sacrifice themselves if need be'.

"The *Typos* prefers to stick to heroic legends and recall the exploits of Leonidas at Thermopylae and ancient Hellenic victories over the Persian host, proclaiming that 'the Greek nation is more than united and has never submitted since it appeared in history'.

"No doubt the Greek papers exaggerate. We understand the bellicose spirit by which they are so generously animated. We do not understand quite so well this inclination to abandon themselves utterly to Utopia, an Utopia which borders upon the ridiculous. They would do well to lay aside literature and heroic memories in order to fit themselves into the frame of present realities. If in truth Greece does hold aloft the torch of calm and poise, let her make haste to carry it into that Albanian territory left under her dominion, in order to illuminate the intolerable and dangerous conditions she has created there. If instead of doing that she devotes herself to proclaiming by facile historical improvisations her time-long invincibility, we find ourselves obliged to remind her that Roman Generals more than once forced her to yield. And if she insists on reviving in 1940 the glorious memory of Thermopylae and the Persian javelins, we find ourselves obliged to remind her that the weapons with which nowadays wars are fought and won are armoured cars, aircraft, and guns of heavy calibre. In these polemics, which from now on serve no purpose, the poise and moderation of which Greece boasts herself to have been the repository for three thousand years should no longer be found wanting."

Sulla no doubt was the Roman General particularly in Mussolini's mind—Lucius Cornelius Sulla, who swept North Africa and sacked Athens. The most terrifying aspect of this immense tragedy in which humanity now plays is that the two chief villains are figures of comedy. Melpomene holds before her face the mask of her sister Thalia, and two buffoons lead the dance of death.

Soon after this, the *Hestia* was denounced again for its provocation of Italy in reminding the young officers of the Hellenic navy on the occasion of their taking the oath of loyal service that they must do honour to the fair fame of Greek seamen and show themselves worthy of the country's noble maritime traditions from the Argonauts through Themistocles and Salamis down to Coundouriotis and Cape Helles. Mr Politis found it really strange that a simple evocation of the battles of Salamis and Helles should be stigmatized as provocation. True, the table of dates in the Duce's history would have had to take him back to the time when half Italy was Magna Graecia to find comparable prowess at sea, but as a *casus belli* the expedition that sailed from Iolkos in search of the Golden Fleece would seem inadequate in 1940.

On September 14th Mr Politis had a conversation with Mr Anfuso, Count Ciano's *chef du cabinet*, about the unimpeded passage of Greek commercial vessels to Alexandria. Mr Anfuso was at pains to impress on the Greek Minister the care Count Ciano had devoted to this question.

"Naturally enough, indeed," the Director said, "seeing that we have no desire to upset the people of Greece against whom we have no ground for complaint. What we do complain of is the way the Greek Government persists in its Anglophile tendencies. Please note," he went on, without heeding his visitor's gesture of protest, "that I am expressing only my personal opinion at this moment, and not speaking in my official capacity. I am not going to formulate concrete grievances, but the attitude of the Greek Press, for instance, does not suggest friendly feelings towards Italy."

Mr Politis replied that in view of the encouragement given in Italy to abuse of Greece in the Albanian Press, it was hardly reasonable for the Italian Press to accuse Greece of provocation when the examples of Miltiades or Themistocles were extolled to the present generation.

"Ah, but it's when such allusions are seen in the frame of British propaganda that words like these acquire importance they would not possess in themselves," Mr Anfuso objected.

A week later, Mr Politis was advising his Government that Greece had reason to be thankful to the famous Hodza for his part in clarifying Italian designs. Nevertheless, paradoxical though it might seem, the fact that Italy had had to withdraw from the affair of the Albanian brigand with some damage to her prestige had increased the danger to Greece. Vanity had been wounded by the hilarity which the Hodza drama had aroused. Fascism never forgave those who laughed at it, and would never forgive Greece for supplying the laugh. "It will seize the first opportunity to be revenged", Mr Politis wrote. "To the original hostility has been added the rancour caused by loss of prestige. . . . It is certain that we are approaching a decision, in a few weeks. We shall either have to face very grave events or we shall enter a period of less tension."

Four days later on September 24th Mr Politis had heard from a sure source of accurate information that Germany was opposing any plan to liquidate Balkan questions if it might involve military complications. On the other hand, Germany could not oppose any Italian efforts to achieve her aims by diplomatic methods, and indeed would be compelled eventually to support such efforts up to a point.

This communication from the Greek Minister was an echo of

Ribbentrop's visit to Rome and of Ciano's visit to Berlin. The Tripartite Pact between the Axis and Japan was staged for September 27th. Germany for the moment was preoccupied with her plans for the complete occupation of Rumania. Russia was evincing signs of restlessness. Mussolini must wait for Greece.

In Athens hope of a German veto on the Italian project was still green. A representative had been sent to Berlin at the end of August with a view to negotiations later about a new clearing agreement. Germany, which had already bought the Greek tobacco crop, was now buying up the currants of Crete where commercial emissaries were busying themselves over more than currants. We can detect in that telegram from Mr Politis a tactful warning to General Metaxas against undue optimism. And it may be more than a coincidence that the German Consul in Salonika, speaking at a dinner he was giving in honour of the Fair, should say on the very day after this warning was despatched how anxious he was to express the appreciation of the German people for the pacific efforts of the great statesman who directed the policy of Greece.

"We are convinced," he declared, "that in spite of the tempest which rages in Europe and round Europe peace will be preserved for the people of Greece, who have our complete sympathy."

In the September number of the review *Espansione del Impero* an article appeared pointing out the terrible threat to Italy of British naval bases in Greece:

> "In the eyes of the perspicacious Foreign Office Greece, whose aggrandisement after the war of 1914–18 had been beyond every hope and every merit, should serve as a counterpoise to the influence of Italian power in the Near East and in case of war provide bases for the British fleet. That was why the English have always egged on Greece to make stupid claims on the Dodecanese. . . . Italy can never allow Greek bases to be used by the British navy. Should that happen, or perhaps just before it does happen, Italy's action will be crushing and taken without wasting torpedoes on an old and innocent Greek ship."

Alas, the perspicacity attributed to the British Foreign Office was as imaginary as Hoggia's patriotism, and like Hoggia the Foreign Office during the years that succeeded the First World War was headless. If Greece had been built up as a counterpoise to Fascist imperialism Italy would never have entered the Second World War;

and if the Italian Government, even before Mussolini was in control, had been punished for dishonouring its signature to a solemn agreement, the Dodecanese would have been handed over to Greece in recognition of the justice of these 'stupid claims'. The last British statesman who divined what Greece might one day mean to Britain was Mr Lloyd George. The Italians whom he had outmanœuvred at conference after conference during the war and then once more at Versailles did not appreciate the difference between a Welshman and an Englishman; and they never believed in the gullibility of British statesmen until Mr Chamberlain visited Rome. After Mr Churchill took the helm, however, nothing could have persuaded Mussolini that the British would not seize the first favourable moment to occupy the harbours and islands of Greece. Beginning to despair of intimidating Greece by threats, he concentrated upon persuading Hitler to allow him to have recourse to action.

It seems certain that the attack on Greece was decided upon at the meeting between Hitler and Mussolini on the Brenner on October 4th, and equally certain that the pair felt confident that Greece would not resist a display of armed force. The world heard a comic echo from that colloquy on the Brenner when Mussolini announced that Hitler had granted him the privilege of helping in the aerial offensive against Britain. The cur had wagged a propitiatory tail and had earned a pat from his master. Mussolini offered Hitler that Italian squadron which was shot to pieces over the Thames less than a fortnight later as some fawning pimp of Santa Lucia whispers to a fish-eyed German tourist of the maiden tribute he can procure him from the Neapolitan slums.

For the rest of that October information reported a steady increase in the concentration of Italian troops along the frontier, and reconnaissance flights by Italian planes were made daily all over Greece. On October 13th the Greek Minister in Budapest telegraphed:

I learn from an absolutely reliable source that in the Hungarian Ministry of Foreign Affairs they consider the attack of Italy on Greece imminent.

On October 21st the Greek Vice-Consul at Santi Quaranta telegraphed:

Military forces in this region have been moved up towards our frontier.

On October 23rd, the Greek Minister in Rome telegraphed:

> *Rumours of an imminent attack on us continue. A military source of information fixes the date for action to be launched against Greece between the 25th and 28th of this month.*

On October 25th the Greek Minister in Berne telegraphed:

> *Information from Berlin says the attack against Greece is a matter of days.*

On October 25th the Greek Consul-General at Tirana telegraphed:

> *Transport is being requisitioned. Movements of individuals from place to place have been extremely difficult. Telegraphic communications are being obstructed. From the Italian General Staff here officers are leaving for Argyrocastro. The general impression is that we are on the eve of Italian action.*

On October 26th the Greek Minister in Rome telegraphed:

> *The Air Ministry has suspended the service between Athens and Rhodes.*

On that day the Stefani Agency was publishing stories about Greek bands penetrating into Albanian territory, and on October 27th a fantasy was invented about Greek or British agents trying to blow up the harbour-master's office at Santi Quaranta. Now, these tales were never exploited and were therefore quite unnecessary in view of the date of the Italian attack. It seems possible that the date originally chosen was October 31st and that this was put forward to October 28th in order that the Romagna blacksmith could present Hitler with 'something attempted, something done' when they met at Florence on the morning of the 28th. Moreover, October 28th was a holy day in the Fascist calendar and was celebrated as the anniversary of the March on Rome in 1922. Until then it had been an inauspicious date, being the most disastrous day of the Caporetto rout.

There was no Italian in attendance when on October 23rd Hitler made that long journey to visit General Franco on the Hispano-French frontier or on October 24th when he met Marshal Pétain at Montoire. Mussolini may not have felt completely at ease about either of those meetings, even if they were agreed upon between him and Hitler as necessary to the grand strategic plan for the Mediterranean which they had decided to follow, and which will be discussed in due course. The bogy of French and German cooperation which had been haunting him ever since the Armistice may have made him particularly anxious to anticipate by an enterprise of his own anything like the surrender of the French fleet to Germany and the immediate fall of his own stock in consequence. In the event he need not have worried. Neither General Franco nor Marshal Pétain was anxious to share in the glory of driving the British out of the Mediterranean.

If that sudden change in the date be accepted as a fact, the party given to prominent Athenians by Count Grazzi at the Italian Legation on October 27th may have to shed some of its picturesque treachery. The Italian Minister may have been just as unaware then as his guests of what was being planned in Rome. Possibly he did not receive his instructions until the telegram from Rome was decyphered in Athens on that very Sunday. Be that as it may, shortly before three o'clock in the morning of October 28th General Metaxas was woken by the ringing of the telephone. When he picked up the receiver he heard a voice he did not recognize:

"Ici le ministre de France qui désire vous voir immédiatement."

General Metaxas, supposing that the French Minister had something of extreme urgency to communicate, told him to come along to his house. A few minutes later General Metaxas went down in his dressing-gown to open the front door and found that his visitor was the Italian Minister bringing with him this ultimatum:

"The Italian Government has had to take notice from time to time, during the present conflict, of the way in which the Greek Government has adopted and maintained an attitude which is at odds not only with the normal relations of peace and good neighbourliness between two nations, but with the duties incumbent upon the Government of a neutral State.

"From time to time the Italian Government has found it necessary to recall the Greek Government to the fulfilment of its duties and to protest against their systematic violation, a violation particularly grave inasmuch as the Greek Government has allowed its territorial waters, its coasts and its harbours to be used by the English fleet in the course of warlike operations, has facilitated the refuelling of British airplanes, and has permitted the organization of a military intelligence service in the Greek Archipelago, all against Italy. The Greek Government is perfectly aware of these facts which have been the subject of diplomatic *démarches* by Italy to which the Greek Government—and it should have

taken into account the grave consequences of such an attitude—
has not responded by any measures to protect its neutrality, but,
on the contrary, has increased its assistance to the British armed
forces and its collaboration with the enemies of Italy.

"The Italian Government possesses proof that this collaboration
has been foreseen and arranged by the Greek Government itself
through military, naval, and aerial understandings. The Italian
Government is not referring only to the British guarantee accepted
by Greece as a part of action directed against the security of Italy,
but to express and precise engagements entered into by the Greek
Government for the purpose of placing at the disposition of the
Powers at war with Italy important strategic points in Greek territory, by which is understood air bases in Thessaly and Macedonia,
designed for an attack on Albanian territory.

"The Italian Government must remind the Greek Government of the provocative action carried on with regard to the Albanian Nation, by the terrorist policy which it has adopted with
regard to the population of Tsamouria and by the persistent
efforts to create disorders along its frontiers. On that account the
Italian Government was compelled—but uselessly—to remind the
Greek Government of the inevitable consequences which such a
policy would entail where Italy was concerned.

"All this can no longer be tolerated by Italy. The neutrality
of Greece has become more and more a pure and simple pretence.

"The responsibility for this situation falls primarily on England
and on her intention to involve more and more countries in
the war.

"The Italian Government considers it obvious that the policy
of the Greek Government has been and is directed toward trans-
forming Greek territory, or at least to allow Greek territory to be
transformed, into a base for warlike operations against Italy. This
would only lead to armed conflict between Italy and Greece, a
conflict which the Italian Government has every intention to
avoid. Consequently the Italian Government has decided to
demand from the Greek Government—as a guarantee of Greece's
neutrality and as a guarantee of Italy's security—facilities to
occupy with its armed forces, for the duration of the present conflict with England, certain strategic points of Greek territory.
The Italian Government demands that the Greek Government
shall not oppose this occupation and shall not obstruct the free
passage of the troops intended to effect it. These troops do not
come as enemies of the Greek people, and the Italian Government
has not the slightest intention by this temporary occupation of
certain strategic points, dictated by necessity as it arises and having

a purely defensive character, to prejudice in any way the sovereignty and the independence of Greece.

"The Italian Government demands that the Greek Government shall immediately give their military authorities the necessary orders to ensure that this occupation can be effected in a peaceful manner. If the Italian troops should meet with resistance, such resistance will be broken by arms, and the Greek Government would have to assume the responsibility for whatever consequences might follow from it."

"What exactly are the strategic points mentioned in this communication?" General Metaxas asked.

"I cannot tell your Excellency. My Government has not informed me." The Italian Minister paused for a moment, in some embarrassment. Then he remembered that in Fascism decency was a sign of weakness. "I only know that the ultimatum expires at six o'clock this morning," he said.

"Then this communication is a declaration of war by Italy on Greece."

"No, Excellency, an ultimatum."

"It is tantamount to a declaration of war."

"But you will give the facilities my Government requests?"

"No," said Metaxas, and with that negative the little General unified Hellas beyond his most sanguine hopes as a political craftsman, expunged the blots upon his own career, and added to the world's oldest and richest roll of honour another immortal name.

CHAPTER FIVE

THE Proclamation of the Prime Minister to the Greek people:

October 28th, 1940

"The moment has come for us to fight for the independence, for the integrity, and for the honour of Greece. Although we have observed the strictest neutrality, with absolute impartiality towards all, Italy, denying to us the right to live the life of free Hellenes, demanded from me at 3 o'clock this morning the surrender of portions of the national territory, to be chosen by herself, and informed me that her troops would move forward at 6 A.M. in order to take possession. I replied to the Italian Minister that I considered both the demand itself and the manner of its delivery as a declaration of war on the part of Italy against Greece.

"It is now for us to show whether we are indeed worthy of our ancestors and of the freedom won for us by our forefathers. Let the entire nation rise as one man. Fight for your country, for your wives, for your children, and for our sacred traditions.

"Now the struggle is for very existence. Νῦν ὑπὲρ πάντων ἀγών.

JOANNIS METAXAS."

The Proclamation of His Majesty the King to the Hellenes:

"The Prime Minister announced to you a short while ago the circumstances which have compelled us to go to war in reply to Italy's threat to suppress the independence of Greece. At this solemn moment I am confident that every Greek man and woman will do their duty to the last and will show themselves worthy of our glorious past.

"With faith in God and in the destiny of the Race, the Nation, united and disciplined as one man, will fight in defence of hearth and home until final victory..

"Given at the Palace of Athens, October 28th, 1940.

GEORGE II."

First War Communiqué of the General Staff, October 28th, 1940:

"Since 5.30 this morning Italian military forces have been attacking our advanced units on the Greco-Albanian frontier. Our forces are defending the soil of the country."

On that October morning the people of Athens woke to the shriek of sirens and the angry ominous clangour and tolling of the church bells: πόλεμος! πόλεμος! πόλεμος! War! War! War! Two-hundred thousand times more swiftly, and ah, how much more easily than Pheidippides, who had to run a hundred and fifty miles in forty-eight hours to give Sparta the news of the Persian landing in Euboea, the Athens wireless could give in a moment the news of the Italian invasion to all Hellas, and as a single soul all Hellas answered. From the olive-groves of Mytilene, from the vineyards of Samos, from the high pastures of Arcadia and the stubble-fields of Thessaly, from the tobacco factories of Thrace and the mart of Salonika, from busy Patras and quiet Naupaktos of the rust-red walls, from Thebes and Corinth and Sparta, from the Ionian Isles and the Cyclades and the Northern Sporades, from Marathon and Salamis, from Crete the cradle of our Europe, and from countless streams and vales and moun-tains sacred to memory, consecrated by legend, and immortalized by history the Hellenes came to take their stand against a nation which had betrayed its own glorious past and reverted to barbarism—eight million free Hellenes against forty-five million Italian slaves. And had not those free Hellenes themselves been at the mercy of a dic-tatorship for four years? That cannot be argued here. Whatever the merits or faults of the régime of the Fourth of August achieved by the *coup d'état* in 1936 of John Metaxas, whatever its justification or lack of justification, the unanimous echo with which Hellas re-peated that 'no' he gave to an embarrassed Italian diplomat in the small hours of that October morning was the echo not of a dictator's command but of a patriot's confidence. If John Metaxas had answered 'yes' he would have been swept away by the wrath of a proud people within a day.

The darkness and chill of that three o'clock were symbolic of that dark and chill hour of human history in which the liberty of Europe seemed to be expiring. Poland had been bestially mangled. Fin-land had been overpowered. Norway had been overwhelmed. Denmark had surrendered. Holland and Belgium had been trodden underfoot. Hungary and Rumania lay prone like two serviceable prostitutes. France had cried 'enough'. Yet Greece, disdaining the darkness and the chill, gave an answer which must outlive even the unimaginable touch of time. We who heard the news in Britain, we fighting on in that dark hour alone, grasped the dear small hand

Marshy Swamps between Jannina and Kalpaki

Greek Cavalry in Albania

of Greece offered to us in the darkness, and found a new faith in the ultimate invincibility of free men.

There is no doubt that neither Mussolini nor the General Staff of the Italian army expected even as much resistance from Greece as they had received from the few Albanians loyal to King Zog when Albania was 'conquered' on Good Friday in 1939; and as no army in Europe fights better than the Italian when serious opposition is lacking, there seemed every reason to anticipate a well-organized and picturesque triumph.

As early as August at the time of the *Helle* outrage the Greek Consul-General at Tirana had notified the Ministry for Foreign Affairs in Athens that Italian propagandists addressing the Albanian Civil Guard had announced their country's intention to make a present of Epirus to Albania because Greece would not offer any more resistance than Denmark had offered to German demands. At first, probably with German encouragement, Italian diplomacy had been obsessed by the fancy that General Metaxas would lend his influence to a benevolent neutrality in favour of another authoritarian State. When it became increasingly obvious that, with Germany remaining in the background so far as Greece was concerned, General Metaxas was unwilling to accord any particular advantages to Italy over Great Britain and was even likely to resist open violence, Italian fancy veered toward hopes of a revolution in Greece against the Fourth of August régime under the shock of invasion. It was significant that during the first few days of the war the Italian Press and Radio were most insistent upon the divided state of popular opinion in Greece. It was reported that dissension had broken out in the Government. The Crown Prince Paul was said to have declared himself eager for an understanding with the Axis powers and to have been banished to an island, while numerous arrests had been made in Athens. That the wish for such a revolution had begotten the fancy of it was clear from the preparations made to administer a country at the mercy of civil strife. The Italian bureaucrats followed the army toward the Albanian frontier as sedulously as the Italian whores. The Bank of Italy was getting ready to send funds to Jannina, the first military objective. Special units were to be entrusted with the distribution of food and clothing in the wake of the advancing forces. Leaflets in the Greek language were printed to reassure the natives, who it was presumed would be duly struck with terror at the sight of the tremendous invaders.

"The Italian soldiers are chivalrous and generous", proclaimed one of the playbills of the *pagliaccio* Mussolini, bundles of which would be found within a month in the hangars of the captured aerodrome at Koritza undistributed as yet by the Regia Aeronautica.

"Fear nothing for your houses, for your property, or for your women. Honour the puissant Italian army which will bring order and justice to your country. The Italian army marches toward its goal and nobody will be able to stop it."

On the face of it there were strong grounds for confidence. At the outbreak of hostilities the Italian forces in Albania consisted of the Ninth and the Eleventh Armies under General Visconti-Prasca and amounted in all to 300,000 men, among which were many of the best of Italy's troops. The front along which this force extended was roughly about ninety miles divided into three main sectors. The most southerly of these, the Epirus sector, ran from the sea to Jannina and, low lying in the extreme west, was crossed by the river Kalamas. The central sector was occupied by the great mountainous mass of the Pindus. The northern sector was concerned with Koritza on the Albanian side of the frontier and with Florina on the Greek side.

In the Epirus sector the Italian's disposed of the 23rd Ferrara Division of so-called Mountain Infantry, the 51st Sienna Division, and the Centaur Armoured Division. Besides these there were the 6th, 7th, and 19th Regiments of Cavalry, and the 3rd Regiment of Grenadiers, with eighteen batteries of heavy artillery. To contest the advance of this force there was only the 8th Division of the Greek army not at full strength.

The troops on this sector had been dosed with that rhetoric which is all too facile in the Italian tongue. When these troops were so soon retreating from Greek territory there fell into the hands of the Greek High Command an Order of the Day indited by the General Commanding the Ferrara Division on the evening of October 26th. This effusion not only offers a typical example of the turgid balderdash on which the people of Italy have been nourished since they made rods for their own backs by surrendering to the lictor's bundle or *fascio* that is the emblem of Fascism, but it also offers irrefutable proof that the attack upon Greece had been planned as long ago as April 1939.

66

CHAPTER FIVE

To the Ferrara

For nineteen months in this tough and rugged land of Albania we have been tempering our weapons and our hearts, straining toward the goal now in sight. Bound tightly in one fascio of energy and will, infantry, blackshirts, artillery, engineers, let us all, Italians and Albanians, direct our gaze towards Epirus.

We shall make green again the laurels of the Ferrara.

In this certainty, the slogan of the struggle that shall end in Victory yells to you:

"Our Day is come . . . and we must prevail."

L. Zannini,

General Officer Commanding.

If words could kill, General Zannini would have been a formidable adversary indeed.

In the Pindus sector reinforced by an extra regiment was the renowned 3rd Division of Alpini—the Iulia, with one machine-gun battalion, and a considerable strength of mountain artillery. They were opposed by one regiment of Evzones not at full strength and one battery of artillery.

In the Koritza sector was the Sixteenth Army Corps of the IXth Army consisting of the 19th Venice Division, the 29th Piedmont Division, and the 49th Parma Division, with three Albanian battalions, the 101st Machine-gun Battalion, fourteen batteries of heavy artillery, and one tank regiment. The Italians were opposed by the 9th Greek Division and one Brigade, neither at full strength.

Nobody who has read the account of the diplomatic exchanges between Greece and Italy that preceded over so many months the final act of shameless aggression will be astonished to hear how pitiably outnumbered the Greek forces on the Albanian frontier were. In the effort to preserve the country for peace General Metaxas had taken a very grave risk. In public speeches Mr Winston Churchill had several times warned the smaller neutral nations of the danger they ran from the Axis; but he was hardly likely to succeed in persuading small neutral States to heed a warning of his to which his own country had turned a deaf ear for so long, and in no single instance did Great Britain attempt to exert pressure. With complete truth Mr Churchill could declare in the House of Commons on November 5th, 1940: "We have most carefully abstained from any action likely to draw upon the Greeks the enmity of the criminal dictators. For their part, the Greeks have maintained so strict a neutrality that we were unacquainted with their dispositions or their intentions."

It will be more convenient to discuss at greater length the guilt of Germany when the time comes to write of that country's final plunge into eternal infamy. Meanwhile, it should be noted that for some days after the ultimatum Berlin appeared to encourage the idea that an arrangement could be reached between Greece and Italy through the mediation of Germany. In private conversation Prince Erbach-Schönburg, the German Minister in Athens, was at pains to dissociate his country from the action taken by its partner and to insist that the friendly relations between Greece and Germany were not in the least impaired by such action. A spokesman for the German Legation told the Athens correspondent of the United Press that there was no quarrel between Germany and Greece, and that even if Germany approved of the action taken by Italy, German and Greek relations could be maintained as they were. Finally, with an optimism inspired either by courtesy to an ally or by credulity in that ally's martial equipment, this spokesman declared that "Italy would be solely responsible for the military side of the conflict".

It is significant that until the afternoon of October 29th the German Press kept silence about what had happened in Greece. This silence can be explained only on the supposition that Berlin still believed in the possibility of an arrangement by which a tractable Greece could be exploited in the Axis interest without the bitterness of fighting, for it is hard to believe that the silence of Berlin was the embarrassment of shame. It is indeed the ἀναίδεια and ὕβρις, the shamelessness and insolence of the German people as a whole which challenge Nemesis and make an attempt to differentiate between good and bad Germans an unprofitable expense of sentimentality. Probably even in Rome it was hoped for two or three days that Greece would listen to Axis reason, for it was not until November 2nd that the Stefani Agency denied the possibility of settling the conflict by negotiation. Nevertheless, on November 6th the official German Agency D.N.B. was still speaking of contacts which had been made with a view to an arrangement between Italy and Greece. This was at once contradicted by the Stefani Agency, which declared that Italy had no intention of engaging in *pourparlers* with a view to peace and that the war machine having been set in motion it could not be stopped until the conflict had been decisively settled. After this communiqué the official German Agency brought the discussion of a possible approach to peace to an end with these words:

"Italian political circles declare that, military operations having been rendered necessary by the rejection of the Italian ultimatum, no change can be effected in the situation except through the military standpoint, that is to say through the cessation of the Greek opposition to the Italian occupation of certain bases or through the development of the operations."

In other words, Greece must accept Italy's ultimatum delivered ten days before. One asks what information the German Minister in Athens was sending to the Wilhelmstrasse about the spirit of the nation to which he was the accredited representative. Could he have given the faintest hope to Ribbentrop that such a nation would parley with the Italians, he who had seen politics turn in one blinding flash to polemics as the white-hot fire of patriotic reality consumed the quarrels and resentments, the vendettas and recriminations and schisms and revenges which had lasted in Greece since that October in 1915 when the better half of Hellas knew that mobilization to help Serbia was a farce? Did Prince Erbach dare to suggest to Berlin that *this* mobilization was a farce, when soldiers were so eager to reach the front that they were often two days ahead of their commissariat, marching on empty stomachs, and when every private car in Athens was filled with young men who could not reach the mobilization centres fast enough for their longing to be within a bayonet's thrust of the invader?

"Near Kozani we overtook column after column of marching troops and long lines of plodding burros. They were swinging northward toward Florina and had been travelling like this for several days, but the soldiers shouted and waved at us as we crawled past. They were bright-eyed, wiry-built men. They looked strong, all right, even if most of their uniforms were rumpled and messy and seemed about two sizes too big for them. 'Poor devils,' we said. 'What chance have they got against the Italian army? Maybe the Fascists' mechanized divisions are a third of the way to Athens already.' But these little Greeks, like the people in the villages, didn't seem at all worried. They kept going, up and up."

Thus wrote Leland Stowe,[1] the American correspondent, after

[1] Leland Stowe, *No Other Road to Freedom*, p. 176.

driving from Bucharest to Athens at the news of the Italian onslaught.

No doubt his belief at that time in the inability of the Greeks to resist that onslaught for any appreciable time was shared by the vast majority of onlookers. Those of us who had had personal experience of Greek valour and resolution, of Greek readiness to die for an idea, and of Greek selflessness when the cause was manifestly something greater than the individual, who in Greece as befits a nation with such a past is not easily persuaded to sacrifice his individuality, we had no doubt at all that man for man the Greek soldier was better than the Italian. But since the Nazi hordes swept into Poland events have not allowed the individual to be even a cog in the huge and horrible machine of modern war: he is no more than a minute drop of the fuel which propels it. We knew that the Italian High Command would attempt a *blitzkrieg*, and in Britain our hopes sank when we considered how little we could do to avert the success of such a *blitzkrieg*. Graziani with a great Italian army had invaded Egypt. The British forces had had to evacuate Somaliland. The German air attack upon Britain had been broken, but the threat of invasion was still imminent. The whole of our plan for defending the Mediterranean had been destroyed by the surrender of France and the intervention of Italy. We had failed to give enough material aid to Poland, Norway, Holland, and Belgium to prevent their being overwhelmed. The German taunt that British help was fatal to those who accepted it rang ever in our ears. Yes, there was some justification for the spirit of bouncing confidence wherein the Italian High Command began its *blitzkrieg*. The bombastic phrases with which from his balcony Mussolini would proclaim a week or two hence the Italian conquest of Greece must have been already shaping themselves upon that mountebank's tongue.

On October 29th the first communiqué from Italian General Headquarters was published:

"Yesterday at dawn our troops in Albania crossed the Greek frontier and penetrated enemy territory at several points. The advance continues. Our air force, in spite of unfavourable atmospheric conditions, has repeatedly bombed the military objectives assigned to it, obtaining hits on the buildings and platforms of the railway station at the port of Patras and starting fires. It has also bombed installations along the Corinth Canal, the naval base at Preveza, and installations at the Tatoï airport near Athens. All our planes have returned to their bases."

CHAPTER FIVE

Among the military objectives successfully bombed at Patras were many children who had run into the street to cheer the planes which were carrying the Greek colours. This was an ignominious habit of the Regia Aeronautica even before the attack on Greece. Some time previously, an Italian seaplane carrying Greek colours had come down in the sea by Cephalonia, which accounted for the ability of the Italian General Staff to believe that British destroyers flew the Greek ensign to avoid the danger of being brought to action by the Italian navy. With so little of which to be proud, perhaps the lack of pride should not be counted too hardly against an Italy mentally affected and morally corrupted by twenty full years of Fascism.

That much was expected from the activity of the Italian air force in the way of shattering the spirit of the Greek population is evident from the plan of the Italian offensive. The fact that, except for occasional attacks on places of military importance like Salonika, most of the Italian bombing was directed against country districts in the interior of Greece southward was an indication of the direction of the main thrust of the invaders. The obviously suitable ground for the *blitzkrieg* on the theory of which General Visconti-Prasca, the Commander-in-Chief of the Army of Albania, had written a book published in 1935, was in the Koritza sector, and it was generally believed beforehand that the main Italian thrust would be made here. The capture of Florina, a town of 20,000 inhabitants, would open the way to Salonika. Salonika was joined to Florina by a railway and by a good road some eighty miles long. The fall of Salonika would involve all Macedonia and isolate the Greek forces in Thrace, and though there was no immediate prospect of any such moves being made, it would effectually forestall any attempt by the British to land troops at Salonika. It would be the old Roman road to conquest for the legions marching eastward from Dyrrhacchium. There were many who believed that Salonika was an objective of such predominant importance that the Italians might even violate Yugoslav territory by taking advantage of the Monastir Gap to turn the Greek position by attacking it in the rear of its right flank. It may be that the dropping of bombs on Monastir by Italian planes on November 7th and 16th was an experiment to test the reaction of Yugoslavia and estimate the probable effect on public opinion there of a more extensive violation of the country. Moreover, on both occasions these attacks on Monastir followed immediately upon

71

successful actions by the Greek forces in the Koritza sector.

The Italian plan was soon revealed to be more ambitious. It was to strike at the heart of Epirus and, by seizing Jannina and Metsovo, to make the fullest use of the Albanian port of Santi Quaranta which was linked with Jannina by road. Jannina and Metsovo were the keys to Larissa and the plain of Thessaly and ultimately to Athens itself. No doubt, with the rapid advance on which the Italians counted, the complete occupation of Greece was expected to be achieved before any British aid could arrive.

So, when the command to advance was given at dawn on October 28th, one column moved into the low-lying country along the coast to outflank from the south the Greek positions round Jannina; a second column, with which was the Centaur Armoured Division, advanced toward the upper reaches of the Kalamas, with Jannina as the direct objective beyond; and a third column made a daring thrust through the great mountainous mass of the Pindus in order to reach at the earliest possible moment the strategically important town of Metsovo about twenty-two miles east of Jannina. This last operation was the most difficult and from the point of view of the Italian plan of campaign as a whole the most vital to its success. With the fall of Metsovo Jannina would be isolated, the communications of the Greeks could be cut and Thessaly could be overrun. Finally, a fourth column based on Koritza moved slowly along the Yugoslav frontier toward Florina.

At first the Italian advance proceeded smoothly enough. Philiata, nine miles beyond the frontier, was occupied by October 31st, and simultaneously the river Kalamas was crossed and bridge-heads were established on its southern bank. By November 2nd Italian cavalry patrols were reported in the neighbourhood of Jannina. Next day the Italian communiqué from headquarters announced that "Italian troops having by a daring manœuvre overcome numerous defensive lines heavily mined and strongly protected by obstacles" were moving on Kalibaki. This place should not be confused with Kalabaka, which lies east of Metsovo at the junction of the road south from Florina with the road running east from Jannina to Larissa. Kalibaki if not so important as Kalabaka was important enough, and it was soon in Italian hands.

While this was happening on the Italian right, in the centre the Alpini of the Iulia Division had crossed the wooded heights of

Grammos and Smetika on the northerly slopes of the Pindus and had penetrated as far as Samarina and Distrato to within scarcely more than ten miles of Metsovo. Such was the confidence of the Italian High Command that supplies were dropped in Metsovo from planes under the impression that the Italian troops were already in occupation.

At first the forces at the disposal of General Papagos, the Greek Commander-in-Chief, were obviously strong enough to fight only delaying actions as they fell back before the weight of the principal Italian thrust in an effort to hold it up long enough to give the main forces of the Greek army time to mobilize and concentrate. Yet these delaying actions were fought with so fierce a determination not to yield more than the barest minimum of the sacred soil to the invader that at no point was there anything in the nature of a break-through. With bayonet and grenade in hand-to-hand fighting, the outnumbered soldiers of Hellas defied the new Barbarians. The little Greek air force, equipped with planes already long out of date, flew as Zetes and Calais flew in pursuit of the Harpies to attack the loathed Italians that preyed upon children and shepherds. Not for them was the undefended village in the Thessalian plain, not for them the hospital, the school, or the church. Outnumbered by six to one, those heroic Greek pilots attacked the aerodromes of Koritza and Argyrocastro and hoped that the R.A.F. would soon send them what help it could spare.

And the Greek forces were not falling back all along the line. In the Koritza-Florina sector they attacked the enemy, drove him from strong positions at the bayonet's point, penetrated three miles into Albanian territory, and took as prisoners 9 officers and 153 men. This success was announced in a communiqué from Athens on November 1st. The peaks of mountains near Lake Presba were occupied. These positions astride the frontier were of great strategic importance because they commanded the whole of the defile through which runs the road from Koritza to Florina, and thereby made possible the development of the operations against Koritza later on.

This early success in the northern sector of the front coincided with announcements in the Italian Press of a concentration of Italian troops at Koritza designed to carry out a great offensive against Salonika by way of Florina. On November 5th the Greek High Command announced that after a successful attack "Greek troops had occupied another series of well-fortified heights in Albania. Guns, mortars, many machine-guns, much material and some prisoners had been taken. Sections of the enemy in retreat had been attacked by his own armoured cars." Whether this last achievement of the Italians was due to nervousness, over-confidence in the impossibility of an Italian retreat, or merely to incompetence, is not known. On the same day as this successful little operation by the Greeks, a despatch of the United Press from Rome declared that well-informed opinion in the Italian capital considered that the operations along the Yugoslav frontier in the direction of Salonika were the most important. If Salonika fell into Italian hands the whole of Thrace would be cut off and communications between the mainland of Greece and several of the islands would be seriously threatened.

If this despatch was inspired by the Italian Intelligence it was no compliment to the intelligence of General Papagos. Could even the Italian Intelligence Service, which, unless it has greatly improved since the First World War, is credulous, inaccurate, and petty-minded, have supposed he was capable of being deceived by this chatter when at that very moment the crux of the original Italian offensive had been reached in the grim recesses of the Pindus? The Greek High Command had its own hopes of an offensive in the Koritza sector when the most serious threat, that of the Iulia Division to Metsovo, had been averted.

Three battalions of Evzones [1]—it is a commonplace of war correspondents to compare them to the Guards, but in truth they should be compared to the Highland regiments of the British army—three battalions had fallen back before the advance of a crack Italian division of Alpini, contesting the issue desperately all the way. The Alpini pressed on along the valleys, the Italian planes bombing before them. Konitza, not to be confused with Koritza, was captured and many other villages. By November 9th the Iulia was within ten miles of Metsovo and the only pass from Epirus into Thessaly. The Evzones holding the approaches were in a bad position, for the Alpini had broken their centre. It was now that General Papagos gave the order that the Evzones were to take up positions on the ridges of the mountains on either side of the three defiles by which the Iulia was closing in on Metsovo. This manœuvre was to be

[1] There were five regiments of Evzones in all, and normally one was allotted to each of the five Army Corps.

carried out urgently at all costs and it was to be carried out regardless of whether supplies could reach the men entrusted with so desperate a task.

We may pause for a moment to marvel at the way in which events were to give the Greeks an opportunity of repeating the tactics by which both Marathon and Salamis were won, for when this war shall have run its full course it may well be decided that the manœuvre which broke the Iulia in the Pindus had consequences as important for mankind as those two victories against the Barbarians of two and a half millenniums ago. The Athenian centre gave way at Marathon and the Persians were caught by the two wings of the Ten Thousand. The centre of the Hellenic fleet backed away at Salamis as the Phoenician and Ionian fleets swept in through the channels, and they were shattered by the two wings, one led by a trireme of Aegina, the other by a trireme of Athens.

During that night of November 9th–10th the Evzones climbed the mountains to establish themselves on the ridges above the valley of the Sarandoporos. During that night, old men, women, and children of the Pindus villages dragged up supplies and ammunition. The heroines of Suli and Parga in the War of Independence lived again in these heroines of the Pindus. At dawn the signal was given for the counter-attack. Shouting their war-cry of 'Aera! Aera!' 'Wind! Wind!', the Evzones swept down upon the flank and rear of the Alpini. The crack Division cracked. The retreat was sounded. The retreat became a rout. The Iulia fled. The renowned Alpini flung away their arms and abandoned their wounded. Many were drowned in the swollen waters of the Aoos. Those who could not run fast enough surrendered, and surrendered crying, 'Bella Grecia!' to appease with a pretty phrase and a compliment the redoubtable foes by whom they had been broken. With these two words the Division named after the greatest Roman of them all acknowledged that the grandeur of Rome was dead, the glory of Greece alive.

It was regrettable that the refusal of the Greek authorities to allow war correspondents at the front during that first crucial fortnight meant that no adequate account of what had happened in the Pindus was given to the world of free men.

"A large number of Italian prisoners, among them several officers, have been taken in the Pindus region; a quantity of material of every kind has fallen into our hands." Thus did the Greek High Command in its communiqué of November 10th announce the first serious military check which the forces of the Axis had received since the Germans invaded Poland. It emulated a little too carefully the terseness of Sparta. Newspaper readers who were accustomed to hear a wretched game between two teams of hired football-players described as epic could not appreciate such laconic phraseology.

On November 13th another communiqué announced : "The Italian Alpini Division, hard pressed, continues to fall back in the direction of Konitza".

The retreat of the Alpini from the Pindus at once affected the columns operating to the south. That same day the Greek High Command was able to announce that the Italian forces which had pushed on across the Kalamas were falling back and that Greek forces advancing northward had reached Mazaraki, seven miles south of the river. Two days later the Italians had recrossed the Kalamas and were still falling back. Simultaneously with this withdrawal by the extreme right of the Italians the forces which had advanced against Jannina also fell back, and by November 16th every village they had taken was again in Greek hands. The invaders in their panic disgraced themselves by carrying off hostages from the villages they evacuated. It was with this column that the Centaur Armoured Division was operating. The Centaur tanks were not a success. The country was unsuited to tank tactics, and a great number ran into a ditch which had been dug for them, with humiliating results. The first help that came from Britain was effectively used against these Centaurs. Anti-tank rifles were flown from Egypt to Patras and flown by Greek planes on to Jannina, whence they were at once sent up to the front. It was not surprising that the discomfiture of the Centaur Armoured Division should have inspired one of the comic artists of Athens to mock the Italians with a cartoon representing the defeat of the Centaurs by the Lapithae. The human part of every Centaur was portrayed as a Bersagliere and the cruppers of the miserable beasts were being prodded by the bayonets of jeering Lapithae in Evzone uniform as they galloped away . . . but not from Thessaly into the recesses of the Pindus like the original Centaurs. These modern Centaurs were chased farther.

By November 18th not a single Italian soldier was left alive on Greek soil.

CHAPTER SIX

LET it not be forgotten that, while the Italian Army of Albania was being so ignominiously expelled from Greece, Wavell's Libyan campaign and Cunningham's naval victory off Matapan were both in the future. Even the destructive raid by the Fleet Air Arm on the base of Taranto was not made till November 11th. When this immense war shall have become a memory, nay, when it shall have become a mere tale of old unhappy far-off things and battles long ago, it will be Greece who for ever in the pages of history will be accorded the honour of having been the first State to shatter the legend of Axis invincibility.

The shock to the confidence of the Italian people was sudden and sharp. For eighteen years the wordy warfare of that Bombastes Furioso to whom it had entrusted its destiny had reverberated from the Alps to the Apennine and boomed from the Adriatic to the Tyrrhenian. The eruptions of this pocket Vesuvius had seemed to express the travail of an Italy in the throes of a second renaissance. Dazed by rhetoric and bombast, the people of Italy had supposed that Mussolini's war against Greece would be a repetition of his war against Corfu. The shameful result made it necessary for the Duce to explain even to the cowed population he possessed like an unclean spirit what had happened to make his refurbished Italy the butt of two hemispheres.

As usual the wind-galled hack Virginio Gayda was saddled with the responsibility of public opinion, and as early as November 12th the mouthpiece of Mussolini was writing in the *Giornale d' Italia* that Italy had made no preparations for a war against Greece.

"We were only really able to prepare," he wrote, "after October 28th, the day on which war was declared."

It is not worth wasting ink on the overwhelming evidence which contradicts this lie, to support which the Italian Press could offer nothing better than the Italian General Staff's ignorance of the climate and geography of Epirus. To their surprise they had discovered that it was no country for motorized warfare, that roads were few and far between, and that the weather was horrible. The articles of Gayda were used as fig-leaves for these innocents.

Six days later Mussolini himself appeared on his balcony to explain why Italy had suffered such a reverse. He rebuked those armchair strategists who stuck little flags on maps and talked about a *blitzkrieg* in Greece, where the mountains of the Epirus and the marshy valleys did not lend themselves to such a style of warfare. Then he dared to bellow:

> "This famous Alpini Division, the Iulia, which is supposed to have suffered such enormous losses, which is supposed to have fled, and which is supposed to have been pulverized by the Greeks, has just been inspected by General Soddù. After this inspection General Soddù telegraphed me as follows on November 12th: 'I have visited the Iulia Alpini Division this morning. I must send you word, Duce, of the magnificent impression made upon me by this superb unit, prouder and stronger than ever, with its ranks of Alpini carved out of granite'."

The Duce omitted to point out to his audience that the very fact of General Soddù's presence in Albania to replace General Visconti-Prasca was itself a proof that something had happened to the Alpini in the Pindus to make it necessary for the relieving General to inspect them on the wrong side of the Greek frontier. It is unusual for shock troops to administer the shock to their own commanding officer.

Mussolini concluded what was perhaps even his most successful effort to make words take the place of deeds by promising his audience the compensation of an ultimate victory. "We shall break the back of Greece," he roared.

The proofs that about this time the Duce appealed to Germany for help to extricate him from the mess in which he was sprawling are not yet available; but the meeting between Field-Marshal Keitel and Marshal Badoglio which was held at Innsbruck on November 15th could hardly fail to suggest that the discomfiture of the Italian invaders at the hands of Greece had made an examination of the military situation in the Eastern Mediterranean an urgent necessity. At the time it was generally believed that the project of bringing Bulgaria in to attack Greece was under examination and that this was abandoned under pressure from Russia, which was as anxious as the Axis had originally declared itself to be to localize the Balkan conflict and prevent its extension to Yugoslavia or Turkey. Knowing as we do now that it was Hitler's plan to attack Russia in the spring, we can see how inconvenient to German military plans would have been any premature warning to Russia of future intentions. No doubt, the possibility of really substantial British help to Greece was carefully weighed and it was decided that for some months British help need not be considered as a serious threat. Such aid was in fact beyond the power of Britain to offer. As things were, the Greek Government was concerned to demand the minimum of help from Britain in the hope of averting the menace of German help to Italy and the British Government was equally concerned not to press more than that minimum upon the Greek Government in the hope that nothing would be allowed to weaken the position in Egypt.

The Italian retreat after the Pindus disaster had left Greece confident of being able to deal with the invader provided that the invader did not summon those hordes from the north to do his work for him; and the Italians consoled themselves with the theory that a disorderly retreat all along the line which left a great deal of war material in the enemy's hands was in fact one of those strategic withdrawals carried out according to plan with which the literature of modern warfare is so familiar. The Italian Press was full of what would happen to Greece presently when conditions were more favourable to the manœuvres of the Italian motorized divisions. What the Italian Press failed to appreciate was that the spirit which had inspired a little country to defend itself so superbly would not be content with defence, but that it would inspire with equal ardour a well-conceived and pertinaciously executed offensive.

It must be borne in mind that this offensive had already begun when advantage was taken of the failure of the Italian forces to make an energetic bid for Florina to occupy the mountains which commanded the road between that place and Koritza, and that while the enemy was falling back in the Jannina sector after the defeat of the Iulia in the Pindus, Greek pressure in the Koritza sector was being intensified continuously. Cautious to the point of dullness though the Greek communiqués were during those critical days at the beginning of the third week in November, the Italian Press was accusing them of "a high power of invention"; and in fact even the best-disposed military critics were inclined to suggest that the rapidity and the completeness of the Greek advance in the northern sector was too good to be true. The speed of the Greek mobilization during those first three weeks and the transport of the troops to the front line was indeed a miraculous feat.

There was a noticeable tendency in current criticism to attribute the success of the Greek mobilization to the discipline secured by an authoritarian régime. It would do the memory of General Metaxas an injustice not to admit the value in a military emergency of having as head of the Government a statesman of exceptional military experience who was a strategist of some note; but it would be a very gross exaggeration of the benefits conferred by the Fourth of August if that date received the slightest credit for the resistance offered to Italian aggression by the people of Greece. Metaxas will always deserve the honour of rejecting the Italian ultimatum, but it must be repeated that if he had accepted it he would have been swept from office by the fierce wind of public indignation, and eternal ignominy would have been his portion in Hellenic history.

The Greek mobilization was to a large extent improvised, and that such an improvisation could be achieved was due to the passionate will of the people of Greece to resist the Italian onslaught. The Greek army was able to go into action so soon and the units of that army were able to attain their full war-time strength so soon because the wider groupings of peace-time were abolished on the spur of the urgent moment and the men belonging to them were hastily concentrated at one point. It was no doubt lucky that the Regia Aeronautica attached more importance to terrorizing the civil population than to destroying roads and bridges or bombing the troops moving north; but the incompetence of the Italian air force does not detract from the feat of improvisation which allowed the Greek High Command to change so swiftly from the defensive to the offensive. The original mobilization provided for seventeen divisions of infantry and one of cavalry. Of these the 1st, 2nd, 3rd, and 4th Divisions were entrusted with the advance in Epirus, while in Western Macedonia the 9th Division which started the offensive in the Koritza sector was quickly reinforced by the 10th, 11th, 16th, and 17th Divisions.

On November 18th, the same day as Mussolini was bragging in Rome of Italy's intention to break the back of Greece, a communiqué of the Greek High Command announced that fighting was going on all along the front from Epirus to the mountainous region to the east of Koritza and that heights of the very greatest military importance had been occupied in the face of vigorous enemy resistance in which his air force had played a conspicuous part. The action of the Regia Aeronautica alluded to was that of the dive-bombers trying to drive the Greek troops from the positions in which they had established themselves. The mountainous region is that known as the Marova. On November 19th the Greek troops on the Marova were repelling enemy counter-attacks and occupying new positions. Fighters of the diminutive Greek air force shot down seven Italian dive-bombers and two fighters. Greek troops were penetrating into Albania in the Epirus sector and enemy supply depôts at Erseka and Borova were destroyed.

On November 20th bayonet charges were driving the Italians from their positions round Koritza, and the Greek communiqué paid a tribute to the desperate Italian defence. That same day in the Marova the Greek assaults upon the Italian mountain strongholds were renewed with ever-increasing ardour and the Greek air force shot down eleven enemy planes without loss.

On November 21st the communiqué of the Greek High Command announced dazzling fresh successes for the troops in the Marova, from the greater part of which the enemy had been dislodged, so that the Greek troops were now advancing along the western bastions. Retreating enemy columns were bombed and machine-gunned by the Greek air force.

That same day the Italian High Command announced that repeated attacks by the enemy had been broken up by the stout resistance of the Italian troops.

Twenty-four hours later the Italian High Command had to announce that Koritza had been evacuated and that the Italian losses had been considerable.

It was on the morning of November 22nd that, after a hard struggle lasting for nine days, the Greek forces entered the largest town in Albania where, so hasty was the Italian evacuation, a great quantity of arms, stores, and equipment fell into their hands.

The Italian Press was hard put to it to explain away the Koritza disaster, and a diverting example of the working of the Fascist mind is provided by the simple pride with which the Minister of Information in Rome drew the attention of a conference of foreign correspondents to the frankness with which the Italian High Command had admitted the fall of such an important place. There was the proof of the Duce's pudding of rhetoric he had emptied from his balcony into the open mouths of his admiring followers. Had he not asserted on November 18th that the communiqués of the Italian High

Command were the simple truth? Did not these communiqués lay as much stress on the knocks the Italian forces were receiving as upon the blows they were giving? What the Minister of Information failed to point out was that the communiqué which admitted the loss of Koritza failed to point out that the Italian Ninth Army had suffered a heavy defeat in a battle lasting nine days. Indeed the communiqué went beyond a *suppressio veri* with an *affirmatio falsi*, because it stated explicitly that the forces defending Koritza consisted only of covering troops from the two divisions which were extended along the Greco-Albanian frontier in the northern sector.

In point of fact the Ninth Army, which was commanded by General Vercellino, formerly commander of Mussolini's pet Army of the Po, had been heavily reinforced immediately after the defeat of the Iulia Division in the Pindus; for the offensive in the Koritza sector against Florina and Salonika, which military opinion had generally expected would be the first thrust of the invaders when they advanced into Greece at dawn on October 28th, was then accepted as the most promising strategic move. The Italian Press had tried to hearten the public by declaring that this forthcoming offensive would lead to the decisive battle which would settle once and for all the Italo-Greek problem, and the American correspondent of the United Press who was with the Italian army was allowed to report that this offensive was likely to decide the fate of Greece. The Venice, Piedmont, and Parma Divisions had been reinforced by the 2nd Triestino Alpini Division, and the 53rd Arezzo Division, by the 4th Regiment of Bersaglieri, by the Independent Taranto Battalion, and by the 109th and 166th Blackshirt Battalions. The 101st Machine-gun Battalion and the fourteen batteries of heavy artillery had also been heavily reinforced, and there was strong air support. There were, too, a number of tanks and armoured cars; but the terrain was not favourable to the useful exploitation of these, and they can be left out of the odds against the Greek forces.

Immediately after the fall of Koritza the Italian Radio started a war of words with the B.B.C., which it accused of making an exaggerated fuss about the operations proceeding in Albania.

"We are content at this stage of these operations," Radio Roma declared, "to observe that Italy will be able to despatch all the troops necessary to force a decision in Albania whenever she wants to, but it is considered valuable to have compelled the Greeks to quit the advantageous positions which they originally occupied and to have brought them to battle in a sector chosen by the Italian High Command. Once upon a time in Epirus there was a king called Pyrrhus who had to fight against the Romans. During the first part of the struggle his task seemed relatively easy. He defeated the Romans, but in doing so his army sustained such losses that what was left of it was comfortably annihilated by the Roman legions in the battles which followed. The exhaustion of the enemy is sometimes more advantageous than a speedy victory. Italy can wait, secure and confident, for the final result. The people of Italy are well aware that the Italian army has always known how to extract the maximum of profit from its victories."

The cynic has been able to observe with a sneer that the reputation the British enjoy for not knowing when they are beaten has too often led to their glorifying a shattering reverse with the attributes more usually associated with a signal victory. Nobody, however, has been able to accuse the British of trying to pretend that a Corunna or a Mons or a Dunkirk was anything except an enforced retreat. It requires the ingenuous vulgarity of the *mezzosignore* attitude of Fascism to be afraid of accepting a defeat with dignity or grace.

The Iulia Alpini Division which, as its conquerors would be the first to recognize, had fought after the first panic a rearguard action of praiseworthy determination in retreat, was made a figure of fun by being decorated for having been compelled to change its position and face continual bayonet charges no less than sixty times. Yet, during this change of position, which was a euphemism for a rapid if not absolutely headlong retreat, the Iulia always outnumbered its pursuers by two to one.

The war of words conducted by the Italian Press and Radio and indeed for that matter by General Ubaldo Soddù who had replaced General Visconti-Prasca, resembled that of Mr Snodgrass on the occasion of Mr Pickwick's arrest in Ipswich on suspicion of planning to fight a duel: "Mr Snodgrass, in a truly Christian spirit, and in order that he might take no one unawares, announced in a very loud tone that he was going to begin, and proceeded to take off his coat with the utmost deliberation".

The retreat of the Italian troops on the Koritza front was considered in authoritative Roman circles as a mere episode in a plan of campaign the final result of which would be known in a few weeks. The whole operation was in the safe hands of General Soddù and the preparations for it were being pushed forward as energetically as possible in order to allow for a speedy offensive and assure its success.

General Soddù, the Assistant Chief of the General Staff and Under-Secretary of State for War, was one of the Duce's most trusted collaborators, and everybody in Rome felt that he had the situation well in hand. So did General Soddù himself. In the order of the day which he addressed to the Italian Army of Albania as soon as he arrived to take over from General Visconti-Prasca, he beat the big drum outside his mountebank's tent and proclaimed in words that should have been set to music by Leoncavallo: "Our mission is quite settled. We must give the Greek army the lesson which it deserves. We must demonstrate to it that in spite of its courage it will have to yield before the implacable will and power of Fascist Italy's armed forces."

On November 28th General Soddù gave an interview to the correspondent of the United Press in which he announced an Italian offensive on a grand scale by New Year's Day at the latest. This was not to be a *blitzkrieg*. *Blitzkriegs* were at a discount in Rome since the abortive effort of October 28th. This was to be a slow and methodical advance in the course of which the Italians would apply a special strategy based upon the experience they had gained in Abyssinia and in Spain.

By December 1st competent opinion in Rome had decided that the Greek advance had been definitely checked all along the front. The Italian forces had consolidated south of Argyrokastro a powerful defensive line supported by heavy artillery and nests of machine-guns. Other strong defensive positions had been established near Koritza and Konisopolis. The forty thousand Fascist labourers who had been working on the roads of Albania had been engaged on these fortifications. Powerful reinforcements had reached General Soddù, and a grand enveloping movement might soon be expected.

On December 1st Radio Roma announced the completion of the defence in the mood of an athlete who has stepped back a pace to break the record for the long jump:

> "All the audacity of the enemy will not be enough to persuade him that the obstacles in the way of his advance from now onwards can possibly be surmounted. This stabilization of the defensive link, however, is only the prelude of the great Italian offensive which will be launched at the first opportunity."

CHAPTER SEVEN

WHEN Mr Winston Churchill told the House of Commons that General Metaxas had asked Sir Michael Palairet, the British Minister in Athens, for help in accordance with the guarantee offered and accepted by Greece after Mussolini's assault on Albania, he did not give his listeners the impression that such help was likely to be embarrassing in its generosity.   Britain would do as much as she was able to do.   At that moment the threat of invasion, although much less acute than it had been, was still alive, and the decision taken earlier to reinforce General Wavell in Egypt was still regarded by many experts of strategy as a mistake.   There was a body of military opinion which believed that the right plan for Britain was to remain strictly on the defensive, accumulate armament and equipment, and allow Germany to expand for years if necessary until she overreached herself and exposed her heart to a knock-out blow.   It is an open secret that the decision to hold Egypt and if possible strike back at Marshal Graziani's invading Italian army owed almost everything to Mr Churchill's own imagination and resolution.   The attack on Greece came at the moment when hopes of successful offensive action in Egypt were rising, and it was obvious that any help to Greece must be at the expense of the Imperial forces in Egypt.

And when we think of those five squadrons of the R.A.F. which were all that could be spared from Egypt, we have to remember at the same time that even that amount of help was for some time handicapped in its efficacy by the fear of provoking Germany which animated the Greek Government.   Throughout that glorious November and December of 1940, when the country burned with a white-hot fire of determination to rout the Italian invader, the hope was still unduly cherished that if Germany intervened it would be to negotiate honourable terms from which Greece would be left securely at peace.   This hope was steadily encouraged by German diplomacy for reasons which we can now appreciate, but which were by no means so obvious at the time.   During the First World War Greece had been split into two camps by Venizelos' conviction of an Allied victory and an equally strong conviction that the economic welfare of his country in the future depended upon that victory. He was opposed by a large body of opinion which was convinced that the war would end either in a German victory or in a stalemate and that the economic welfare of Greece in the future depended at least as much upon Central Europe as upon the Maritime Powers. A similar cleavage of opinion had existed in Italy where King Victor Emmanuel had supported the popular emotion which took the country into war, whereas in Greece it is on the whole fair to say that King Constantine had done his best to cool it with the misgivings he shared with his General Staff. If the British Government had given to pro-Entente Greece, which represented at the most conservative estimate at least four-fifths of the population, the fullest practical support instead of abandoning it to a military and diplomatic exploitation by France, it can be declared with utter assurance that the unhappy political strife which rent the country for exactly a quarter of a century from October 1915 to October 1940 would never have developed. As it was, that sublime sacrifice to the purest patriotism made by those soldiers of Hellas who followed Venizelos, Coundouriotis, and Danglis to Salonika was made . . . no, not in vain, for a pen held by the fingers of one who assisted at that sacrifice refuses to write the words . . . let it be said rather, was made without securing to their country the gathering of those fruits so many died to ripen.

The point it is desired to make in thus referring back to the First World War is that the neutrality party of that time tinged, deeply enough in parts, with Germanic colouring, controlled Greece at the outbreak of the Second World War in the person of its most representative figure; and it is reasonable to suppose that General Metaxas *was* inclined at first to accept the suggestion put forward by the German Minister in Athens that provided British help did not extend beyond the reinforcement of the small and gallant Hellenic air force, Germany would intervene only with the object of re-establishing peace in the Balkans. Otherwise it would be difficult to find an excuse for the refusal of the Greek High Command that autumn to allow the R.A.F. squadrons to use any of the aerodromes in the north. Neither the aerodrome at Tatoï (renamed Menidi) nor at Eleusis was suitable as a base from which to bomb Durazzo and Valona.

As it happened, the fear of provoking German offensive action that seemed uppermost in the strategic use made of the R.A.F. squadrons was not unwelcome to the British High Command, which was in no position to take full advantage of the situation created by the Italian invasion of Greece either on land or sea or in the air. In justice to both the Greek and the British Governments it should be remembered that in the autumn of 1940 neither of them knew what we all know now, that is the vital importance to Hitler of securing his flank before he could launch his attack on the Soviets he had planned for May 1941. That he did not anticipate having to come to the rescue of his ally is most probable, and to that extent the assurances of his representative in Athens were no doubt sincere. It is even conceivable that, if Mussolini's reputation in Italy would have allowed it, Germany might have tried to secure a peace and gambled on the ability of Greece to preserve her neutrality after a return to the status quo. However, the crushing defeat of Marshal Graziani and the possibility of a complete Italian collapse made any idea of intervening except with force of arms ridiculous, and before General Metaxas died he had faced the fact that a German attack was ultimately inevitable. He must also have faced the fact that some of the Greek officers and Greek politicians whom his régime had favoured at the price of leaving Venizelist officers and politicians in retirement or exile were less likely than himself when the testing hour was upon them to stand firm.

If we consider the dictatorships which have been the outstanding feature of the last two decades we shall note that a man like Mustafa Kemal was able to impose his character upon his country and reform it out of the abundance of his own vitality. As much may be said for Mussolini, but with this difference that he is himself a coward at heart and has communicated this cowardice to the Italian people, so that he and they are gnawed by a continuous moral and mental indigestion which tries to obtain relief by an excess of flatulent assertion. Hitler on the other hand is the incarnate expression of a nation which has felt itself perpetually thwarted through the centuries in the revelation of its own genius. It is futile to attempt to differentiate between Hitler and the people for whom he now speaks and acts, and in Hitler's hesitation to attack Greece directly we may discern the uneasy conscience of the German people.

Metaxas was one of the pedagogic dictators, a combination of a Salazar and a Pilsudski without the larger qualities of either. He was essentially a petty man, and the narrowness of his outlook may be judged by his refusal to allow a performance of the *Antigone* without cuts made to suit the politics of the moment or by his banning of the Funeral Oration of Pericles from school texts of Thucydides on account of its democratic philosophy. Nevertheless, he was a patriot who, by recognizing in the final test that his country was greater than himself and by bowing instinctively to what he apprehended must be the will of Hellas, rejected the Italian ultimatum and thus allowed himself to be absorbed in the unity he himself could never have achieved by youth movements and road-building and beating up communists and exiling Liberal politicians to islands.

Nevertheless, that unity must be comprehended as the result of Italian action. It would not have happened if that ultimatum had been presented by the German Minister and rejected. The commercial links which had been forged with Germany had woven too strong a chain for many of the influential sections of Hellenic society. This is not to suggest that General Metaxas would have surrendered to such an ultimatum, and certainly not that the people of Greece would have tolerated such a surrender. There would not have been, however, such an absolute unity of purpose as consolidated in one moment a nation which had been politically restless for twenty-five years. It is tragic that certain Greeks have been able to reconcile with their consciences the task of cooperating with the two evil powers in temporary possession of Hellas; but the material for that tragedy was gathered long before, and it is one of the ironies of history that Metaxas himself had been one of its most assiduous contributors.

Press correspondents who have written about events in Greece have expressed severe criticism of the toleration extended to German intrigue, espionage, and propaganda during the months before it became necessary for Germany openly to come to the rescue of Italy. The British Legation has been censured for its failure to support the claims of Venizelist officers who in spite of the unified nation were not always given the commands their ability deserved, and for its blindness to the elements, particularly conspicuous in Athens, which because they were fervidly anti-Italian were by no means fervidly pro-British. British propaganda was by unanimous testimony ludicrously wanting in efficiency and efficacy. Whether with all the straw required there would have been British diplomats or propagandists capable of making good bricks is a matter of opinion: the matter of fact is that there was a grave shortage of straw and in such circumstances speculation about the expertness of the brickmaker becomes irrelevant.

It is typical of the Ethelred spirit which haunts British military plans for the first year or two of a war that, although as much R.A.F. help as could be spared from Egypt arrived on the scene in time for the first communiqué about its activity to be published on November 7th, the herald of a British Military Mission did not reach Athens until the day on which the church bells were ringing for the fall of Koritza on November 22nd. This was Lt.-Col. Stanley Casson, who writes:[1] "I had chafed to come sooner, but the organization of such a mission and its transport had taken up all the time. For you have to work hard to catch up with the aggressors."

This excuse is as loyal and lame as that of a schoolboy shielding his companions. Why was such a mission not organized as soon as Italian intentions were revealed by the outrage of August 15th? He would be an able propagandist indeed who could make anything of such reprehensible dilatoriness. That British Military Mission should have been waiting for the turn of events in Cairo by the middle of October and it should have been established in Athens by November 1st at latest.

Fortunately the R.A.F. had been in action before the British Military Mission arrived. Otherwise German propaganda might have suggested that the help asked of Britain did not begin to arrive until it was certain that Mussolini would not reach Athens first.

Mr Leland Stowe, the distinguished American correspondent, asks,[2] "How and why did the little Greek army drive the Italians back and backward, scoring one astonishing triumph after another?"

And this is how a man who had seen the war in Finland, Norway, and Rumania before he reached Greece answers that question with six reasons in the order of their relative importance:

"1. The fighting hearts of the entire Greek people.
2. The extraordinary unity of the Greek people.
3. The remarkably high calibre of the Greek General Staff, combined with the fact that virtually all officers, from the rank of lieutenant-colonel upward, were fighting in their fourth war.
4. The startling inefficiency of the Italian General Staff and the extremely poor direction of the Italian air force.
5. Pronounced lack of combative spirit and an understandable lack

[1] *Greece Against the Axis*, p. 12.
[2] *No Other Road to Freedom*, pp. 184-5.

of conviction (even respect for what they were commanded to do) on the part of the Fascist soldiers.

6. The highly important aid given by the British air force and British naval units where the Greeks most needed help."

Bright in the ever-lengthening scroll of honour, glory, valour, and skill which adorns the records of the R.A.F. during the Second World War stand out the names of those squadrons which helped Greece during the last two months of 1940. There was 211 Squadron of Bristol-Blenheims, 84 Squadron of Blenheims, 80 Squadron of Gloster-Gladiator fighters, 70 Squadron of Wellingtons, and 30 Squadron of fighter-bomber Blenheims. The sumtotal of the figures only just misses adding up to the mighty year of Salamis.

Here is the first communiqué about their activities published by the Press Bureau of the Greek Legation in London on November 7th:

"We are informed authoritatively that a formation of bomber aircraft of the British air forces in Greece yesterday, November 6th, carried out a most successful raid on an enemy aerodrome at Valona on the Adriatic coast in Albania. Enemy aircraft on the ground were bombed and machine-gunned, and a large number of airmen standing on the tarmac were also attacked. A number of bombs were seen to obtain direct hits on aircraft which were completely destroyed and near misses severely damaged other aircraft. British aircraft were attacked by enemy fighters without effect, all British aircraft returning safely to their base. One air-gunner was killed by a stray bullet. The leader of the formation on returning to his base reported, 'We took the enemy completely by surprise and were able to make our runs over the target without interference. Our observers watched bombs bursting among the aircraft on the ground and very heavy damage was inflicted.'

"The military funeral of the air-gunner, the first R.A.F. casualty of the war in Greece, took place at the British cemetery in Athens to-day. King George of Greece was represented and General Metaxas, President of the Council, General Papagos, the Commander-in-Chief of the Greek Army, Air Commodore J. H. d'Albiac, Air Officer commanding British Air Forces in Greece, and many high officers of the Greek Army and Air Force were present in person."

The first official communiqué from Headquarters of the R.A.F. in Greece was not published until November 12th:

CHAPTER SEVEN

"A most successful operation was carried out during the night of November 11th–12th. Durazzo, a port of the Albanian coast, was completely gutted and the fuel depôt destroyed. Three fires that were started on the jetty later merged into one, and our pilots saw the fires still burning when they were a hundred miles on their homeward flight. In a night raid on Valona all bombs were observed to fall in the target area, and what was probably a munitions dump was seen to blow up. Yesterday the dock area at Valona was attacked again, salvoes of bombs falling on the jetties and also in the centre of a large building. The heavy anti-aircraft fire was not effective, and from all these operations our aircraft returned safely."

These two communiqués serve to illustrate what was the main task of the R.A.F. during the first two or three months of the war in Greece. The Italian supply ports of Durazzo, Valona, and Santi Quaranta were continually bombed by day and by night.

The unwillingness of the Greek High Command to allow the R.A.F. squadrons to use the northern aerodromes meant that for all too long they carried out their operations from Menidi (Tatoï) and Eleusis, the two big aerodromes near Athens. Here they were in full view of any curious spectators who cared to investigate their activities, and on more than one occasion the German Intelligence organization was able to warn the Italians beforehand of raids. Added to that was the accurate check which could be kept of casualties. The greatest disadvantage of all, however, was that the Blenheims operating from this unnecessarily remote base could only just manage to reach their targets and return without refuelling. The conditions in which some of these flights were carried out over country as inimical as any in Europe to operations by air can be summed up in the description of a Blenheim's return from a raid on Valona given by Flight Lieutenant A. Bocking, D.F.C., a Canadian of 30 Squadron, which is quoted by Mr T. H. Wisdom in *Wings Over Olympus*:

"The weather was even stickier than usual, and as we were at 7,000 feet, with mountains 9,000 feet high around us, we had to go up through the cloud. We tried to get above it, but at 16,000 feet ice was forming on the wings, and the controls began to get very heavy. The cockpit was full of snow; it was difficult to see; then glaze-ice, the most dangerous sort, began to form. Just as we were wondering whether it would be necessary to jump we found a hole in a cloud, quite a tiny affair, and we came down through it and steered course for home. One of the other two pilots found the same hole, but the crew of the third aircraft were not so fortunate. The sergeant-pilot had taken his machine up through the cloud to just over 20,000 feet, but at that altitude the machine was wallowing, and now and then slipped back into the cloud, whereupon ice immediately formed. The pilot struggled again and again to bring his aircraft into clear air above the cloud. Suddenly, probably owing to the formation of ice in the air-intake, one engine cut out. The Blenheim went into a spin at once. The pilot ordered the crew to jump, and then it was discovered that the observer's parachute pack had been thrown by the whirling machine into the well and was out of reach. The pilot and air-gunner stayed with the observer. Still spinning, the aircraft came down through the cloud into clear air at 7,000 feet, and they found themselves in a narrow valley with mountains rising sheer on either side of them. The pilot, righting his aircraft, made a 'dead-stick' landing in a tiny field, the only possible landing-ground for miles around."

Raids on the Albanian supply ports were the main activity of those first five R.A.F. squadrons, but they also gave valuable help to the Greek forces advancing upon Koritza by destroying bridges to impede the progress of Italian reinforcements, and on several occasions they were able to drop supplies when Greek regiments in the mountains were cut off from communication by snow blocks on the narrow tracks.

The climatic and geographical conditions in which the Greco-Italian war was fought have exhausted the epithets of the most hardened journalist. That part of Albania in which the two armies were campaigning consists of a series of deep valleys running north-west and south-east between mountainous ridges rising to six thousand feet. Farther north along the coast there is a wide belt of low-lying ground, and in the extreme south-west opposite Corfu a much narrower and less extensive stretch of lowland along which the motorized right flank of the Italian army had advanced into similar country across the Greek frontier. Toward the east of the country the mountains grow higher and wilder, with the two great lakes of Ochrida and Presba beyond separating Yugoslav Macedonia from Albania and Greek Macedonia.

Even in summer such country might have puzzled a more competent invader than the Italian. In late autumn and winter it defied him. Those deep dark valleys and ravines along which swirling torrents roared were not made to be violated by motor-transport, and the ridges were swept by icy winds and savage blizzards. It was on those snow-covered ridges that the Greek soldiers fought. The pack-horses froze in their shoes. The mules lay down and congealed where they lay. Nevertheless somehow the mountain batteries were dragged to the next position, and from spur after spur, from high top after high top, the Italians were driven from their fortified positions. The slogan of the Evzones was heard upon the blast, 'Aera! Aera!', and down below in the valleys the Italian troops hearing it fell back in haste to avoid being cut off.

After due tribute has been paid to the skill with which the Greek commanders carried out the strategy allotted to them by the High Command, after due tribute has been paid to the feat of improvisation by which the Greek army was mobilized and concentrated along that fearful front, and after due tribute has been paid to the timidity of a hostile air force which never attempted to make those congested roads northward impassable but preferred to bomb undefended villages, there remains an immeasurable tribute to pay to the simple Greek soldier whose self-denial, audacity, endurance, and valour offered the world an example of military virtue which has never been surpassed. He fought from icy dawn to icy dusk, that simple soldier, on a handful of olives and a chunk of bread. For warm clothing he had to substitute the warmth of his love for Hellas. For shelter from the wind in night after night he had nothing except a hole dug in the drifted snow. He had to drag guns up precipitous slopes on which the pack-mules lost their footing. Mention has been made of the women and children and old men of the Epirus villages who helped with the transport. They were animated by the same spirit as inspired the soldiers. The measure of what the Greeks achieved may be estimated by the failure of the far better equipped enemy. The superlatives of horrifying description with which the Italian Press and Radio excused the failure of their troops provided a more eloquent eulogy of the ability of the Greek soldier to surmount the unsurmountable than even his most devoted sympathizer could indite. Fascism was able to supply the trappings of efficiency, but it was unable to supply the individual with the ardour, courage, and endurance of the will without which theoretical discipline was vanity. It was the hasty opinion of the superficial observer that the Greek triumph was evidence of the value of a totalitarian régime. In point of fact some of the determination of the simple Greek soldier to eject the Italian invader was sharpened by the conviction that in striking at him he was striking simultaneously at the régime of the Fourth of August, by which a nation of individualists had felt itself oppressed since the *coup d'état* of General Metaxas imposed it on them.

It is not desired to labour this point, but it is of immense importance to the future of mankind that the ever-darkening prospect for the liberty of the individual, which is already visible upon the post-war horizon, should be lightened by the beacon that was kindled in Hellas during those last two months of that disastrous year of 1940. Let there be no mistake. The Hellenic defiance was for humanity a second Marathon, and when the clamour of this huge and hideous war shall have died away that is how that defiance will be regarded in the serene air of history. This contemporary chronicler at least has no hesitation in anticipating that view by affirming that if Greece had yielded to the confident demand of the Italian recreants from liberty the whole course of events would have been changed, because Russia would have been crushed during the autumn of 1941. It was Greece which saved the soul of man; it was once again that small sea-girt mountainous country where liberty was originally conceived, liberty rather than forsake which Themistocles declared the Athenians would forsake Hellas itself. And it was the simple Greek soldier who saved Greece. The skilful strategy of Metaxas, the rapid improvisation of the Greek General Staff, the mobility of the Danglis-Schneider mountain-gun, the generosity of the civil population, the enthusiastic reinforcement of the R.A.F., none of these would have been of the least avail unless every man in the ranks had been able to feel that he was all Hellas in himself and, what was more, shoulder that responsibility as resolutely as he shouldered his rifle.

CHAPTER EIGHT

THE fall of Koritza evoked from the Italian Press and Radio threats thick as leaves in Vallombrosa of what Italy was going to do to Greece when the Italians following a strategic plan had withdrawn far enough to lure the Greeks away from the strong positions they held. From the Greek High Command it evoked merely the laconic announcement that the advance of their troops was continuing all along the front. The Italian Ninth Army had been compelled by the hasty evacuation of Koritza to retreat in two portions, one taking a northerly direction along the valley of the Shkoumbi in the direction of Elbasan, the other moving westward along the valley of the Devoli in the hope either of joining up with the northerly portion or falling back on Berat. This double retreat was announced by the Italian High Command as a movement of troops being carried out with a regularity of cadence which the enemy had tried in vain to interrupt. To extend the musical simile, the two portions of the Italian Ninth Army were performing a dispirited duet marked *presto* in the score, the failure to interrupt which was a tribute to the speed at which it was being played. By November 24th Greek detachments pushing rapidly on up the Shkoumbi valley were on the outskirts of Pogradetz, a little town about eighteen miles north-north-west of Koritza in the highlands above Lake Ochrida, while the Greek cavalry in pursuit of the Italian retreat along the valley of the Devoli entered Moschopolis. This village is famous in the annals of liberty, for it was here in the mountains that a printing-press was started just after the War of Independence to publish the Greek classics. Lying about ten miles west of Koritza it had been awarded to Albania by the boundary commission.

The strategic withdrawal of the sundered Ninth Army involved the Italian Eleventh Army in another strategic withdrawal southward. It fell back toward Argyrokastro, and by November 27th the Greeks were fighting near Delvino on the road that links Argyrokastro with Santi Quaranta, the most southerly of the three Albanian supply ports.

On November 30th Greek forces entered Pogradetz and pushed on immediately in the direction of Elbasan; simultaneously in the central sector they were pressing the Italians back along the Devoli valley toward Berat. It is due to the retreating forces to note that the communiqués of the Greek High Command testified to the stubbornness with which the Italians were now contesting the Greek advance, making use of fortified positions in the hills and being helped by the ever increasing severity of the weather which laid a heavy strain alike on the Greek transport and on the endurance and valour of the Greek soldiers. The lines of communication were often lines of dead pack-horses and mules, and often the Greek forward troops amid the snows of the high tops went without their rations for four or five days at a stretch. Sometimes the Italians would hold a fortified post on a mountain spur, and the Greek forward troops would have to drag their mountain batteries into position to shell them out of it. At other times the Italians would be driven out by assault with hand grenade and bayonet. Thus height after height was seized and held, always with the intention of outflanking the Italian positions above and closing the entrances of the valleys so that Italian troops below had to abandon such valleys before their communications were cut. The configuration of the country, with the valleys running north-west and south-east, allowed the frontal advance, which was steadily pressed along the ridges, to swing continuously round toward the west and thus threaten the Italian forces with envelopment by reaching the coast in their rear and capturing Valona. "The movements were thus in the nature of sickle-shaped drives through the mountains", Lt.-Colonel Casson has recorded,[1] "each separate move swinging slightly round to its left flank. There was no such thing as a continuous line. All the Greek positions were strong points—mobile strong points."

The terror which this almost supernatural-seeming Greek advance struck into the guilty hearts of the Italians was reflected in the habit the latter made of carrying off from the villages they evacuated hostages from the Orthodox inhabitants whether Greek or Albanian. It can only be presumed that they hoped in some way to protect themselves by this device. What her lovers had regarded as the most civilized nation in Europe horrified those lovers by behaviour copied from that most barbarous nation in Europe with whom she had made her despicable alliance.

But although the Italian High Command could copy the German

[1] *Greece Against the Axis*, p. 41.

A Greek Airman

Mountain Artillery Pack Mules

Infantry attack in the Snow

Tough Greek Soldiers

method of making war upon non-combatants it was quite unable to copy its master in the more important task of making war upon combatants. Mussolini's *blitzkrieg* was planned on the assumption that there would be no combatants. The presence of such an unexpected obstacle wrecked it. The *blitzkrieg* had been planned so carefully that no allowance had been made for any possible change that might have to be made in order to suit unforeseen circumstances. The Regia Aeronautica, for instance, continued to bomb undefended villages in the path of the invaders as if the invaders really were advancing. There was nobody in the Italian High Command with enough imagination to perceive that from the moment the assumption of non-resistance was shown to be unjustified it was essential to use the Regia Aeronautica to deal with the altered situation. That it was vital to impede the Greek mobilization if the *blitzkrieg* was to proceed as smoothly as had been presumed was apparently never recognized. The plan had laid down that the Regia Aeronautica was to terrorize the civilian population. So off flew Bruno Mussolini to lead a squadron upon the desperate adventure of bombing the school children of Patras and off flew the ineffable Ciano to lead another squadron in an attack upon Salonika. And while the exploits of these two wretched braggarts and *mascalzoni* were being advertised in the Italian Press, which twenty years of Fascism had reduced to the condition of toilet-paper for the Duce's verbal diarrhoea, the roads northward congested with Greek troops, lorries, and pack-transport were never once bombed. The plan of the *blitzkrieg* had not provided for such an operation. The Italian navy was equally unenterprising, and the transports from the islands were never seriously threatened by the enemy's warships.

The whole blame for the failure of the *blitzkrieg* was laid upon the weather and the absence of good roads in Epirus. Yet the losses sustained by the Greeks were far heavier from the weather than from the Italian artillery or such squadrons of the Regia Aeronautica (not led by Bruno Mussolini or his brother-in-law the Count) as tried to bomb them among the rocks of the mountains. Everywhere the Greeks had the worst of the weather because all the local actions by which they advanced into the enemy's country were fought on the heights, and they were without shelter and often without food until they could expel the Italians from their fortified posts and gain their shelter and the food they left behind them. That the lack of good roads in the Epirus should have been put forward seriously as an excuse for the failure of the *blitzkrieg* is one more example of the schoolboy intelligence to which Fascism so nearly approximates. Obviously the configuration and the development of the country through which the Italian advance had to be made must have been available in maps and reports of the *Servizio di Informazione* for that branch of the Italian General Staff which dealt with operations in the field.   It is true that after the fiasco Italian propaganda alleged that the check was itself clear proof of the lack of preparation for any aggression against Greece and by implication therefore of any intention to attack Greece until it was forced upon Italy by Greek double-dealing with the British; but we do not require the documentary evidence which rebuts such an argument, for the Italian intentions had been self-evident for a quarter of a century.

In April 1917 the present writer was noting in the forlorn hope of impressing the Foreign Office:

"Of the confusion, political and diplomatic, which followed hard upon December 1st (1916) the Italians have taken the fullest advantage.   They have established themselves firmly in Corfu; they have overrun Southern Albania; they have so denuded the Epirus of foodstuffs as to make their occupation even of Jannina perfectly feasible, and, having established themselves as firmly in Greece as the French, they are now looking across the Aegean towards Asia Minor. . . .

"In the Dodecanese the Italians everywhere decry the notion that the Greeks have any national sense and insist that the Greeks are only Greeks in so far as they belong to the Orthodox Church. . . . Whatever the French may have done to outrage the susceptibilities of the Greeks, they have never struck at the roots of national life in the shameless way in which a nation entering this war with the cry of *Italia irredenta* has struck.   Already there is a proposal afoot to enrol the population of the Dodecanese in the Italian Army, and already a deliberate attempt is being made to starve Calymnos, the most uncompromisingly Greek island of all in the Dodecanese. . . .

"It is scarcely too much to suppose that Italy, in seeking to replace Austria in Europe, will return some years after the war to her former alliance with Germany, and it will obviously be a great danger to the future peace of the Levant if Germany achieve her ambitions in this direction through the help of Italy."

It is as well to remind contemporary opinion that the Italian ambition to dominate Greece is not just one of the unpleasant products of Fascism. The abortive *blitzkrieg* of 1940 is only one more incident in a very long tale.

No, it was not lack of preparation which upset that *blitzkrieg*, but the failure of the Iulia Division to reach Metsovo and thus open the way to Thessaly for the motorized forces of the invaders. That battle in the valley of the Sarandoporos is seen to possess more and more the attributes of a decisive battle as one examines it, although it would be premature to award it all the attributes until the issue between Germany and Russia, which as these words are written is still in the balance, has been decided. What the Italian High Command had failed to appreciate was that, unless their motorized forces could move steadily on, such forces were likely to become an unwieldy handicap. And this they did become in the event. The armoured cars and tanks and lorries hampered the mobility of the Italian troops in every valley along which they were fighting; they even hampered the mobility with which they were able to retreat and were responsible for many of the prisoners the Greeks were able to take. Dependency upon mechanical transport and tanks and air support coupled with the corrupting effect of the Fascist training upon individual initiative and self-sufficiency had deprived the Italian soldier of his qualities as a fighter until he turned like a rat in a trap, when he fought well. It was not a piece of idle rhetoric which claimed that one Evzone was worth six Alpini. The Italian soldier was morally, physically, and mentally the inferior of his Greek opponent, on whom the influence of authoritarian theory had not had time to make itself felt for the worse. Another decade of the Fourth of August régime might have reduced the Hellenic nation to a condition nearer to that of the Italian nation; but four years of it had been faintly beneficial. This could be urged with equal truth of Fascism. Let it be repeated that as a tonic Fascism like arsenic or strychnine in minute doses can be useful, but it is a stimulant which taken to excess over a long period is ultimately lethal.

Nevertheless, it would do a grave injustice to the skill and courage with which the Greeks fought that campaign in Epirus and Albania if the inferiority of the Italians in that mountain-warfare were to lead to the belief that they were so many poltroons. The Greek communiqués repeatedly testify to the valour and tenacity with which their opponents contested the ground. Undoubtedly a large proportion of the Italian officers are surpassed only by the Rumanians in their lack of every military virtue; but if well led, the simple Italian soldier, even after twenty years of Fascism, is capable of putting up a much better show than is generally believed. It must be emphasized once more that the Greek soldier was not only fighting in the conditions which were best suited to display his qualities as an individual warrior, but that every single Greek soldier was animated by that conviction of being all Hellas in himself, and not merely all Hellas of his own time but all Hellas of three thousand years. If a man in his passionate resolve to defend his wife and his family and the olives of home feels himself to be one of Miltiades' Ten Thousand or one of Leonidas' Three Hundred as well as a Klepht of the War of Independence, and perhaps adds to this the practical experience gained from fighting in four wars, not to mention the conviction that he is opposed to a foe of a lower breed than himself, he will be a formidable adversary indeed, and it will take more than the facile and sonorous exhortations penned by generals or officials of the Fascist party to withstand him. The strategy and the tactics of the Greek High Command were perfectly adapted to the warfare they had to wage and the most effective use was made of the material at their disposal; but far-sighted strategy and cunning tactics would have been useless without men who were capable of outdoing the most sanguine theory with what seemed a superhuman practice. It was impossible to demand too much of those Greek soldiers. Without hope of reinforcements or relief, subsisting for days on end upon the meagre fare they could carry themselves, their only protection against the snowstorm and the icy wind a single blanket, they fought their way onward along the spurs and ridges six thousand feet up, dying up there for Hellas and thinking as they died, some of the olives of home, some of the bells of goats and sheep in the pastures of Arcadia, some of a foam-laced strand beside the blue Aegean, some of the jangle of the Athenian streets, some of the brawling of a stream in Thessaly.

It was by the efforts of such men that on December 4th the Greek Evzone regiment which had won the great victory in the Pindus occupied Premeti where the Aoos (Viosa) flows swiftly north-west toward the low country above Valona. Two days later the passage of the Bistritsa was forced in spite of the enemy's tough resistance, and Santi Quaranta (Haghioi Saranda) was entered. That forcing of the passage of the Bistritsa had involved a Greek battalion in wading for three hours in icy water, starting at 4 A.M. This, the most southerly supply port of the Italian armies in Albania, lies at the head of the narrow strait which divides Corfu from the mainland. The Italians burnt the town before evacuating it and abandoned in the harbour the half-submerged wreck of a destroyer which had been sunk by the bombs of the R.A.F. Not the least ridiculous piece of braggadocio perpetrated by the Duce had been his attempt to change the venerable dedication of this port to the Forty Saints to a less venerable dedication to his favourite daughter Edda, the wife of Ciano. The old journalist in Mussolini should have been wise enough to avoid such an opportunity for wit at the expense of a young woman whose reputation was not of a kind proof against the all too obvious ribald comparison.

With Santi Quaranta in Greek hands and Delvino falling into their hands the next day, Argyrokastro, the base of the Italian Eleventh Army, was threatened from three quarters, and on December 8th the 'silver fort' was occupied.

The Italians stood at last on a line stretching from Khimara on their right flank to the high ridge between Elbasan and Lake Ochrida on their left. The key to this line and northern Albania was the gorge of Tepelene, the old stronghold of Ali Pasha, which runs east and west above the road from Jannina to Berat and commands the road from Argyrokastro to Valona. This was roughly the same line as the Austrians held during 1916.

Much had been heard from the Italian Press and Radio about the strategic withdrawal which after luring the Greeks from their own advantageous positions was to be transformed into an irresistible and overwhelming counter-attack; but the achievement of this new line did not suggest that high military circles in Italy considered it a complete triumph. On December 6th Marshal Badoglio resigned from his exalted position and was succeeded by General Ugo Cavallero as Chief of the General Staff. The next day General da Vecchi resigned from his post as Military Governor of the Dodecanese and was succeeded by General Ettore Bastico. And on December 8th Admiral Cavagnari, Chief of the Naval Staff, resigned. Something was seriously wrong with the Italian High Command. It was impossible any longer to hide from the Italian public that the attack on Greece had been a complete fiasco. And then on December 9th the British offensive in Libya began, and for week after week the Italian public was to receive news of nothing but defeat.

CHAPTER NINE

WE have heard one of the mighty voices of Liberty speak in the mountains of Greece: the voice that spoke from her sea rang out in tones of equal resolution. What else was to be expected from a nation whose chief naval base is the dockyard of Salamis, a name famous in history two millenniums before Portsmouth or Brest were dreamt of?

At the outbreak of war between Greece and Italy the Royal Hellenic Navy consisted of the following units:

A. One 10,000-ton armoured cruiser, the *Georgios Averoff*, which had been built in 1911 and was therefore a veteran of four wars. She had been modernized in 1925–27 and carried four 9·2 guns, eight 7·5 guns, six 3-inch guns, and five 3-inch A.A. guns. As the flagship of Admiral Coundouriotis she had played the chief part in keeping the Turkish fleet out of the Aegean in the war of 1912, and the victory she was instrumental in gaining off Cape Helles had been commemorated in the name given to the light cruiser *Helle* which was sunk by Italian treachery off Tenos on August 15th, 1940.

B. Ten large destroyers, six of which were modern ships and four old but modernized in 1924–26.
Two *King George* class (1938) of 1350 tons with a speed of 36·5 knots.
Four *Coundouriotis* class (1929–33) of 1375 tons with a speed of 40 knots.
Four *Aetos* class (1912) of 1050 tons with a speed of 31·5 knots.

C. Six submarines built between 1925 and 1930, all of which were in fairly good condition.
Two *Katsonis* class (1926) of 605 tons carrying four 21-inch torpedo tubes.
Four *Proteus* class (1927–28) of 735 tons carrying eight 21-inch torpedo tubes.

D. Thirteen torpedo-boats built between 1908 and 1915, but re-fitted and partially reconstructed in 1926–30.
Two *Sphendoni* class (1918) of 400 tons with a speed of 30 knots.
Two *Nike* class (1908).

Two *Pergamos* class (1917) of 250 tons with a speed of 26 knots.

Three *Khios* class (1917) of 250 tons with a speed of 26 knots.

Four *Aigle* class (1912) of 125 tons with a speed of 23 knots.

E. Two Thornycroft motor torpedo-boats built in 1930.

F. Thirty auxiliary craft including a repair ship, depôt ships, mine-layers, minesweepers, etc.

G. Three squadrons of naval cooperation aircraft consisting of Ansons, Dorniers, and Fairey III F seaplanes which were under the orders of the Admiral commanding the fleet for reconnaissance and anti-submarine controls.

The main fleet base was Salamis Dockyard, and there were secondary bases at Salonika, Volo (with an even older history in the annals of the sea than Salamis, for it was from here that the Argonauts sailed), the two entrances of the Euboea Straits, and the western approaches to the Gulf of Patras. For its organization and fighting efficiency the Greek navy had had the advantage of a series of successive British Naval Missions which had been lent for thirty years. It has already been noted that Mussolini as early as 1926 agitated with the Greek Government for the withdrawal of the British Naval Mission, which he regarded as a hostile influence to his ambitions in the Eastern Mediterranean.

At the outbreak of the Second World War the Greek Mercantile Marine, which had been reduced to 250,000 tons by the First World War, had a total gross tonnage of 1,800,000, which was exceeded in the Mediterranean only by the French and Italian merchant fleets.

The first task of the Hellenic navy when Italy attacked Greece was the escort and protection of the convoys of troops and material, not only from the islands but also from ports on the mainland, to the mobilization ports of Salonika and Volo in order to avoid the congestion of the roads leading northward to the frontier. This operation lasted from October 28th until November 15th by which date the mobilization was completed, and it was covered at long range by the British fleet in the Eastern Mediterranean which prevented any attempt by the more powerful units of the Italian battle fleet to intervene in force. Nevertheless, it has to be remembered that the main base of the British fleet was at Alexandria, which is a long way from the Aegean, and that the Italians could dispose of a number of fast cruisers and large modern destroyers conveniently based at Taranto and also at Leros in the Dodecanese. Fortunately the dismal lack of audacity which characterized the Italian navy during the First World War had been handed on as a pusillanimous tradition to the Second World War and, incredible though it may seem, not one of these bold heirs of Venice and Genoa ventured to engage the escorting Greek destroyers. A few submarine attacks were made on convoys, but as the submarines did not venture to operate in the daylight it is not astonishing that these attacks were all quite harmless.

Toward the end of the Greek mobilization the Fleet Air Arm and the R.A.F. made its devastating raid on Taranto with torpedo-carrying aircraft, and the losses incurred by the Italian navy on that November night provided a further powerful stimulus to inaction.

After the mobilization was completed the Hellenic navy was kept busy protecting the long and what so easily might have been the very hazardous sea communications. Most of the supplies for the Greek army went by sea to Salonika and Volo which saved the road transport by greatly shortening the distance to the front. Most of the ocean-going cargo ships of the Greek Mercantile Marine had already been time-chartered to the British Government, and a comparatively small number of these transported war material and supplies from Britain and America to Egypt whence they were escorted to the Piraeus by Greek destroyers in cooperation with units of the British Eastern Mediterranean Squadron. Besides war material, foodstuffs had to be sent in bulk to Greece, which could grow only enough cereals to last its population for six months, and that fact has to be noted (it seems so coldly!) at a moment when Greece is starving.

The activity of the Hellenic navy was not restricted to escort duty. Within forty-eight hours of the Italian ultimatum two Greek destroyers, the *Spetsai* and the *Psara*, island names commemorating naval exploits of the past, steamed through the Corinth Canal and down the Gulf of Patras to reach the Albanian coast opposite Corfu. There they shelled for two hours the right flank of the Italian army which was moving toward the Kalamas. No Italian ship was sighted. During the night of November 9th a division of destroyers under Rear-Admiral E. Kavadias, the Commander-in-Chief of the Greek fleet, carried out a reconnaissance almost up to the mouth of the Bay of Valona, and once again no Italian ship was sighted. In the second half of December a strong force of light cruisers and destroyers from the British Eastern Mediterranean Squadron steamed as far as Durazzo while heavier units bombarded Valona and did a great deal of damage. Greek destroyers followed this up with two more raids, during the second of which, on the night of January 5th–6th, they bombarded Valona once more.

The naval advantage that accrued either to Great Britain or to Greece from the position brought about by Italian aggression was nothing like as great as it might have been if a realistic and far-sighted policy of cooperation between the two countries had been steadily pursued for many years previously. The keynote of Venizelos' idea was struck as far back as December 1912 when he discussed with Mr Lloyd George, Mr Winston Churchill, and Prince Louis of Battenberg the question of leasing Argostoli to the British Admiralty as a naval base. Venizelos believed that the future of Greece depended on her own naval strength, which would be unassailable so long as British naval strength was maintained in the Mediterranean.

What British naval strategists, or rather what British foreign policy of which British naval supremacy has always been the only practical implement, failed to make provision against was French defection and Italian hostility. The *rapprochement* with Turkey was delayed too long, and when that *rapprochement* was finally brought about it was brought about without making an attempt, and thus doubling its effectiveness, to include Greece as a partner in the alliance that resulted. There is no doubt whatever that, if British policy had interested itself in the restoration of King George II of the Hellenes some years earlier and had offered Greece the full advantages of a firm defensive and offensive alliance, by which is to be understood the necessary economic support as well, the elements in Greece which opposed a restoration could have been swayed to take a practical view of its advantages and the dissensions which were rending the country internally could have been healed. This is not the place to pass in review the unimaginative series of improvisations which has characterized British foreign policy since the First World War; but when a mighty empire based on sea-power hands over to jellyfish statesmen the sea it should rule it must expect to suffer the consequences; and among many consequences the almost complete inability of the British navy to take advantage of what the precipitation of Greece into war offered for a display of naval strategy must be counted as perhaps the greatest.

If the British navy had possessed a base at Argostoli it is doubtful whether Mussolini would ever have risked that attack on Greece; but if he had, he would never have been able to reinforce or supply the Italian armies in Albania, and such a failure, it is not too fanciful to speculate, might have involved an invasion of Italy by British forces which would have changed the whole position in the Mediterranean.

In this matter of interference with reinforcements and supplies it is worth noting what was effected by the six small submarines of the Hellenic navy, though their exploits were carried out at a date later than the narrative has reached.

On the morning of December 24th the *Papanikolis*, commanded by Lt.-Commander Iatrides, a sister ship of the *Katsonis* and one of the two older and smaller submarines, attacked a convoy of six Italian supply ships escorted by six destroyers. The *Papanikolis* fired four torpedoes and dived immediately to 170 feet. Three explosions were heard before the depth-charges began to burst all round the Greek submarine. This was the beginning of a hunt which lasted all day, in the course of which the *Papanikolis* escaped northwards into the Adriatic. On the next day, which was Christmas Day, the *Papanikolis* turned southward and succeeded in getting through the straits of Otranto, although she was sighted and repeatedly bombed by enemy aircraft. Later it was established that she had sunk two large Italian transports laden with troops and war material—the *Lombardia* of 20,000 and the *Liguria* of 15,354 tons gross.

Soon after this the *Katsonis*, commanded by Lt.-Commander Spanides, attacked an Italian oil-tanker off Durazzo, and when the torpedoes were fired the submarine broke surface to engage the enemy ship, which was armed with two guns and manned by a crew of the Regia Marina. Instead of counter-attacking the *Katsonis* before she could bring her single 4-inch gun into action, the crew of the tanker took to the lifeboats and left the *Katsonis* to sink the tanker at leisure.

On December 29th the *Proteus*, commanded by Lt.-Commander Hadjicostantis, attacked a strongly escorted enemy convoy and succeeded in sinking the troop-transport *Sardegna* of 11,452 tons gross. Unfortunately the Italian destroyers of the escort succeeded where they had failed with the *Papanikolis*. It was claimed by the Italian Radio that the Greek submarine was rammed by an Italian destroyer and that after coming to the surface she subsequently sank. No lives were saved, and the Italian version of the attack has never been confirmed.

On the night of January 28th, 1941, the *Papanikolis* sank a supply ship of 10,000 tons, and on February 23rd a heavily laden transport was sunk by the *Nereus* (Lt.-Commander Brasidas Rotas). Just a month later, on March 23rd, the *Triton* (Lt.-Commander G. Zeppos) sent to the bottom the 5000-ton ship *Carnia* and hit with a torpedo another ship, but without sinking her.

The sixth submarine of the tiny Greek flotilla, the *Glaukos*, had to wait until November 10th, 1941, to take her toll of enemy shipping, on which date she torpedoed off Herakleion in Crete a heavily laden Italian supply ship of 3000 tons which was presumably sunk.

The Adriatic offers particularly difficult water for submarines to operate in. The entrance is only forty miles wide, and the coasts on both sides were commanded by the enemy. The clear waters of that sea add to the difficulty of submarines by the opportunity they afford to air observation. Nobody who can appreciate the difficulty of successful submarine action in the Adriatic will allow their admiration of the Greek submarine commanders to be qualified by the natural contempt they may feel for their unseamanly opponents. Even Italian destroyers supported by aircraft can be very formidable when there are as many available in a small area.

That they were able to sink only one Greek submarine in five months as an offset to the 70,000 gross tons lost by the Italian Mercantile Marine is a tribute to the audacity and seamanship of the little submarine flotilla of the Royal Hellenic navy, and the careful staff-work of the Naval Staff under Rear-Admiral A. Sakellariou.

The greatest disappointment to those who had hoped that the opportunity offered by the attack on Greece would lead to a determined attempt to eliminate the Italians from the Dodecanese was what seemed the lack of any idea that the Italian occupation of the Dodecanese might be a menace in the near future either to Cyprus and Syria or to Crete and Egypt. Obviously the Hellenic navy was not strong enough to undertake such offensive action without powerful support from the British naval forces, and the necessary information is not yet available on which a critic of strategy would be justified in expressing an opinion. It must be presumed in the absence of such information that no operation on a large scale was feasible in the Dodecanese, and that the bombing of enemy aerodromes in Rhodes,

Leros, Casos, Carpathos (Scarpanto), and Astypalaea (Stampalia) represented the maximum offensive effort possible.   Nevertheless, the comparative immunity which the Italians enjoyed in the Dodecanese is an exasperation to look back on.   One asks how far it was due to what seemed a lack of coordination at that date between the three arms of the fighting forces.   When the time comes to record what happened in Crete in May 1941 we may be disagreeably astonished to hear that a few more guns of heavy calibre might have prevented the capture of the Maleme aerodrome in the west of Crete, and we may be not less disagreeably astonished to learn how little could be done during the six months that were available to put that strategically vital island in a condition to beat off the German and Italian attack. Furthermore, even if we recognize that an operation against Rhodes and Leros was beyond the scope of the forces at the disposal of Greece and Britain, it is difficult to believe that the Italian garrison of Astypalaea would have offered an infrangible resistance to a resolute assault.   However, it must be repeated that such criticism is dependent for its justification on what could be done with what there was.   We may very well hear one day that with the supplies available it was miraculous that so much was done.

Perhaps some of the acute sense of frustration that must have been felt by the Dodecanesian exiles on the mainland of Greece was reflected in the action taken by Dr. Vasili Verghis and fourteen of his Dodecanesian compatriots on the night of November 17th–18th. Dr. Verghis secretly hired a small motor-boat in which his expeditionary force sailed from a bay on the mainland and landed upon the islet of Agathonissi about a mile from Leros, the Italian naval base with which Great Britain had allowed Mussolini to challenge her Mediterranean strength and menace her Mediterranean security.   On this islet Dr. Verghis and his fourteen companions attacked the post of the *carabinieri* and took prisoner the *maresciallo* in command and three of his men with all their arms.   After this the naval post on Agathonissi was attacked and three Italians were killed, among them the officer in charge.   Then Dr. Verghis and his party sailed back to the mainland with the four captive *carabinieri*.

According to the Greek communiqué the Italians supposed that the enterprise of Dr. Verghis undertaken entirely on his own initiative was the prelude to a great Greek military campaign against the Dodecanese, and for the whole of the daylight of November 18th the garrisons of the various islands remained at the alert. When darkness fell, the destroyer flotilla wrote a glorious page in Italian naval history by venturing forty miles away from its heavily fortified base at Port Laki in Leros in order to shell the undefended town of Tigani on the south coast of Samos. Several shells were fired without causing material damage and after the bombardment the destroyers steamed back at full speed to their base. Italian planes next morning dropped bombs both on Tigani and Port Vathy on the other side of Samos.

In February 1941 hopes of vigorous action against the Italians in the Dodecanese were raised again when an Admiralty communiqué announced that the island of Castellorizo or Castelrosso had been occupied by British forces, which included four destroyers and some fighter planes; but a day or two later it was announced that these British forces having achieved their purpose had evacuated the island. Castellorizo, three and a half miles long and hardly a mile and a half across at its widest, lies eighty miles east of Rhodes and barely three miles from the coast of Anatolia, and in spite of its small size, its barrenness, and its lack of springs, the island used to maintain a Greek population of between six and seven thousand, nearly all the males of which were mariners and as good as any to be found in all the Mediterranean. No doubt that population has been much reduced by the Italian policy of ruthless expulsion which has been practised against the Greek inhabitants of the Dodecanese for the last thirty years. Yet Castellorizo itself is not one of the Dodecanese Archipelago, and why the Italians were allowed to seize and occupy it in 1918 is a gloomy mystery, because the fortification of Castellorizo and the construction there of a seaplane base should have seemed too defiant an indication of Italy's aggressive schemes in the Eastern Mediterranean to be tolerated.

It was the destruction of this seaplane base which was the object of the British naval operation early in 1941. How successful it was has not been made known even eighteen months later. At the time the Italian Radio supported by the German stations claimed that the expedition was a fiasco and that the British flag flying over Castellorizo was captured by the relieving Italian force. No communiqué about this ambiguous affair was published by the Greek High Command.

There was nothing ambiguous about the offensive action taken by those five squadrons of the R.A.F. which were in Greece during the last two months of 1940. They were much handicapped by the denial of forward bases due to the fear in Athens of provoking the Germans; but by the end of December the two fighter squadrons were allowed to use the aerodromes at Larissa, Trikkala, and Jannina. In spite of the serious disadvantage of still having to work from Menidi (Tatoï), the bomber squadrons continued to attack the Italian supply ports of Durazzo and Valona whenever the weather allowed. Thirteen destructive raids on Valona were carried out in December alone, and the popular appreciation of what these young airmen were doing for Hellas was intense. Brindisi and Bari were also attacked, and there is no doubt that the Italians were severely hampered both in the transport of troops and supplies. The effect of this on the operations was gratefully perceptible, and reinforcements were frequently rushed direct from Italy to the front line not only by Italian planes but also by German troop-carriers. Besides the raids on the supply ports, Italian troops and communications in the Tepelene sector were attacked and much damage was inflicted. On one of these attacks by the bombers of 211 Squadron escorted by the Gladiators of 80 Squadron a large formation of C.R. 42 and G. 50 fighters was encountered, of which eight were definitely shot down and seven more probably shot down. This was achieved without loss to the Gladiators, a wonderful tribute to the skill and daring of the British fighter pilots when pitted against the latest Italian fighters with fighters of their own that were on the verge of obsolescence. On December 21st nine of these Gladiators intercepted a large enemy bomber formation escorted by fifty C.R. 42 fighters. On this occasion eight of the enemy were shot down with three probables for the loss of two British pilots. It is melancholy to have to record that the Italian airmen made a habit of machine-gunning the British and Greek pilots when they baled out; but when Marshal Balbo was lost to the Regia Aeronautica a tradition of chivalry died with him. It has been impossible to find a single instance of *signorile* behaviour by Italian airmen in Greece or Albania. Generally speaking, it can be said that Fascism has proportionately a much larger representation in the Italian air force than in either the Italian army or the Italian navy, and the deplorable example of men like Bruno Mussolini or Ciano has been widely copied. On Christmas Day some of the bombers of 84 Squadron dropped presents for the children of Corfu as a token, in the words of Air Vice-Marshal

CHAPTER NINE

d'Albiac, the A.O.C., in a message to the Nomarch of Corfu, of "our admiration of your courage in the face of heavy and constant enemy attack and an appreciation of your kindness to our airmen who had to land in Corfu".

Some hours afterwards the defenceless island was heavily bombed by the Italians, and such an outrage on Christmas Day is typical of the profoundly anti-Catholic spirit of Fascism which has now desecrated with violence and treachery three of the holiest days in the Church's calendar.

During that December Air Vice-Marshal d'Albiac in the course of a talk to the war correspondents about the war said: "Flying conditions in Greece are more difficult than anywhere in Europe. The weather changes with great rapidity, making accurate forecasts impossible, and the nature of the country does not always allow landings when pilots are unable to regain their bases. Ice formations are another difficulty. Instruments freeze, and air-screws get a covering of ice which makes it difficult to maintain sufficient altitude to clear the mountains. The temperature is never more than 28 degrees, and sometimes goes to minus 50 degrees. Those conditions, as well as the restricted number of air-bases available to the R.A.F., make the operation of a large air force in Greece during the winter impracticable, but I believe that the R.A.F. will be greatly reinforced when the weather improves."

Air Vice-Marshal d'Albiac was an optimist.

CHAPTER TEN

THE second phase of the Greek offensive begun after the fall of Koritza and Argyrokastro—the two forward bases of the Italian Ninth and Eleventh Armies—made the counter-offensive on which the Italian Press and Radio still harped an impossibility, at any rate for a long time to come. The chief objectives of this offensive were the port of Valona on the Greek left, Berat in the centre, and Elbasan on the right. The fall of these places would open the way across low-lying country toward Tirana, the capital of Albania, and Durazzo, the chief supply port, and ultimately to a reasonable hope of throwing the Italians into the Adriatic, not to mention the opening-up of that sea to British naval action.

There has been a tendency in one or two books about the war in Greece to suggest that if the second phase of the Greek offensive had been pressed with the vigour and determination which marked the first phase there would have been a reasonable chance for the line of the river Shkoumbi to have been reached before the end of 1940. It has even been suggested that the German influence on certain political circles in Athens was sufficiently powerful to lead General Metaxas to encourage a deliberate slowing-down of the forward movement.

An accusation like that cannot be rebutted authoritatively at a time when so much material, both documentary and human, is not at the disposal of the chronicler. On the face of it, however, there is not the slightest need to look beyond the obstacles which confronted the Greek armies for an explanation of the slowing-down of their effort. In the first place the Italian defensive line was an extremely strong one. Their right flank rested on the old Acroceraunian mountains under their modern names of the Lugara, Chika, and Griva ranges, with strongly fortified positions round Khimara. Nearer to the centre the gorge of Tepelene with the strong point of Klisura at the head of it and the great mountainous mass of Tomor presented a formidable barrier. And the Italian left flank rested upon other mountains between Elbasan and Pogradetz. Added to the natural strength of the Italian line was the ever increasing difficulty of the

112

Greek Soldiers leaving for the Front

The Greek Army celebrates its Easter Festival

supply problem. Indeed, unless the Greek troops had been able to
help themselves from time to time to the supplies of the enemy the
tempo of the offensive would have been much slower. It must be
remembered that very little material British aid apart from those invaluable R.A.F. squadrons had as yet reached Greece.

Finally, there was the weather which throughout that December
grew more savage.

The Greek advance was slow, but in view of the complete inability
of the Italians to launch any except small local attacks it could be
called sure. Columns on the Greek right had penetrated the upper
valley of the Shkoumbi after gaining a foothold upon the mountains
which command the road to Elbasan. In the centre Greek forces
had advanced beyond Moschopolis and were beginning to threaten
Berat. By December 10th a column had reached the valley of the
Usum, a tributary of the Semeni on which Berat itself stands. Other
Greek forces were gaining ground on the heights of Tomor.

Farther north an attack on Valona was developing along the valley
of the Aoos (Viosa) where the road runs from Argyrokastro, but the
approaches to this road are covered by the gorge of Tepelene which
overhangs the road from Jannina to Berat to the east of it, and there
was no chance of a serious threat to Valona until Tepelene fell.

Still farther south Greek forces advanced from Santi Quaranta to
occupy Porto Palermo on December 13th. After this they met with
strong resistance from the Italians on the hills above Khimara. The
Regia Aeronautica was particularly active in this direction, and the
road to Khimara was heavily bombed all the time. Finally in a
desperate attack the Evzones took Mount Peluri by storm on December 20th and four days later, on Christmas Eve, Khimara fell. The
153rd Battalion of Blackshirts, which had been specially flown over
from Italy to defend Khimara, surrendered to a man (29 officers and
677 rank and file). The honorary commander of this battalion was
none other than Roberto Farinacci of ill fame, the former secretary
of the Fascist party. The colonel of the Second Battalion of the
Second Regiment of Bersaglieri together with his staff were also
captured. The town was entered by a young Greek naval officer,
himself a Khimariot, with twenty-five gendarmes. Khimara, although awarded to Albania, is as purely Hellenic a town as exists,
and the inhabitants have kept the old Doric accent. When Constantinople fell in 1453 and the Turks overran Greece, Khimara

alone held out and refused to recognize the conquest. Expedition after expedition against the town failed, and it was not until after the fall of Venice that Ali Pasha was able with the consent of Napoleon to attack this ancient stronghold of liberty from the sea. After a heroic resistance Khimara fell, and many of its citizens were killed or exiled. Nevertheless, Khimariots played a great part in the War of Independence and again in the Balkan Wars of 1912. It will be intolerable if after this war Khimara is not restored to Greece.

Although the Italian Press made light of this Greek success by claiming that Khimara itself was a small place of no importance, its capture increased the threat to Valona by the tactics of infiltration in the now familiar style of Greek mountain warfare. Such infiltration, provided that the strongholds of Tepelene and Klisura at the exit and entrance of the gorge could be overcome, would make Valona untenable.

And in spite of the paralysing cold, the blizzards, the inadequate clothing of the troops, the loss of transport in a savage country where the mules would be swept over precipices by the wind or collapse on their haunches and freeze to death, those Greek columns winding among the mountains continued their offensive, and seldom a day passed without loss of men or material to the enemy. His mountain artillery was steadily being driven back out of range of the roads so that the main Greek forces could advance along them. If only it could be considered certain that the Germans would not intervene to save their allies it could look certain that Durazzo would be as fatal to Mussolini as Dyrracchium once upon a time to Pompey, and that the whole gimcrack edifice of Fascist Imperialism would crash. But would Hitler leave Mussolini to his fate? The arrival of Stukas in Sicily early that January was of ill omen for such an intention.

On the first day of the New Year General Metaxas, as Minister of War and the Marine, sent the armed forces of Hellas this message:

"Heroic fighters by land and sea and air, commanders, officers, non-commissioned officers, soldiers, sailors, and airmen, the Christian festivals and the New Year find you with arms in your hands engaged in a very hard struggle for the defence of the country. Hard though that struggle may be it has been filled with glory and with victories. The whole Hellenic people regards you with admiration and with pride. You are the manifestation of the nation's strength and the defenders of its existence.

There is nobody in Greece who does not think of you continually, at every moment of the day and night. Your fathers, your mothers, your wives, your children, your brothers, your relations, your friends, men and women one and all stand at your side and pray to God for you, proud of your heroic deeds, of your victories, of the glorious end of those who fall on the field of battle to live eternally in the memory of the nation. Every man, woman, and child of Greece, and my own self who follows your exploits with so much pride and satisfaction, we wish you from the bottom of our hearts a new year rich in triumphs and victories. We await your return full of honour and glory when you have destroyed our perfidious enemies and gained a solid assurance for the future of a strong and indomitable Greece."

Alas, even yet that return is awaited, and he who wrote those words would live to witness only one more of those heroic exploits of the army of his pride. Through those first days of January the Greek forces drew nearer to Klisura, and after repelling six fierce Italian counter-attacks on January 10th they charged down from the heights upon the burning remains of what General Soddù, who had himself drawn the plan of the fortifications, considered an impregnable position. Klisura, he had assured Rome, would be the tomb of the Greek army. Instead it was to be the pyre of General Soddù's reputation.

Three days after the fall of a place which the Balkan Correspondent of *The Times* declared could have been defended by a handful of men merely by hurling rocks down upon their assailants General Ubaldo Soddù was recalled and the command of the Italian armies in Albania was handed over to General Ugo Cavallero, who had succeeded Marshal Badoglio as Chief of the General Staff. The capture of Klisura cost the Greeks heavily, and the fall of Tepelene eleven miles away at the other end of that terrific gorge evaded their achievement.

In the moving words of Mr Leland Stowe:[1]

"If we had waited for the capture of Tepeleni what a dreary, freezing, unbathed, hungry, heartbreaking winter we should have spent along the savage Drina Valley. Tens of thousands of nameless Greeks did that, keeping alive on round chunks of hard bread, dried figs, and an occasional strip of salted mackerel. Hundreds of them remained on the blizzard-swept heights of the Nemeroka

[1] *No Other Road to Freedom,* p. 245.

range, attacking and edging forward night after night, until their feet were fearfully frozen. In the big schoolhouse-hospital, far down the valleys in Jannina, a great many men lost one foot or both. Some lost their legs. The feet of some quadrupled in size from the swelling and were dyed an ominous purple-black which extended far up their legs. . . . But for all their heroism and sacrifice, Tepeleni could not be taken, not before Spring in any case. Mussolini had been crushingly defeated. Nevertheless, the gods of ice and snow had saved Tepeleni, Valona, and Durazzo for the Fascists."

But, when the snowy couch of Arethusa in the Acroceraunian mountains should melt, would the Italians be able to make their counter-offensive without German help? Throughout that ghastly winter this was the question which stalked like a cold spectre at the back of the north wind.

Down in Athens many of the strong men of the Fourth of August still hoped for the miracle of a kindly German intervention, and the German Minister enjoyed himself in encouraging those vain dreams. If Prince Erbach-Schönburg had been sent packing, the situation in the Balkans might have been precipitated that January to the disorganization of the German plans. What happened in Belgrade at the end of March might then have happened earlier. Turkey might not have signed the non-aggression pact with Bulgaria. The oilfields of Ploesti might have been bombed effectively from Salonika. . . . Dreams, dreams. British armed strength was still in the throes of the improvisation rendered inevitable by years of *laissez-faire*. It was easier to prolong this *laissez-faire*, at any rate for a short while in Greece, and excuse it with the plea that the Greeks themselves did not want to imperil their chance of escaping a German attack by allowing a powerful British Expeditionary Force to land at Salonika. And the same *laissez-faire* was content to postpone the strengthening of the Cretan aerodromes because the Greeks did not want it. Was not their refusal to allow the R.A.F. the use of the northern aerodromes a welcome proof of this?

On January 10th a great British convoy which had been heavily attacked by the newly arrived Stukas in the narrow waters between Sicily and Tunis reached the Piraeus. Its escort had meant the loss of the cruiser *Southampton* and serious damage to the new aircraft-carrier *Illustrious*; but the great convoy, bringing with it the first real military aid to Greece, did make its port with only a few ships missing. The cloth which had been meant for the Home Guard went to the Greek army, and the Home Guard was proud and glad to be without uniforms for such a reason; Bren gun-carriers, tanks, shells, and supplies of all kinds, food, equipment, and medical stores were safely unloaded on the Piraeus quays.

Yet no mention of this great convoy's arrival was allowed by the Greek censorship to appear in the Press because such action by Great Britain might be considered provocative to the Germans. That this convoy was by no means welcome to the Germans was clear from the efforts they had made to prevent its getting through the Mediterranean. Those Stuka bombers did more damage in a couple of hours than the Italian navy and air force had managed to do in six months.

Yet it is not fair to be for ever sneering at the Italian navy. Only three days before that great convoy reached the Piraeus there was a particularly audacious action by Italian naval forces based at Port Laki (Porto Lago) in the island of Leros. Between the Greek island of Amorgos and the equally Greek island of Kalymnos, too long in Italian hands, there lies an islet called Kynaros, the only inhabitants of which were a shepherd's family numbering five persons. In the small hours of January 7th two Italian destroyers arrived off Kynaros and two hundred soldiers were landed. This force opened a fierce fire with machine-guns and rifles for half an hour at two men, who managed to hide themselves in a cave. When the resistance of Kynaros had been quelled the landing-party searched the shepherd's huts without doing any damage, and then at ten o'clock re-embarked on the destroyers, which steamed off at full speed to the safety of Port Laki thirty miles away. This brilliant little exploit will surely always take a very high place in the annals of the Italian navy, as its reply to the attack by Dr Verghis and fourteen Dodecanesians on Agathonissi, when four carabinieri were captured and three Italian sailors killed.

On January 13th General Wavell flew from Cairo to Athens. In Libya, where Tobruk was hard pressed and likely to fall very soon, the prospect of presently reaching Benghazi was good; but rumour was insistent that German armoured divisions were on the verge of crossing the Danube, and the prospect of indefinitely staving off a German attack on Greece by way of Bulgaria was not at all good. Obviously the vital decision about Greece's attitude toward a direct

German threat had soon to be taken, and if it was Greece's intention to defy that threat it was necessary to plan the strategy by which such defiance could be given effect.

Whatever may have been the hope of Metaxas for a British Expeditionary Force strong enough to defy the Germans by an occupation of Salonika, there must obviously have been severe limitations to the numbers which General Wavell felt able to spare from the Forces under his command in Africa, and with the steadily increasing strength of the Luftwaffe in Sicily there was little chance of getting reinforcements on a large scale through the Mediterranean. The discussion of the future must have been greatly complicated by the uncertainty about Hitler's object in attacking Greece and about the attitude that would be taken by Yugoslavia and Turkey toward aggression by way of Bulgaria. There was a faint hope that Russia, alarmed by the German advance down the Danube, would cry 'halt' to any extension of Hitler's Balkan projects, but apparently there was not the slightest inkling that these Balkan projects were a necessary preliminary to an attack on Russia itself planned for the month of May. The strategists, professional and amateur, were still obsessed by the theory of the pincer movement against the Suez Canal, and there was a tendency to regard Greece as a battlefield only from this angle and therefore to lose sight of the alternative method of helping Greece, which was an immediate attack upon Sicily that if successful could have been developed into a full-scale invasion of Italy. It is difficult to believe that if there had been the faintest prevision even of the possibility of that tremendous move which Hitler had already planned against Russia the course adopted would have been the one that was. In the end the British aid to Greece took on the appearance of a romantic and generous gesture, and it was as such that Mr Winston Churchill presented it to the British public and the House of Commons after a fiasco as complete as the attempt to help Norway in the previous April. There was nobody in Great Britain who did not desire with passion that Greece should be aided at whatever the cost, and therefore it was all too fatally easy for the British Government to shroud mistakes in a golden haze of sentiment.

It can be taken as certain that the Germans were extremely anxious not to see a large British Expeditionary Force landed at Salonika. The efforts made to persuade the Greeks that if British aid did not

extend beyond a few squadrons of the R.A.F. operating from bases
in the south of Greece Germany would not intervene were a proof
of this. Therefore, in view of that anxiety, which we can well
understand now when the attack on Russia is history, it would seem
that a large expeditionary force was our right policy. If Great
Britain had been in a position to equip and ship half a million troops
to Salonika in the autumn of 1940 there is no doubt that it would
have been the right move to make, and it is inconceivable that fear of
the effect on the Germans of such a move would have deterred the
Greek Government from acceding to it. In the event Great Britain
could have landed a well-equipped expeditionary force of half a
million men upon a planet as easily as at Salonika in the autumn of
1940, and those who criticize the Greek Government for its de-
ference to Germany must remember the disheartening effect of
Ethelred the Unready's personality. Moreover, it is certain that
Germany superstitiously did not like the idea of violating Greece,
and it is at least imaginable that if matters had not gone wrong for the
Germans in Belgrade, and if Britain had restricted her help to R.A.F.
squadrons, Germany never would have invaded Greece.

It seems unlikely that General Wavell was over-sanguine about
the strength of British aid to Greece, and possibly some reflection of
his own dubiety may be discerned in the accounts put out by the
German wireless of the discussions during those January days, by
which General Metaxas was supposed to have staggered out from
the final meeting of the military chiefs groaning, "This day Greece
is lost". That the German Intelligence in Greece thought it worth
while to offer this melodramatic tale as credible is evidence if not of
acute disagreement in Athens, at any rate of a certain amount of mis-
giving about the future. But why did the German propaganda
machine bother to put out this sensational version of the discussions
in Athens? Presumably in the hope of dissuading Greek opinion
from putting any trust in British promises, and thereby getting this
German unwillingness to intervene in Greece with armed force encouraged by the Greeks themselves. It is to be noted that when
British troops did begin to arrive in Greece during the month of March
the German wireless was sedulously exaggerating their strength. No
less than 200,000 were announced to be in Lemnos by the beginning
of April when the revolution in Belgrade had made it clear to the
Germans that they must attack Greece. And even then they were

seeking the justification for an action they superstitiously disliked having to take.

If the German intention to attack Russia in May (*not* June) had ever been considered as a remote possibility, the whole of British strategy in the Mediterranean might have been changed accordingly. As it was, the threat of that pincer movement against Suez destroyed any hope of embarrassing German strategy by an audacious counter-plan. Whether lack of equipment made even the least audacious counter-plan not worth discussing must remain a matter for speculation at present.

On January 17th General Wavell returned to Cairo. Five days later, on January 22nd, Tobruk fell. The British and Imperial troops were pressing on in Libya, but news reached Athens on the day General Wavell left that a German armoured division had crossed the Danube by covering with sleepers the lines of the Cernavoda railway bridge, which could only mean a direct threat either to Greece or to Turkey by way of Bulgaria, Rumania having become by now a German area of concentration.

It was on January 20th that Mussolini travelled to Berchtesgaden. At first Hitler had visited him. Then they had visited each other in the Brenner Pass. Now he had to visit Hitler. It would probably be exaggerating to call the change of place a deliberate humiliation of the Italian dictator, but it did mark with absolute precision the condition of tutelage to which Mussolini had reduced himself and his country. It can be presumed that the Duce invited the Führer to have confidence in the Italian offensive that was presently to be launched by the new commander-in-chief, General Cavallero. It can be presumed that stress was laid on those seven fresh divisions which by sea and air had reached Albania. We can speculate further-more that Hitler laid down as his condition for helping Mussolini to recover from the mess which the Italian commanders had made of the Libyan and the Albanian campaigns that, if at any given moment it was considered necessary, the Italian fleet should be sacrificed in order to get the reinforcements and supplies across to Tripoli. With plans in Bulgaria and Yugoslavia well forward, it is difficult to believe that Hitler was anxious to invade Greece if Mussolini could produce any remotely feasible plan to carry through the job of immunizing the threat to the German flank when the move against Russia started.

As usual the Axis Press and Radio insisted upon the complete accord about the future conduct of the war which the two dictators had achieved in the course of the long discussion between them lasting into the small hours of January 21st. It seems as certain as anything can be without an authoritative revelation of what did take place at that meeting that Hitler promised Mussolini his diplomatic assistance in solving the unpleasant Albanian puzzle, together with tanks and aircraft and perhaps, more important than either, enough German personnel to galvanize his troops for the task of preventing a British conquest of Tripolitania. Mussolini on his side no doubt promised Hitler that the efforts of German diplomacy should be strengthened by an Italian offensive against Greece in the spring.

During that second fortnight of January General Metaxas was ill. His illness was a well-kept secret in Athens. On the early morning of January 30th the leader of Greece died. The cause of his death was heart-failure after a slight operation on the tonsils. To what extent the last days of the little General were darkened by the shadow of coming events can only be speculation. He must have known that those two [1] Greek divisions in Eastern Macedonia and Thrace were utterly inadequate to oppose successfully those German divisions which in steadily increasing strength were concentrating in Rumania. He must have known that the Metaxas Line defending Kavalla was more imaginary than real. He must have known that the failure to fortify the gap between Guegueli and Lake Doiran might lead to the isolation of the Greek army in Eastern Macedonia and Thrace. What he had feared as a possibility in 1915, and feared so acutely that he preferred to resign from his post rather than be involved in preventive action, he must have feared even more acutely as a dreadful probability in 1941. Fortunately among the few diplomatic documents which were saved by the Greek Government from that disastrous April of 1941 there are three or four available which provide proof that by whatever dark forebodings about the future the mind of Metaxas was oppressed he was resolved to carry to its logical conclusion the 'No' he gave to Italy by an equally firm 'No' to Germany.

The first of these documents is a memorandum written by Metaxas himself on December 20th, 1940, after the only visit he received from Prince Erbach-Schönburg, the German Minister in Athens, since the Italian aggression. The purport of this visit was the

[1] The 7th and the 15th Divisions of the Fourth Army Corps commanded by Lt.-Gen K. Backopoulos, and known as the Army of Eastern Macedonia.

question of commercial relations between Greece and Germany, but when these had been discussed Prince Erbach, in a private capacity, went on to discuss the war. Here is the note of this conversation made by Metaxas:

" 'We sustained,' I said, 'an entirely unjustifiable attack, although we had done everything possible to maintain the strictest neutrality. I can now disclose to you that we declined to afford the British even those facilities that are permitted by the fundamental rules of international law, and they accepted this without protest, showing thereby a thorough understanding of our position. Consequently, there was no justification whatsoever for the unprovoked attack. But the Italians wished to conquer Greece. For that reason Greece rose up as one man, and we shall resist until the end, that is, until Italy has been expelled from the Balkans.' Prince Erbach thereupon asked whether our alliance with Great Britain was directed against Germany also. 'If you touch us in the Balkans,' I replied, 'it certainly is.' 'We do not propose,' the Minister replied, 'to cause you any trouble in the Balkans; Germany will do nothing that might harm the interests of Greece.' Next, wishing to make the discussion more general, he asked for my views as to how the war with England would end. 'On that question,' I said, 'I cannot continue our conversation, because we are allies of England, and it is not possible for us to deal with such a subject in our conversation.' "

The second document is a telegram of the Greek Ministry of Foreign Affairs to the Greek Legation in London dated January 5th, 1941:

"Please see Mr Eden and stress to him the very grave danger for all the Balkans that is created by the concentration in their direction of German forces. In the event of an attack, even if she remain alone, Greece will for certain resist to the end."

Presumably General Wavell's arrival in Athens on January 13th was the result of the interview between the Greek Minister and the British Foreign Secretary, and on January 15th Metaxas noted in a memorandum:

"No case can arise of our making a separate peace with Italy; that can never happen, even if we obtain a guarantee from Germany. The reason is that I do not trust Germany. I do not believe that the Italians torpedoed the *Helle* without the knowledge of the Germans: I do not believe that the Italians invaded Greece without the assent of the Germans, and I anticipate the materializing of an attack on Greece by Germany, *to whose every proposal I shall oppose the same refusal that I opposed to the Italians.*"

This was followed on January 18th, 1941, by a formal declaration made by General Metaxas and communicated to the British Government:

> "We have not the slightest intention of provoking a German attack. But if such an attack materializes we are determined to oppose it in every way possible and at any sacrifice."

The determination to resist violent action by Germany and to refuse any separate peace with Italy guaranteed by her accomplice was expressed in unequivocal language; but it is not quite clear what Metaxas understood by "provoking a German attack". The answer might well be that he did not know himself; but it is difficult to believe that by a less direct method of communication than that of a private discussion with Prince Erbach General Metaxas was not made aware of the German point of view. Certainly, during that November and December of 1940, the responsibility for refusing the use of the northern aerodromes to the R.A.F. was Metaxas' own. This does not mean, however, that a heavy weight of responsibility does not rest upon the British Government also for accepting such a refusal merely because the negligence of men entrusted with the safety of their country before war came had made any excuse for inaction welcome to the Government which inherited the burden of such negligence.

There seems little doubt that Hitler was still hoping to avoid a direct attack on Greece when Metaxas died, and there is reason to suppose that the death of General Metaxas may have been as much of a shock to the Germans as it certainly was to his own people and to his British allies. It would be absurd to feel any confidence in an opinion founded upon the extravagant assertions of the Italian Radio. Nevertheless, there is a measure of significance in the accusation that the death of Metaxas was an achievement of the British Secret Service, because, even if the Axis was beginning to lose hope of conquering Greece without the armed intervention of Germany, the fact that such a tale was put out proved that the Axis propagandists believed they could plausibly present the dead dictator as one in favour of a settlement by compromise.

It is to be noted that while the Italian Radio was hinting at foul play, the German Radio was sedulously spreading tales about the prospect of German mediation between Greece and Italy.

We who now know why all those German divisions were being concentrated in Rumania, aware though we may be of the necessity to Hitler of securing his right flank, should not overlook that intense desire of his to avoid invading Greece. In the month of January he was already certain of immuring Bulgaria in that great European brothel in which Slovakia, Hungary, and Rumania were already serving. He was confident of shortly adding Yugoslavia to the list of inmates. And he was apparently not without hope of persuading Turkey to accept the post of eunuch doorkeeper. It must be presumed that, provided he could deter Metaxas from encouraging or even accepting British aid beyond the few squadrons of the R.A.F. already in action, it was the intention of Hitler to leave Greece to his accomplice. Italy could be more effectively helped in the German interest by sending tanks to Libya and Stukas to Sicily. Moreover, there is no doubt that Mussolini did believe in the ultimate ability of the Italian forces to carry through a grand offensive from Albania and that for the sake of his own prestige he was anxious to avoid the taunt of succeeding in this only with the assistance of a German force operating through Bulgaria.

It will not detract from the honour by which Metaxas' name should always be surrounded in Greek history to admit frankly that he felt it his duty as a clear-sighted strategist to strive to the last against any military move by his British allies which would precipitate offensive German action without guaranteeing the necessary strength for an adequate defence. There can be no attempt to apportion the blame for what happened in April 1941 until further authoritative information is available; but the soldier of Hellas, to whom Metaxas offered immortal fame when alone in the small hours of that October night in 1940 he rejected the Italian ultimatum, is justified in the belief that the General would not have been found wanting in the agony of that April of 1941. Of him as of another Hellenic commander about whom controversy once raged it could be said:

οὗτος Ἀδειμάντου κείνου τάφος, οὗ διὰ βουλὰς
Ἑλλὰς ἐλευθερίας ἀμφέθετο στέφανον.

This is the tomb of that Adeimantos through whose counsels Hellas put on the crown of freedom.

CHAPTER TEN

The legless soldiers of Hellas in tattered uniforms who now drag themselves about the streets of Athens selling matches do not turn one reproachful glance toward the great cypresses of the Athenian cemetery in which what was mortal of Metaxas rests in peace. They gave their frostbitten limbs to their country as free men. They saved not only their own souls but the soul of Europe itself.

The immediate effect of the death of Metaxas upon the Greek army has been well expressed by Stanley Casson:[1]

"A period in modern Greek history was over; a new and unknown period was to start. There was a certain bewilderment in the air, but no trace of alarm and none of fear. The Greeks pulled themselves together, and you could feel them saying to themselves: 'Now we have lost a fine leader we must do all the more by full co-operation and increased energy to make up for that loss. Perhaps we may do even better than he did.' I have never seen such resolution, such authentic natural discipline and such determination. It was about this time that one of the Greek commanders of a fort on the Macedonian frontier called his three hundred-odd men together and addressed them: 'The Germans,' he said, 'are over the hills away to the north. They may soon attack our fortresses. How many of you are married men?' About ninety put up their hands. 'I give all the married men now two months' leave if they care to take it, and I will replace them with unmarried men. How many of you wish to leave?' No one answered and no one took his leave. Later that fort was assaulted and attacked without respite by the Germans and most of its defenders were killed. But the fort never fell. The Germans got into Greece, but hardly any of the Greek forts were captured. That was the spirit of the Greeks, a spirit which it is hard to analyse and hard to explain; but in different ways all Greeks shared this strange and exalted determination. It was the most inspiring thing I have ever known."

And now for a sentence or two let the pen in which the ink has so often run dry waiting for words with which to express due homage to a little nation of heroes pursue a dream of when the war is over. In a valley of the Pindus stands a great Doric temple open to the four winds the roof of which covers the bones of the unknown warrior who died in the snows of Albania for man's freedom, and for his country's virtue. And let the frieze round this temple show forth a procession of heroes—the fighter pilots and merchant seamen of

[1] *Greece Against the Axis*, pp. 74-5.

Britain, the American marines and airmen of Wake Island, the gunners of Malta, the schoolmasters of China, the Highlanders who stood at Tobruk and Singapore, the Polish sailors of the submarine *Orzel*, the Russian defenders of Sevastopol and Stalingrad, the Fighting French and Czechs and Dutch and Belgians and Norwegians, the men of Yugoslavia who by a supreme effort dragged their country out of a morass of ignominy, and leading this procession let there be carved an Evzone and a Cretan, the eldest European sons of that Liberty whose two mighty voices are of the mountains and the sea. Aera! Aera! Wind of Freedom!

CHAPTER ELEVEN

A SUPERFICIAL view of the situation might suggest that the logical step for King George II of the Hellenes to have taken after the death of John Metaxas was to assume autocratic power for himself. It has been reported by correspondents that this was the solution which would have been most acceptable to the British Legation in Athens and therefore presumably to the British Government.

The King himself was unwilling to follow this course. Instead he called upon Alexander Korizis, the Governor of the National Bank of Greece, to succeed John Metaxas as Prime Minister, which was as good a choice as could have been made from the supporters of the Fourth of August régime. There were many who deplored that the opportunity was not taken to form a National Government representative of Hellenic unity; but truly representative National Governments are hard to form in the most favourable circumstances, and the King no doubt considered the moment too urgent and the situation too grave for experiments. In a proclamation that followed the nomination of Korizis to succeed Metaxas he laid stress on the continuity of the new Government's policy, and if this proclamation displeased many by reaffirming the King's support of the Fourth of August régime it was surely justified by reaffirming at the same time the determination of Greece to maintain the struggle against aggression.

The choice of Alexander Korizis may have been the best that could have been made; but it did not disturb that great commonplace of history which denies the possibility of sustaining a tyranny or a dictatorship in the succession. Acquiescence in the infallibility of one man, unless it is an infallibility nurtured by an appeal to a supernaturally conferred right such as the Stuarts failed, the Romanovs succeeded, in imposing upon their subjects, always means that to win such acquiescence the tyrant or dictator must surround himself with less able and less forceful associates, and it is among those that the successor has to be sought. An incomparably greater man, Venizelos, had been as much at the mercy of this rule as Metaxas himself. Yet in some directions Korizis showed a finer appreciation than

Metaxas of what was wanted to protect his country against the storm, the clouds of which were already beginning to darken the northern sky. No suspicion was attached to him, as whether or not deserved it certainly was attached to his predecessor, of extending but a half-hearted cooperation to his British allies. No suspicion was attached to him of desiring to keep the King in the background. One of his first actions on assuming office was to promote a Royal visit to the front, which nobody can suppose was not made long before except by the influence of Metaxas. What Korizis lacked was the energy of will, the ardour of imagination, the courage of decision, and the fearlessness of responsibility which an unexpected action demands and without which there was by now no hope of effective cooperation against Germany. This is not to suggest that Metaxas possessed all those qualities. He did possess, however, a knowledge of strategy and, since October 28th, 1940, a prestige the moral support of which the country required if it was to confront the German attack in a spirit not of fatalistic valour but of plenary confidence.

On February 8th, 1941, Alexander Korizis confirmed the declaration of Greek policy made by his predecessor to the British Government: "We remain steadfast in our firm resolve to resist a possible German attack at the cost of any sacrifice, hereby renewing the declaration made on January 18th by the late Premier Metaxas."

On the following day Mr Winston Churchill in a public speech gave a solemn warning to the Bulgars of what would be the result of putting their aerodromes at the disposal of German military engineers and mechanics with a view to aiding German offensive action by way of Bulgaria.

Meanwhile, toward the end of January General Ugo Cavallero, who had succeeded General Ubaldo Soddù as Commander-in-Chief of the Italian armies in Albania, had launched a new offensive, no doubt at Mussolini's orders after the Berchtesgaden colloquy. The Italians had been heavily reinforced, the new divisions crossing by night from Bari, Brindisi, and other ports in Southern Italy, and landing at Valona. German troop-carriers with German pilots also brought troops from the aerodrome at Foggia. Strong additions were made to the motorized forces and also to the air force, to which was attached a German mission.

A captured order of the day penned by Major-General E. Bancale, the Commander of the VIIIth Army Corps, suggests that the Italians took this offensive very seriously:

> *Officers and men of the VIIIth Corps,*
>
> *In the severe fighting which has taken place up to now, rendered still more severe by the remorseless hostility of the elements, you have given a shining example of the incomparable fighting qualities of the Italian soldier.*
>
> *The enemy has already been destroyed. Cut off from his bases of supply, he has nothing left to make existence or advance possible.*
>
> *One further blow, which we shall now administer, will in the present situation assuredly overthrow his fortunes. With that exalted confidence which overcame all the enemy's advantages of equipment and turned to our account everything that was in his favour, you must now concentrate all your energies and all your unconquerable courage into one superlative effort, and conquer inflexibly even to the supreme sacrifice. If any man of the enemy dares to approach you, let out your furious battle-cry: "No one passes here". Plant the blade of your bayonet in his breast, and turn him to flight.*
>
> *All Italy is present before your eyes, strong and firm and full of confidence in her noblest children.*[1]

The Italian offensive lasted for ten days; but every attack was broken by the defence, and it petered out without impressing itself on a single Greek communiqué issued while it lasted. The measure of its ineffectiveness may be gauged from the fact that the historian dependent only upon those communiqués could not possibly deduce from them that there had been an Italian offensive. Indeed, all that remains by now of General Ugo Cavallero's offensive is a memory of the rout of the Tuscany Division known as the Lupi di Toscania, the Wolves of Tuscany. It was exactly what ought to have happened to a division named after animals which even in the pack are always afraid of serious opposition; and as the result of this straining after ferocious nomenclature the unfortunate Tuscany Division became a laughing-stock for journalists in every country outside the Axis. The Wolves of Tuscany added the last touch to the contempt with which civilized opinion regarded that unhappy Italy of Fascism which had betrayed liberty.

On their side the Greeks in counter-attacks gained ground at certain points and everywhere kept the initiative; but the strain of the winter had been too heavy for such hardly tried troops to stage a

---

[1] Quoted in *Greece Against the Axis*, Casson, p. 79.

large-scale offensive themselves, and local gains were the most that could be achieved. Valona was threatened from five points, and one column advancing down the Dukati valley between the Lugara and Chika ridges north of Khimara penetrated to within two and a half miles of the bay of Valona, while on February 5th the village of Dorza, on the principal road between Tepelene and Valona, was captured and the enemy's communications cut.

Tepelene itself, however, held out; and, although the heights all round it were occupied one after another by the Greeks, the ancient stronghold of Ali Pasha continued to hold out and bar the way to that decisive advance which would have thrown the Italians out of Albania into the Adriatic.

Since the Italian attack on October 28th the Greeks had captured over 20,000 prisoners, 230 heavy and light guns, 1500 mortars, and an immense amount of ammunition of all kinds. They had suffered scarcely even a minor reverse in the course of the operations. They had endured in conditions vastly inferior to the enemy's the worst winter in Albania within memory. Would Germany stand by and allow the Italians to be humiliated even more completely when the snows melted?

An indication of the growing belief that nothing Greece could with honour do or abstain from doing would avail to influence the German decision was to be found in the withdrawal of the ban placed upon the use by the R.A.F. of aerodromes and landing-grounds nearer to the front than Menidi and Eleusis, and by the reinforcement of the five squadrons already in Greece by four more, two of which, 33 and 112, were Hurricane fighters, the other two, 11 and 113, Blenheim and Wellington bombers.

Early in February 211 Squadron of bombers moved up to Paramythia, a valley in the mountains between Jannina and the coast. This was not an aerodrome but a landing-ground; and it may be noted in passing as an example of the difficulties with which the R.A.F. was faced in Greece that the journey from Menidi to Paramythia, which took just over an hour by air, took seventeen days for the convoy of motor vehicles that moved up the Squadron's gear to its new quarters. 80 Squadron with its Gladiators was transferred to the little aerodrome at Jannina, and presently Hurricanes took the place of these.

A sentence or two from T. H. Wisdom's book *Wings Over*

Olympus [1] gives a vivid impression of those first days at Paramythia:

"A solitary saloon car did duty as our entire transport section. It carried water and tins of petrol, it fetched rations from the aircraft as they arrived from the base, it carted bombs. . . . After a raid the crew, whether squadron leaders or sergeants, bombed up their aircraft ready for the next job. We went to the dumps, piled the rear seats of that sorely-tried saloon with bombs, big and little, drove over to the aircraft, slung them out and fitted them into the racks. Eventually you get used to seeing 250-pounders slung about like sacks of coal, but it's frightening at first."

Lt.-Colonel Casson has recorded [2] the invigorating effect of the arrival of squadrons of Hurricanes over Athens on the sunny Sunday morning of February 16th:

"From now on the Greeks felt that our help was worth having at all costs, but as yet they had not decided to ask us to send more troops or large forces. The total British force in Greece at this time—R.A.F. and supporting army troops—was barely five thousand men."

Those Hurricanes were not less welcome at Paramythia, where six of them arrived the following evening with five Wellingtons. Three days later fifty-one aircraft left Paramythia for the front. Mr T. H. Wisdom writes: [3]

"Twenty Blenheims escorted by our Hurricanes went off to do a job, and then the Wimpeys [Wellingtons] and a Junkers 52— borrowed for the occasion from the Greeks—went up the line to drop food supplies to Greek troops up in the mountains. . . . Then, further to enhance a joyous occasion, twelve PZLs, a queer little high-wing monoplane fighter made by the Poles and sold to the Greeks in exchange for tobacco, took off. The men of the Greek R.A.F., with their tiny ill-equipped air force, were grand chaps. Those PZLs were difficult things to fly, and their endurance was only a little over an hour. . . . The day before two PZLs had, by some slight error of judgment, landed at the same time but in opposite directions. They had met in the middle of the aerodrome . . . with typical enthusiasm, refusing to accept any reverse as a defeat, these chaps got together, dragged in the mangled remains of the two aircraft, still locked in a twisted embrace, and set about making one good aircraft out of the two wrecks.

[1] Pp. 127-8.   [2] *Greece Against the Axis*, p. 82.
[3] *Wings Over Olympus*, pp. 145-6.

"Fitters and riggers toiled all night out in the open, and next morning there was one complete PZL ready to take the air . . . it was tied up with pieces of wire, and one wing-tip was sadly bent, but that didn't deter the pilot . . . those brave Greeks always had our greatest admiration.   You just couldn't get them down."

Honours were equal that day.   The Hurricanes shot down four G 50 fighters "every one off the wing-tip of a Blenheim".   The Gladiators shot down four Italian fighters.   The PZLs shot down four Italian fighters of which "the rebuilt wreck claimed one".

Not one Greek or British aircraft was lost.

There was another good day for the R.A.F. on February 28th when the Hurricanes of 112 Squadron and the Gladiators of 80 Squadron went off on patrol and shot down twenty-seven Italian aircraft within an hour and a half besides severely damaging as many more.

At nightfall of that February day Larissa was destroyed by an earthquake.   In the aerodrome which had just been taken over by 11 Squadron the field was covered with fissures and the hangars collapsed.   The Italians had already bombed Larissa often, and during the fortnight after the earthquake they bombed the city three times, killing many homeless women and children sheltering in shallow trenches.   Outflown and outfought by the pilots of the R.A.F. and the Royal Hellenic Air Force, the Regia Aeronautica emulated in the air their jackal Duce below by taking on the wings of the carrion crow. The habit of machine-gunning pilots who had baled out and were on their way to earth has already been mentioned.   The lover of Italy who tries to console himself with the hope that such allegations are part of the propaganda of hate must remind himself that the martial performance of the Italians against the Greeks never justified the expenditure of any emotion except contempt, and it is fear, not contempt, that imagines atrocities.

It is a pity that the dread of provoking the Germans which so long dictated the policy of the censorship in Athens impeded newspaper correspondents in every direction.   Otherwise the world would have learned more of the heroic part played by the tiny and ill-equipped Greek air force.

At the outbreak of the Greco-Italian War, the R.H.A.F. suffered some initial disadvantage from its size and from the lack of an individual tradition, which it had been prevented by various circumstances from acquiring. The fact that its senior officers were recruited in the main from the old army and navy, although advantageous to cooperation, did not assist the formation of this tradition; and shortage of material, due to the lack of a native aircraft industry in Greece, together with financial restrictions, hampered until quite recently the development of effective striking forces in peace, and increased difficulties of maintenance and replacement during war.

The flying material in use in October 1940 was made up as follows:

1. Two fighter squadrons of Polish PZL aircraft. These machines were obsolete; they were slow, and their wireless communications were unsatisfactory.
2. Three squadrons of light bombers, all of different types (Blenheim, Potez 63, and Fairey Battle). These units were not complete to establishment in point of material; nor were the individual aircraft fully equipped.
3. Two squadrons of army cooperation aircraft, viz. one squadron of modern Henschels, as used in the German air force, and one squadron of Breguet 19s purchased some fifteen years before, with a top speed of less than 130 m.p.h. and ill-equipped.
4. Three incomplete squadrons of naval cooperation aircraft: Ansons, Fairey III's, and Dorniers.

These forces were augmented after the war by certain aircraft made available to the Greek Government by the R.A.F.; but the extent of this reinforcement was of course limited by the strategical situation at the time.

The personnel of the R.H.A.F. was insufficient to provide an adequate trained reserve, and was somewhat naturally deficient in training under war conditions. Nevertheless, morale was extremely high and, in the Greek tradition, all concerned were inspired by a strong offensive spirit, which was the keener after it became clear that Italians were to be the object of their attack.

These special conditions, and in particular the shortage of equipment, placed certain marked limitations upon the tactical employment of the R.H.A.F. For example, the bomber squadrons, owing to lack of sighting gear, could only be used for dive-bombing; and similarly lack of communication, equipment, lubricants, repair facilities, and above all of highly trained personnel, placed the R.H.A.F. under a great disadvantage in comparison with the enemy, while the absence of permanent operational aerodromes and shortage of staff put a severe strain on both officers and men.

In practice, however, the adaptability and high morale of the R.H.A.F. overcame many of these disabilities; and many operations were successfully carried out. Fighter protection was given to ports like Volos and to aerodromes like Larissa. Many successful bomber sorties were continuously carried out over the enemy's rear in Albania. Aerodromes at Koritza and Argyrokastro, ammunition stores at Premeti and elsewhere, and many other strategic objectives were repeatedly bombed. In addition, the Services cooperation squadrons, despite their great inferiority to the enemy, successfully fulfilled their rôles in reconnaissance and other tactical operations over land and sea. Numerous Italian aircraft were destroyed both in the air and on the ground; and at no time could Italy be said to have secured general (as opposed to local) air superiority over Greece.

In the course, however, of these successes, losses of trained pilots and material were incurred faster than they could be replaced; and a strategical reinforcement by fighter squadrons of the R.A.F. was required and effected to make good the deficiency. The results were most satisfactory, and the combined force remained in action until the withdrawal from Greece on April 23rd, 1941.

Mr David Walker, the correspondent of the *Daily Mirror*, has given in his book *Death at My Heels* [1] a vignette of two officers of the R.H.A.F. which with the story of the PZLs already quoted from Mr T. H. Wisdom's book may be accepted as typical of the whole Hellenic Air Force:

"At our hotel were a couple of pilots, a tall bearded Captain, and a stocky little Lieutenant. Every evening at dusk they used to walk quietly into the hotel, order coffee, and sit down to Poker with friends. At ten every night they went to bed. One evening I asked them if I . . . could come out to Koritza airport . . . to watch the life of a Greek squadron at the port.

" 'If you wish to observe the life of a Greek squadron at the port,' said the Captain with a smile, 'you must first obtain the permission of General Tsolakoglou.'

"We obtained permission next morning and . . . walked out to the airport. . . . The barracks still bore the traces of a direct hit by a Greek aircraft which had killed sixty Italian pilots and air gunners. I asked to see the mess and be introduced to the Squadron. I noticed only two Greek machines on the ground—

[1] Pp. 143-4.

both very ancient high-wing monoplanes, looking very dilapidated beside even the destroyed Savoias and Fiats and G 52s. . . .

"We found our old friends . . . still playing cards. These two men, the tall bearded Captain and the stocky Lieutenant, *were* the Greek squadron holding Koritza . . . against the Italian air force in the northern sector. The Captain used his aircraft as a bomber, and after loading it with bombs added old boots, bedroom crockery, anything insulting he could think of to drop on the Italians. The Lieutenant used his machine (I think it was an old Potez) as a fighter. It would not climb high enough to engage enemy bombers, but he used to strafe troops on the ground with his machine-gun.

"Even while we were there the telephone rang and a mechanic answered it. 'Important enemy formations' were on the way. Both of them smiled happily, like children.

" 'You are not to disturb the cards,' the Captain said to me. Mechanics had run out to the machines, which were tied to the ground with rope as there was a highish wind and thin snow. We watched them take off, and in half a minute they were out of sight, in the misty driving snow.

"We waited a long time for them to come back. First the Lieutenant arrived. He had been unable to force his machine to any height, and had seen nothing, but he had had a lovely twenty minutes with a column of enemy troops on the Elbasan road. It was nearly half an hour before the second machine arrived, with the bearded Captain. They wrote out brief reports, gave some instructions to the mechanics, and settled down to cards again. . . .

"A few days later the Captain was killed, shot down by nine Italian aircraft as he returned from a bombing attack he had carried through alone at 300 feet."

It would desecrate the picture of that squadron of two up there in the Albanian snows to print in the same chapter the story of the politicians and royalties who in that fateful February cringed and surrendered to a blood-soaked jack-in-the-box from the monstrous toyshop of Nuremberg. The page must be turned.

CHAPTER TWELVE

IT has already been stressed that the Axis attack upon Greece must be regarded first and foremost as a preliminary to the attack on Russia, and at the moment of writing these words (October 1942) it looks more than ever as if the Axis failure to achieve its hopes will be traced by history to that valley in the Pindus from the ridges above which that regiment of Evzones charged down to rout the Iulia Division of Alpini in the dawn of November 10th, 1940. Should the Axis be finally defeated, that action in the Pindus will count as one of the decisive battles of the world, and in its ultimate influence upon the future of mankind reduce the Battle of France to comparative insignificance.

When, perhaps at the very moment that the House of Commons was wrecked by a German bomb on the night of May 10th, 1941, Rudolf Hess alighted by parachute in a field near Glasgow, there was no glimmer of prescience in Britain about Hitler's Russian project; and even after the explanation of this fantastic embassy had been given it was still possible for the British Prime Minister to rebut the criticism of the House during the Crete debate on June 10th by insisting that the defence of the island during the second fortnight of May was responsible for spoiling a German plan to occupy Syria and threaten Egypt and Iraq. This was true, but it was not all the truth. Mr Churchill himself by this date well knew that the Battle of Crete, as being the culmination of that heroic defiance which began on October 28th, 1940, was less important for what it was preventing in Syria and Persia than for what it was delaying against Russia. It does not detract at all from admiration of the sublime resistance of Russia to recognize that if Greece had yielded in the autumn of 1940 Moscow would probably have fallen in the autumn of 1941, that Rostov would not have been hastily evacuated by the Germans, and that the names of neither Sevastopol nor Stalingrad would have been inscribed imperishably in the chronicle of human valour. If Greece had yielded, the sinister fanatic Hess might have been publicly proclaimed a madman in Germany a couple of months earlier than he was, and by mid-May at latest instead of on June 22nd the *panzer* divisions would have thundered eastward. It is with this fearful protasis in mind that we may contemplate the dark and disastrous apodosis to which it would have led. It is with this fearful protasis before him that the reader who may fancy some philhellene extravagance in the claim made above is begged to note the elaborate pattern of the pall which German diplomacy was embroidering for the coffin of Russia during February and March 1941, and at the same time to dismiss once and for all from his mind the notion that Greece was savaged by Germany merely in order to occupy Syria, penetrate into Iraq, and threaten Suez from the east. In any case the Mediterranean strategy of the Axis had already been wrecked by Greece in the previous November.

By the middle of February the concentration of German troops and aircraft in Rumania had reached such proportions that at long last the British Minister was withdrawn and the blockade imposed, though a declaration of war was to wait for another nine months. Such a concentration could be interpreted as a threat to the Balkans and Greece in particular, as a threat to Turkey, with Syria, Persia, Iraq, and even India as an ultimate objective, and if not as a threat at least as a clear warning to Russia that the Third Reich had no intention of being deflected from the old *drang nach osten*.

Meanwhile the aerodromes of Bulgaria were being gradually occupied by German technicians disguised as 'tourists' and bridges were being built over the Danube along the northern frontier. Hospitals were being prepared and roads were being put in order with signposts at important crossings and junctions marked with directions in German and Bulgarian. Miss Clare Hollingworth from direct observation has recorded:[1]

"At the beginning of January about 800 German troops a day were smuggled into Bulgaria, the Germans choosing the easy flat route by the Black Sea on which Russia had her eye. Half a division of German troops was stationed near Constanza, so that not much notice was taken when every night a train arrived with about 800 soldiers. . . . After detraining they went into the town of Constanza, had a drink and a meal, changed their clothes, and reappeared at the station in mufti three hours later, when they left for Bulgaria. The train went as far as the frontier at Negru Voda, where large numbers of lorries awaited them to take them by night to Bulgaria."

[1] *There's a German Just Behind Me*, pp. 211-12.

In London Mr Churchill solemnly warned Bulgaria against repeating the mistake she had made in 1915, and from Moscow on
February 10th arrived Mr Sobolev from the Soviet Commissariat of
Foreign Affairs to offer, it was reported, a military alliance with
Russia as the result of a conference summoned at Moscow for Soviet
Ministers in the Balkans.   Academic warnings from London and
hesitant overtures from Moscow were as ineffective in 1941 as in
1915 had been the academic warnings from Petrograd and the hesitant overtures from London.   King Boris the butterfly-hunter was
as much convinced in 1941 of a German victory as King Ferdinand
the bird-watcher in 1915.   That King Boris would have found himself at home in England as a country gentleman and that the Nazi
leaders were socially impossible provided inadequate grounds for supposing that he would defy the Germans on the doorstep of his yellow
house in Sofia.   In April 1887 Prince Alexander of Battenberg, who
had abdicated from the princely throne of Bulgaria, said to his sister,
Princess Marie Erbach-Schönburg: "I'm not going to be Bismarck's
tool any longer.   If he wants to reopen the Balkan question, he can
find someone else to do his dirty work."

Prince Ferdinand of Coburg was at that moment as willing to do
Bismarck's dirty work as fifty-four years later in another April his
son would be willing to do Hitler's.   In spite of the denial his Government had issued that German technicians or troops were in Bulgaria,
King Boris allowed Field-Marshal List to set up his headquarters in
Sofia before February was out.   On March 1st Mr Bogdan Filov,
the Bulgarian Prime Minister, was in Vienna where, in the presence
of Hitler, Ribbentrop, and representatives of Italy and Japan, he
signed in the Belvedere Palace the Tripartite Pact and aligned his
country with the Axis.   Forthwith the order was given to the
German troops to march into Bulgaria.   The armoured divisions
moved from the Rumanian Dobrudja.   The Luftwaffe gathered like
vultures on the aerodromes.   Twenty German divisions were mustered, and there would soon be another twenty-three divisions in
reserve in Hungary and Rumania.   On March 2nd Filov informed
the Sobranye that Germany wished to send troops into Bulgaria with
the object of maintaining peace and quiet in the Balkans.   This was
too much for any more optimism in England about the good behaviour
of Bulgaria as the result of King Boris's pro-English sympathies; Mr
George Rendel, the British Minister in Sofia, was withdrawn.   The

Bulgarians sped their parting guest by putting in the luggage a couple of bombs which exploded in the lounge of an hotel in Istanbul and killed two Turkish detectives. On March 6th King Boris formally received Field-Marshal List and on April 3rd he would inspect the German troops under his command three days before they marched against Greece. Long ago the Greeks had a word for such behaviour. It was called 'medizing', and an ignominy was attached to it which none of the city-states that bowed before the Mede ever succeeded in shaking off. It was a taunt which kept its sting. Medizing was rife again that spring in the Balkans. The Nazis communicated the corrupt malady like a venereal disease. Even Turkey incurred a suspicion of having been infected when on February 17th it was announced that a Non-Aggression Pact had been signed at Ankara between Turkey and Bulgaria. The preamble stated that the Pact had been concluded without prejudice to agreements contracted with other countries, and the Pact itself declared that Turkey and Bulgaria regarded it as an unchanging basis of their foreign policy to abstain from any aggression, that they were determined to maintain and develop their mutual confidence still further by good-neighbourly relations, and were ready to seek appropriate means of fostering trade relations between the two countries.

Mutual confidence was apparently not impaired even by the concentration of Bulgarian troops on the Turkish frontier on March 1st.

Without going to the length of suggesting that Turkey medized on February 17th, 1941, it is impossible to pretend that the Ankara Pact was anything less than a conspicuous triumph for German diplomacy, though it were well to add quickly that it is not so difficult to gain diplomatic victories when a prepotent force of arms is available to add point to the argument. The equally conspicuous failures of British diplomacy both in this war and the last have been due rather to the inability of the Armed Services to implement the Foreign Office's threats and demands than to the converse. General Marshal Cornwall and Air Vice-Marshal Elmhirst, discussing abstract strategy and even more abstract divisions and aircraft with the Turkish General Staff in Ankara, could hardly hope to have as much influence over the negotiations between Turkey and Bulgaria as von Papen could exert with those forty-three German divisions gathered in South-East Europe, twenty of them ready to cross the Danube and the flat low levels of the Dobrudja at the very instant the order came from Berlin.

Earnest efforts were made by propagandists to demonstrate that the Turko-Bulgarian Pact was an ingenious device on the part of Turkey to strengthen the ability of Bulgaria to resist German pressure. Allied journalists and broadcasters performed astonishing feats of verbal gymnastics in an attempt to twist themselves into a position from which the Pact might be regarded as a kick in the pants for Ribbentrop instead of a slap in the face for Mr Eden. Reuter discovered in the Pact a definite implication that Bulgaria had no intention of taking any military action and deduced from this that the position of Greece was not affected by it. Even in Athens public opinion was said to be favourably impressed by a diplomatic move which, to quote the paper *Kathimerini*, "would help to re-establish peace and quiet in the Balkans".

Berlin comment declared the Pact meant that Turkey would not intervene against a German advance through Bulgaria. Berlin comment was jubilant. It was also unpleasantly just.

It is certain that Turkey had no idea of playing false to her Greek and British allies. It is equally certain that Turkey would have much preferred to be helpful. The Greeks knew this well. During that dark week in Athens before the end came a rumour that Turkey had declared war on the Axis brought crowds to demonstrate before the Turkish Legation. It was a tribute from the beating heart of Hellas. In choosing the way of appeasement Turkey was following a long-lived fashion, and up to the moment when these words are being written she can claim that in her case appeasement has paid.

Two days after Bulgaria adhered to the Tripartite Pact and while the German troops were pouring over the frontier, a courier arrived by plane at Ankara. He brought with him a personal letter from Hitler to Ismet Inönü in which Turkey was assured of the Führer's benevolence. Honour is not a virtue that Hitler understands or esteems, and too much stress should not be laid upon a mere pledging of his word, but that he should have been put to the trouble even of writing a letter to the head of a State outside the Axis is a measure of the interference with his plans which had been caused by the Greek defeat of his accomplice. However, if Hitler was nervous of the Turks emulating the Greeks and causing further interference, his anxiety was speedily allayed. The Turks were much more nervous of him.

British apprehensions were still of that pincer movement against Suez. When at the end of February Mr Anthony Eden and General Sir John Dill flew off to pull together the Allied front in the Balkans and the Near East, it was generally believed that they reached Ankara concerned above all to ascertain what would be Turkey's attitude toward a German drive through Anatolia. No political journalist speculated whether the trouble Hitler was at to keep Turkey from growing restive might be inspired by the hope of securing Turkish mediation to persuade Greece to come to terms quickly with Italy, or whether Hitler's assurances to Inönü were completely genuine because in very fact he had not the slightest intention of attacking Turkey. If there had been an inkling of what was brewing in Hitler's mind over Russia, would that have changed the plans for the future which were advertised as the fruit of the Ankara conference? The tradition of German stupidity is a sound one; but in this war they have had the advantage of being led by a man with a sense of timing which amounts to genius, and that has offset the stupidity. Accurate intelligence interpreted by swift intuition and acted upon by a fanatical, disciplined, and magnificently trained and equipped army provide between them a formidable combination. At the date of the Ankara conversations the British Government was still relying upon improvisation and the British public on astrology to defeat that formidable combination.

And now we must descend to earth from what in retrospect seems a tour of the clouds by the British Foreign Secretary and the Chief of the Imperial General Staff to note what had been happening in Yugoslavia. According to the speech which Mr Eden made on May 6th in asking for the approval of the House of Commons of the help which had been sent to Greece, the request from the Greek Government to concert measures to assist their determination to resist German aggression reached England on February 8th, the day of the capture of Benghazi. To this the British Government "consented without hesitation, thinking that they would have been greatly to blame if they did not make the attempt to withstand the Germans, superior as their forces were known to be. In this decision the British Commanders in the Middle East fully concurred. Their one chance of success lay in concerted action between Greece and Yugoslavia, but this, in spite of all their efforts, it proved impossible to procure." This allusion of Mr Eden's presumably refers to the declaration of February 8th, 1941, made by the new Premier Alexander Korizis and communicated by him to the British Government: "We remain steadfast in our firm resolve to resist a possible German attack, at the cost of any sacrifice, hereby renewing the declaration made on January 18th by the late Premier Metaxas."

In view of the fact that the British Government had been informed of Greece's resolve to oppose by force of arms a German attack very nearly a full three weeks earlier than February 8th, it is permissible to wonder why Mr Eden took the later date as the decisive moment. On January 18th General Wavell's Libyan campaign was already well on the road to complete success. Tobruk fell on January 22nd. And General Wavell himself had held a conference with the Greek High Command in Athens from January 13th to 17th.

By the time Mr Eden made his offer to visit Belgrade the Yugoslav Government and the Regent Prince Paul were already in negotiation with Hitler as panders for the prostitution of their country. On February 13th Dr Dragiska Cvetkovitch, the Prime Minister, and Mr Cincar-Markovitch, the Foreign Minister, left Belgrade for conversations with Hitler and Ribbentrop at Ober Salzburg. The result of those conversations was not divulged when the two bedraggled Valentines returned; but it was generally believed that they were concerned with facilitating the transport of German troops through Yugoslavia, should it prove necessary. The refusal of the Government to make any statement about its foreign policy was resented by the public and there was considerable unrest throughout the country. Dr Cvetkovitch tried to form a Coalition Government, but the Opposition leaders were unwilling to cooperate. On February 27th the Pact of Eternal Friendship and Permanent Peace with Hungary, which had territorial claims against Yugoslavia, was renewed. By March 1st about a million men had been called to the colours, and the frontiers were manned; but the Germans and Italians had every reason for confidently assuming that in no circumstances would Yugoslav forces be used against them. The flat refusal of the Government in Belgrade to entertain the proposal of a visit from Mr Eden, after the conference in Athens had ended in the confirmation of Greece's decision to resist a German attack, was ominous.

The tour of Mr Eden and General Dill through what to a few

anxious critics was seeming a cloud-cuckoo-land of diplomacy and strategy was so lavishly photographed and written up by newspaper men that one must presume it had raised as high expectations in official hearts as it was intended to raise in those of the general public. It began with a brief visit to Cairo, where a conference was held with General Wavell about the position in North Africa and the situation threatening to develop in the Balkans as a sequel to the German infiltration into Bulgaria and the ambiguous Yugoslav attitude. Then Mr Eden and Sir John Dill flew on to Ankara, where they arrived on February 26th. Here they stayed for nearly a week, so that they were in Ankara when the news came of the adherence of Bulgaria to the Tripartite Pact and of the German troops pouring over the frontier from Rumania. They had only just left Ankara when Hitler's courier alighted there with that autograph letter for the head of the Turkish State. Besides conferring with the Turkish leaders, Mr Eden and General Dill had an opportunity to discuss the situation with the Russian Ambassador in Ankara and with Sir Stafford Cripps who arrived from Moscow. The Soviet Government was becoming a little uneasy about the future, and there was much satisfaction in Allied circles when the Bulgarian view that the entry of German troops would help the cause of peace in the Balkans was not shared by the Soviet Government, and when that disapproval was formally expressed in a communication to the Bulgarian Government. Neverless, it seems certain from the subsequent policy of almost obsequious appeasement pursued by the Soviet Government in the weeks after Germany's attack on Greece that as yet there was no shadow at Ankara of that tremendous event on June 22nd. The strategy of the future in the Balkans must have been related chiefly to that pincer movement against Suez, or a German attempt to reach the oil of Iraq and Iran. Before the visitors left Turkey a communiqué was issued to say that agreement had been quickly reached with the Turkish leaders on all problems of war in the Balkans and the Eastern Mediterranean, and Mr Eden expressed the profoundest satisfaction with his visit.

On March 2nd or 3rd Mr Eden and General Dill flew from Ankara to Athens where they were met by General Wavell. On March 4th a conference was held which did not finish until eleven o'clock that night. Greece was resolved to fight if the Germans attacked. Great Britain was asked to send all the support she could spare. The German Radio warned Greece that she was in a hope-less position militarily, with German forces on her flank. General Wavell flew back to Cairo next day, and on that March 5th the British Military Mission was absorbed in the British and Imperial Expeditionary Force in Greece.

The spirit in which that decision of the Greek leaders was reached at that day-long conference on March 4th, 1941—almost exactly one hundred and twenty years after the outbreak of the War of Inde-pendence—was communicated to the people of Greece and Germany alike in an open letter to Hitler written by Mr George Vlachos, the editor of the *Kathimerini*, in the issue of Saturday March 8th.

This document can be saluted as the noblest affirmation of human virtue which this war has produced. Mr Vlachos had been a loyal supporter of Metaxas, and it was Metaxas who once forbade a per-formance of the *Antigone* because of the defiance of authority voiced by the heroine. Yet, ironically, this open letter of Vlachos has itself a Sophoclean quality.

"*To His Excellency, Adolf Hitler, Chancellor of the German Reich.*

"Excellency,

Hellas, as you are aware, desired to keep out of the present war. When it was unloosed she was scarcely healed of the wounds in-flicted upon her by earlier wars and by domestic strife and faction. She had neither the power nor the will nor the occasion to take part in a war the result of which would without doubt affect the future of the whole world, but which at the beginning did not directly threaten her own integrity at any point. Let us pay no attention to her declarations in this regard, let us pay no attention to the official documents published in the Greek White Book, let us pay no attention to the spoken and the written words which bore witness to her constant anxiety to keep out of the war. Let us pay attention to one fact only. When, after the sinking of the *Helle* by an Italian submarine in the port of Tenos, she found the fragments of the torpedoes and with them the proof that those torpedoes were Italian Hellas was silent. Why? Because if she had divulged the truth she would have been compelled either to declare war or to have war declared against her. Hellas never wanted war with Italy, neither by herself nor with allies, whether those allies were British or Balkan. She wanted only to live as tranquilly as possible in her own little bit of the world because she was worn out, because she had fought too many wars, and because her geographical position exposed her unfavourably alike to the enmity of Germany by land or to the enmity of Britain by sea.

"At the time when the *Helle* was sunk Hellas, besides her own yearning for peace, had a guarantee bearing two signatures: the signature of Italy which guaranteed her against all aggression by Italy and the signature of Britain which was a spontaneous guarantee of Hellenic integrity. Nevertheless, when a little while after the sinking of the *Helle* Italy was displaying clearer signs than before of future aggression, Hellas, now convinced that the first signature was worthless, did not turn as she ought to have turned toward the country which had given her that second signature. She turned—do you remember, Excellency?—toward yourself, and she asked for your protection. What was the answer we were given then? Exactly what was said I do not claim to know, but this I do know, because I heard it from the lips of our late President himself, that Germany replied to our request by advising us not to offer any pretexts—that is to say, not to mobilize—and to remain peaceful.

"We did not offer any pretexts. We did not mobilize. We slept peacefully, or rather we were sleeping peacefully—for that evening we had been dining with the Italians—when the Italian Minister presented his Ultimatum. To whom would you have wished us to turn at that moment? Toward that Italy whose worthless signature we had in our pocket with the fragments of the torpedoes? But the Italians had threatened war. Nay, they had to all intents already declared it. Toward yourself? Alas, on that very morning of October 28th you were in Florence.

"Were we then to stand alone? We had no air force, no munitions, no money, no fleet. So we turned to the signature that was left, to the signature of Great Britain. And the men from Britain, the men whose own motherland was then in flames, the men who were keeping tense watch and ward on the English Channel, the men who, as they told us themselves, had not enough material of war for their own defence, those men came, and they came at once. Without making a bargain or an excuse those men came, and a few days later on the front in the mountains of Epirus where the brutal aggression of the Italians had been launched, there died together soldiers of Hellas and the first airman of Great Britain.

"What happened after that you know well, you and the rest of the world. The Italians have been thrashed. They have been thrashed up there, man to man, by us, the weak and feeble Greeks, not by the British, for no British soldier has set foot in Albania. Yes, the Italians have been thrashed. Why? Because they were without an ideal, because they had no heart to fight, because—but that is another story. In the face of this victory of ours (this must be true because we have been assured of it) you have deliberately remained a spectator. 'This affair' you said, 'does not interest me. It concerns the Italians alone. I shall interfere only when the British army lands in force at Salonika.' We might have asked your Excellency: 'Florence? Is it a fact that on the very day the Italians attacked us you were meeting them on the banks of the Arno and there handed over to them the Hellenes?' But we did not want to ask you that. With those fragments of the Italian torpedoes carefully hidden away we hid away Florence as well, and when indiscreet people brought it to our notice we said, 'Oh, they were not in agreement. The Italians deceived them.' Why did we say that?

"Because that is what we wished to believe. That is what it was in our own interest to believe. So all the while that we were advancing in Albania our relations with Germany went along smoothly. The swastika flew from your Legation on New Year's day, and it flew at half-mast when Metaxas died and your Minister came to pay his respects to the new President of the Council. Commercial intercourse and dealing were renewed, and you yourselves lodged a strong protest when an American paper announced that German tanks had arrived in Albania. We were all happy together over the way things were going in Albania, you as spectators and our allies the British with their air force and their fleet. Only that. You know how earnestly we tried to keep 'only that' a reality. It is enough to say that when a British aircraft crashed at Salonika we asked the British not to salvage it themselves. Why? In order that not even ten British soldiers should put in an appearance at Salonika and that thus all misunderstandings and all pretexts would be avoided. You laugh? How right you are to laugh!

"But while our relations were on this footing and while we preserved a certain equanimity, thanks to the German attitude, you had begun to concentrate troops in Rumania. The first contingent was to teach the Rumanian army, the second was to guard the Rumanian oilfields, the third was to protect the Rumanian frontiers, the fourth . . . but the fourth contingent was 300,000 men. The writer of this letter in his capacity as a journalist visited Bulgaria and covered the very road along which your soldiers are now marching. And when he came back he said to our late President, 'The road to Sofia has just been widened. The wooden bridges have just been strengthened, for the shavings of the carpenters are still scattered on the ground. Evidently the Bulgarians have hastily prepared a road along which an army will pass.'

"And after that what was Hellas to do? Gaze at the Germans on the frontiers of Bulgaria? Count their ships on the Danube? Watch their troops entering Sofia in alliance with the Bulgarians? Hear the Bulgarians growling of their own national claims? And yet preserve that equanimity of ours because we could feel sure that the Germans were at Koula merely to guard the Rumanian oilfields?

"But enough. Forget the past. Let us come to facts. According to every radio station in the world it seems that the Germans now wish to invade Hellas. Why? If an attack on Hellas was from the beginning vital to the interests of the Axis, Signor Grazzi would not have been alone at three o'clock on that morning four months ago. Germany and Italy would have presented themselves together. We must presume that when it was first made the attack on Hellas was not vital to the interests of the Axis. And now, apparently it is. But why? Has the order been given that a front is not to be created in the Balkans against Germany? But such an order could have been inspired only by a fairy tale. Neither the Hellenes nor the British—this was stated officially in the communiqué of March 6th and logic shouts it from the house-tops—nor Yugoslavia nor Turkey has any reason for spreading the war. The war is already big enough for all those countries. Has the order been given, then, with the object of saving the Italians in Albania? But what kind of salvation would that be? The Italians have obviously been thrashed once and for ever, and will not mundane opinion be all the more completely convinced of this thrashing the moment a single German soldier sets foot upon the soil of Hellas? Will not the whole world jeer at forty-five millions of Italians who after attacking our poor eight millions now have to cry for help to another eighty-five millions?

"And if the Italians want to be rescued, why should others come to their aid in this so very humiliating fashion when we could save them ourselves, and save them, moreover, without exposing the creatures to ridicule? Let the Italians get out of Albania. Let them proclaim publicly that they are weary of pursuing us and that satiated with glory they have decided to retire. We will help them.

"But, Excellency, perhaps you will say to us, 'This is all very well, but what about the British?'

"It was not we, your Excellency, who brought the British to Hellas. It was the Italians. And now you wish us to bid farewell to those who were brought here by the Italians. So be it. Let us say farewell. But to whom? To the living, no doubt, for how can we expel the dead?—those who died on our mountains, those who, wounded, fell to earth in Attica and there drew their last breath, those who at a time when their own country was in flames came to Hellas and there fought and there fell and there found their graves. Hearken, Excellency, there are deeds which may not be done in Hellas, and that deed is one of them. We cannot expel either the living or the dead. We will not expel a single soul or body, but we shall stand here by their side erect until the day when the sunlight breaks through the storm.

"Everybody is saying that you are determined to invade Hellas. We Hellenes do not believe it, and in that disbelief we are willing to be accounted simple.

"We do not believe it of your Army, with the long history and the great tradition that even its foes do not deny it. We do not believe that your Army will disgrace itself by such an action. We do not believe that a mighty power armed to the teeth and with a population of eighty-five millions fighting to create a 'New Order' for the world, an Order which we had supposed was to be founded on right, we do not believe that this mighty power desires to attack from behind a little country who is already struggling for her liberty against an Empire of forty-five millions.

"What would your Army do, Excellency, if instead of cavalry and artillery we sent our twenty thousand wounded soldiers in their bloodstained bandages to receive that Army on our frontier? But no, that cannot be. Small or large, such units of the Hellenic army of free men as can be despatched there will stand in Thrace as they stood in Epirus. There they will fight. There they will die. There they will await the return from Berlin of the Runner who came five years ago to receive the torch at Olympia. There they will behold that torch turned into a bonfire to consume with death and destruction this little nation now made great, which has taught all other nations how to live, and will now teach them how to die."

On the day after the publication of this open letter the Italians began their last effort to redeem themselves from universal contempt. Their German allies held back in the hope that they might even now be preserved from a sacriligious violation of the 'haunted holy ground' of Hellas. It was not to be. Nemesis is a jealous goddess. She had marked down Germany for her own. Fascist Italy was too insignificant a victim—not much better indeed than a poor ape awaiting vivisection.

CHAPTER THIRTEEN

IT is now known that Mussolini landed at Tirana from an aeroplane on March 2nd, and we can assume that this arrival was timed to coincide with the adhesion of Bulgaria to the Tripartite Pact and the movement of the German divisions across the frontier. That the German High Command confidently expected any solid results from the Italian offensive blessed by the Duce's own presence in the rear is improbable; but obviously if the twenty German divisions in Bulgaria could escape being called upon to rescue the Italians that would be all to the advantage of time in the launching of the attack on Russia, and it may have been decided that there was just enough bare possibility of an Italian success to make the experiment worth while. A little more pressure upon Yugoslavia would bring that State into line with Bulgaria. Turkey had been effectively neutralized. The success with which supplies and reinforcements were being shipped across to Tripoli was making any further advance by the British unlikely and should keep them too busy for adventures elsewhere. An Italian break-through on the Albanian front would bring home to the Greeks their desperate position, and there was a small but sufficiently influential defeatist group in Greece itself to make the prospect for mediation not altogether unfavourable.

The Duce himself was anxious as much for his personal rehabilitation as anything else for a successful Italian offensive that spring. He had propelled his country into war the previous year in the expectation of a triumph beyond Trajan's before the year was out, and he had to endure instead the destruction of his Imperial dreams by Greece and Britain. He had already had to be helped out of the African mess by his German allies, and if their help was going to be necessary to save him from the Greeks as well he would soon be in a position barely superior to that of Antonescu in Rumania. Hopeful though Mussolini was of restoring his own prestige and readjusting the balance with Germany, he was not sanguine enough to risk incurring fresh ridicule by publicly announcing his tutelary presence in Albania. The butterfly would emerge from its cocoon only if the sky were fair.

The Fascist propaganda machine was set in motion to prepare the Italian people for great events impending in Albania; but not a hint was dropped about the Duce's tour of inspection during the week before the offensive was launched. It was not until early in May, after the armistice with Greece when all was safe, that the news was officially published of Mussolini's personal direction of the operations two months before, with the implication that this offensive had been the primary cause of the Greek collapse and with the assertion that it bore the hallmark of the Duce's military genius. If we substitute 'tactics' for 'genius' we can accept that comment as just. That March offensive did bear the hallmark of the Duce's tactics, which have always resembled those of an old black ram.

Throughout February the Italian armies in Albania had been steadily reinforced by fresh troops transported across the Adriatic, by material of war, and by a concentration of air strength. The Greeks on their side had received as much of the Italian material captured by the British in Libya as was serviceable; but this was all.

The ramming tactics of Mussolini were to be employed on a front hardly twenty miles long stretching from the river Aoos or Viosa to the southern flanks of Mount Tomor; and the point against which his lowered head was particularly aimed was at the three miles between the northerly spurs of Mount Trebeshi and the village of Boubessi, with the object of recapturing Klisura, breaking the Greek line in two, and driving on along the valleys of the Aoos and the Sarandaporos toward Metsovo to effect what the original Italian advance had failed to effect in the previous autumn. As far as can be ascertained, this part of the Greek line was held by troops of the Second Army Corps, which included the 1st, the 5th, the 16th, and the 17th Divisions.

To achieve this ramming operation the Italians had effected an intense concentration of force amounting to seven complete divisions with several other units. Nearly all of these were fresh troops. The seven complete divisions engaged were—of Alpini the 3rd Iulia, which re-formed and brought up to strength was to be given an opportunity to avenge itself, and the 5th Pusteria; of infantry the 24th Pinerolo, the 38th Apulia, the 47th Bari, the 51st Sienna, re-formed and brought up to strength, and the 59th Cagliari. Besides these divisions there were the 41st Regiment of the Modena Division; the 48th Regiment of that 23rd Ferrara Division which had been so roughly handled already; three battalions of Alpini—the Suza, the Valcismona, the Valpescara; the 21st Regiment of Bersaglieri; the 2nd Battalion of the 3rd Regiment of Grenadiers; a battalion of Alpini—the Monteserdino from the 4th Regiment of the Turin Division; two battalions of the 26th Regiment of Blackshirts; and the 152nd and the 155th Battalions of Blackshirts.

The first assault of this very powerful concentration was delivered at dawn on Sunday March 9th; and for seven days the offensive against the Greek positions raged, the greatest intensity of the storm being on the fourth day. That was the day on which Major Pellegrini, the distinguished professor of Naples University and a member of the Fascist Grand Council, was severely wounded and taken prisoner. In view of his serious condition his captors forebore to interrogate him, but of his own accord he muttered, "Things are not going well at all for Italy," before he relapsed into silence. Whatever may be thought of the Fascists, nobody can think without emotion of the courage displayed by the Italian soldiers in desperate attack after attack upon the Greek positions. "They were mown down like ripe wheat," a Greek officer declared. But they returned to the assault again and again. And if we praise Italian courage during those seven days it is to exalt the supremacy of the Greek soldier. All through that ghastly winter he had shown himself a master of attack. Now he proved himself as much a master of defence. Neither the R.A.F. nor the Royal Hellenic Air Force was sufficiently strong to interrupt seriously the operations of the Regia Aeronautica during that seven-day offensive. The Italians were using a very great number of aircraft. The correspondent of the *Lavoro Fascista* telegraphed that never had he seen so many planes in action at once. It was "a veritable tempest of metal and fire", he affirmed. Yet at not a single point throughout those seven days did the Greeks yield one yard. The offensive was utterly broken. The Iulia Division was destroyed for the second time. The tough Sardinians of the Cagliari Division lost over two-fifths of their effective strength. The Apulia Division was so shattered that it was withdrawn and its place in the line taken by the Bari Division. The Duce's concentration of troops that was designed to make German intervention unnecessary and put him on the top of Trajan's column higher than his highest balcony was scattered by the Hellenes, even as the cock's-feathers from the helmets of his Bersaglieri were blown hither and thither by the mountain winds.

The Regia Aeronautica, unable to prevail against the soldiers of Greece, resumed their bombing of the houseless women and children in stricken Larissa. On March 19th the communiqué of the Italian High Command announced, *"On the Greek front nothing to report"*. There was indeed nothing, and because of it on that March 19th the Duce returned to Rome. He had been in Albania with his troops for eighteen days, during seven of which he had rammed 120,000 men against the Greek positions in order to demonstrate his peculiar military 'genius'. Of those 120,000 soldiers of Italy some 40,000 were put out of action, dead and wounded. There were relatively few prisoners. And these men were sacrificed in a supreme effort to rescue Benito Mussolini from becoming the grand butt of history, the comic relief of a mundane tragedy.

While the massacre of that spring offensive was in progress British and Imperial troops were arriving in Greece from Egypt. Most of them disembarked at the Piraeus, though a certain number went to Volo. No transports entered the harbour of Salonika on account of its exposure to action from the Luftwaffe. While the Germans were constructing aerodromes in Bulgaria no suitable answer to that threat was being prepared in Greece. It is difficult to believe that if the R.A.F. had been able to supply the aircraft, the equipment, and the personnel the British Government would not have been able to overcome the Greek dread of 'offering pretexts' to the Germans. Pending information not yet to be had, the responsibility for the failure to counter the German preparations in Bulgaria with similar preparations in Greece cannot be attached either to the Hellenic or to the British Government.

The strategic plan agreed upon between General Papagos, General Wavell, and General Dill had been drawn up on the assumption that Yugoslavia must be counted out as a potential ally and, what was more serious, might even be exploited as a base for military operations by the Germans, using the valley of the Axios (Vardar) and the Monastir Gap through which so often invading barbarians had descended upon Hellas from the north. It was decided to evacuate Western Thrace immediately, that is the low-lying land between the river Maritza on the Turkish frontier and the river Nestos (Mesta), and that such a decision had to be taken was one of the bitter little fruits of that much advertised Ankara conference. If Mr Eden could have brought with him the faintest hope that the Turkish forces on the other side of the Maritza would move, Western Thrace, including the bulk of the civil population, might not have been evacuated. In two small forts, Echinos, north of Xanthi, and Nymphaios, north of Komotini, which guarded the passes southward from Bulgaria, reduced garrisons were left with orders to hold out as long as possible and delay the entry of German forces into Thrace. We shall hear how those little garrisons obeyed their orders and earned such an epitaph as Simonides made for Leonidas and his Three Hundred. With a reverent salute we leave them now on guard.

The centre of the Greek line of defence was to be concentrated in mid-Macedonia, that is along the Yugoslav frontier, and for the defence of Eastern Macedonia it was decided to rely chiefly on the ability of the forts along the Nevrokopi plateau and of Fort Rupel in the Kresna Pass, through which the Strymon (Struma) runs between Mount Beles and the plateau, to delay the enemy's advance southward. The 7th and 15th Divisions were to support these garrisons, but if German pressure should become too heavy it was decided to abandon Eastern Macedonia and Salonika itself in order to fall back on the positions to be established by the British and Imperial troops along the Haliakmon Line.

The British and Imperial troops promised to the Greek High Command at that conference in Athens were to be one British armoured brigade, two Australian divisions, a New Zealand division, and some British Corps artillery. As matters turned out, one of the Australian divisions never left Africa, being kept back to help deal with the first counter-offensive of General Rommel; and of the other Australian division one brigade did not reach the Advanced Base at Larissa until it was time to be on the move in the other direction. The number of British and Imperial troops sent to Greece was 58,000, of whom 23,000 were required to supply and maintain in the field 35,000 combatants.

Official opinion in Great Britain [1] has been somewhat apologetic on the subject of these relative figures:

> "The reader may draw a contrast between all this paraphernalia and the apparent absence of anything comparable on the enemy side. The difference was due to the tasks and the nature of the

[1] *The Campaign in Greece and Crete*, issued by the Ministry of Information for the War Office.

opposing forces. The task of the British army was to establish itself in Greece in order to hold Greece, and therefore it had to compress into the peninsula services which the Germans could spread over a larger space and longer land distances. The Germans were advancing, and, as in France, their spearhead of tanks was far ahead of its rations and lived on the country."

It is a sobering reflection that so hazardous a last-minute effort to retrieve the situation on the mainland of Europe required more than three-fifths of a non-combatant to look after every single combatant. Perhaps the momentary delusion that Hitler had missed the bus in Norway was due to his having left his luggage behind him.

Thanks to the work of the Royal Navy and the Royal Hellenic Navy in escorting the convoys, the whole of the transport of those troops during that March was effected without loss, and a tribute is due to the promptitude with which once the decision was taken the Expeditionary Force left Egypt. By March 13th the headquarters of the British Armoured Brigade between Kozani and Verria were established, and on the following day at Ekaterini the first of the New Zealand battalions just out of the train was marching through the market-place. Lt.-Colonel Stanley Casson records:[1]

"The bulk of the troops were already here on March 16th, twelve days after the undertaking to send substantial help to Greece. I drove down to Piraeus to watch the men land and to see that all was in order from a point of view of security. I made arrangements for their landing to be screened and for strangers to be kept out of the docks."

No criticism of the efficiency of Military Intelligence must be read into the comment that the only part of the world from which those landings *were* successfully screened was the British Isles. No amount of skill at counter-espionage would have been of the least avail at the Piraeus during that March, and numerous Press correspondents have testified to the facilities that the German Legation enjoyed for obtaining and communicating information. An extract from a letter written by a British Gunner officer at the time gives a vivid picture of them:

On arrival (March 20th)
  We docked at Peiraeus about 10 A.M. Almost the first sight we

[1] *Greece Against the Axis*, p. 109.

saw was 600 Italian prisoners coming off a diminutive Greek gun-boat, all in rags, many of them wounded and exhausted by seasickness. They had presumably come all the way round from Albania by sea. And then, as we came into dock, the cheering began. Apart from the few troops, chiefly sappers and R.A.S.C. (and of course the R.A.F.) who had been in Greece all winter, we were among the first British troops to land. It was the beginning of a welcome that never failed in kindness or intensity, from the first drive through Peiraeus and Phaleron to our camp under the slope of Hymettus, right down to the last days when we passed through Athens on our way to the beaches, and drove through crowds cheering and clapping and crying, weeping with pride, distress and sincere thankfulness towards us for the little we had been able to do.

I spent one morning shopping in Athens. Two of us bought walking-sticks for our colleagues: it took us an hour, because every customer who came into the shop, on seeing us, would seize the sticks by the bottom end, cry out in savage tones, "Mussolini! Mussolini!" and then proceed to miss bashing out our brains with the weighted handles by a quarter to half an inch. They were delightfully childish in their enthusiasm over their victories, their joy at seeing us, their seething, scornful indignation that the Italians, of all people, should dare to attack their country. These Mussolini demonstrations became very familiar wherever we went. On our drive up to the north the children used to flock to the side of the road and slit their throats with their fingers as they cried "Mussolini!" and when we halted they would crowd round our guns, pat their muzzles and dance with joy, shouting "Mussolini, Mussolini, boum, boum, kaló, kaló!" But not a mention of Hitler all this time. The German Legation in Athens was of course sending minute reports back to Berlin of every gun and vehicle that was landed. The German Military Attaché, who spoke faultless English, did the rounds of the cafés talking to the British soldiers, asking them their units and where they came from, until the Greek police found out what was happening. The German Legation asked for protection from the Australians. And one night a company of Palestinian Jewish pioneers got very drunk and almost broke in. . . . It was a queer situation. I ran into X. of the Legation. . . . He had many interesting things to say: some of them left me unhappy, and some of his hints about the behaviour of Athenian society were justified by later events. But the atmosphere in Athens was invigorating—grim indeed, but full of pride and confidence. That day I revisited the Acropolis—in battle dress—and thought back to that very different visit four years ago! And I felt thankful that I had been given a chance to do something for a valiant little nation in a great cause.

On the road North

*The first seventy miles were familiar. We drove down Athens'
main street, crowds lining the pavements and cheering. It was
astonishing how quickly a crowd gathered at the first faint sound of a
distant lorry or motor cycle. A gunner regiment on the march is not
a bad sight, and I hope we impressed the German Military Attaché,
who was no doubt watching our progress! . . . On the third day we
crossed the Thessalian plain to Larissa. That poor town was in a
terrible state: in the centre the earthquake hadn't left one house intact.
All were cracked or bulging, and in many the roofs had crashed to the
ground. It was a nice piece of Italian chivalry to bomb the refugees
trying to rescue their poor belongings. . . . On the fourth day we wound
down into the Salonika plain and reached our "permanent" camp
below Edessa. We arrived without a casualty, not a bad effort. It
needed good steady driving to take lorries with three tons of ammunition over those greasy, muddy, stony roads. Spring reconstruction had
only just begun. All along the route women were carting and breaking the stones, helped by children and a handful of able-bodied men.
In every village the population turned out to greet us. Mussolini's
throat was slit with suitably savage gestures (no reference to Hitler).
And as we got further north the children gave us the Nazi salute.
This worried some of our troops a great deal, and one of our sergeants
was most painstaking (and successful) in teaching them to substitute
"thumbs up". When we stopped for the night they swarmed round
us, ready to pounce on our petrol tins, empty bully tins, biscuit tins, any
and every kind of tin. By the end of the campaign I think every
family in Greece must have been eating out of British army petrol tins,
drinking out of them, cooking in them, growing flowers in them, shopping with them. We did well. The rate of exchange started at
five eggs to a tin, 100 tins for a sheep, 60 tins for enough onions or
leeks to feed the battery. We were able to supplement our rations
very nicely. . . . How pleasant to be among a friendly people again.
And they are friendly, these Greeks! And one doesn't always have
to count one's change. . . .*

After reading those words it seems more than improbable that the
Germans, with the means they had of obtaining accurate information
about the dispositions of Greek and British troops, did not know all
about them. Yet there seems little doubt that the Germans did
suppose that British transports were arriving in the great harbour of
Mudros as they had been arriving there in another March twenty-six
years before. The great strength of Britannia has always been the
inability of her enemies to grasp that such a heavy-looking female can

be as stupid as she looks.   The Latins and the Slavs are too clever to
believe it, and the Germans are so stupid themselves that they do not
believe it either.   The Germans, who have a deep aversion from
fighting for a forlorn hope, could not understand the mind of a nation
which was prepared to risk the loss of everything it had gained in
Libya by sending a couple of divisions and an armoured brigade to
contest with twenty ill-equipped Greek divisions worn thin by five
months of desperate warfare the action of twenty German divisions,
many of them fully armoured, with another twenty-three quickly
available, not to mention twenty-eight Italian divisions and, if
urgently required, the whole of the Bulgarian army as well.

The Germans had not learnt their lesson after Dunkirk, and so
once again they hesitated.   They wasted priceless time that March
in making sure of Yugoslavia, convinced that the Greeks would not
have dared to defy them by inviting British aid unless they still
cherished a hope of Yugoslav benevolence.   There was too, probably,
still a lingering fear of Turkish action in spite of that autograph letter
from Hitler to Ismet Inönü.   Hence the additional anxiety about a
concentration of transports in the harbour of Mudros which might
again be bound for the Dardanelles, this time without opposition.
No doubt the announcement by the German and Italian Radio
stations that there were 200,000 British troops at Lemnos was made
to justify the vile crime that the Germans were about to commit; but
it may be that they did genuinely believe, if not in the actual presence
of this phantom armada, at any rate in the possibility of its approaching arrival upon the scene.

The reason why the Italian fleet suddenly made up its mind to
show that the age of miracles was not past by putting to sea on
March 28th is not yet clear.   Of one thing we can be certain, which
is that the astounding spectacle was the result of a German command.
The utter failure of Mussolini's seven-day offensive in Albania had
to be paid for, and the Italian fleet was the price exacted.   One theory
is that the sortie was planned to lure away the British Eastern Mediterranean fleet from the Mediterranean in order that a great convoy
of reinforcements for Rommel should reach Tripoli without interference.   But Admiral Cunningham's ships had been occupied all
that month in escorting transports to Greece and as a result the
Germans and Italians had been able to get their convoys across without undue interference.   Another theory is that the Italian fleet was

ordered out by Hitler to attack the British troopships in the Aegean; but this sounds a very heavy demand to make on such an unseaworthy ally, for it is difficult to believe that an Italian fleet of such potential power could have hoped to operate successfully from a base like Leros unless there was an expectation of such a strong British military force's reaching the Aegean as made any risk worth taking to destroy it. Perhaps the news of the overthrow of the Prince Regent Paul and the sudden reversal of the situation in Yugoslavia was the cause of this staggering display of large-scale aggressive action by the Regia Marina —an action unique in all its history.

It is not within the province of this work to discuss the great naval victory of Matapan, or to assess the importance of the part in it played by the bomber squadrons of the R.A.F. in Greece. The Italian fleet was first sighted by a Sunderland from the seaplane base at Scaramanga, and the Blenheims of 84 Squadron and 211 Squadron, which had performed such splendid service in Albania, together with the newly-arrived 113 Squadron, wrought much execution on the Italian ships, claiming to have stopped the heavy cruiser *Pola* with two direct hits amidships, crippled a light cruiser, and sunk a destroyer. Destroyers of the Royal Hellenic Navy hurried to join in the action. A force of them steamed westward in the hope of intercepting ships of the enemy trying to escape into the Adriatic; but unluckily his line of retreat did not give them an opportunity they so ardently desired. On the other hand, Greek destroyers were able next day to take part in the work of rescuing survivors from the Italian ships, and might have rescued many more if their work of mercy had not been interrupted by the Luftwaffe's dive-bombing. The Greek destroyer *Hydra* brought 112 survivors to the Piraeus. The British Admiral had to withdraw the rescuing ships and send a message to the Italian Chief of Naval Staff giving him the positions of the rafts with survivors. Sir Andrew Cunningham made a signal in which he thanked the Royal Hellenic Navy for the promptitude and speed of their cooperation in action against the Italian fleet.

The pressure from Germany which had performed the miracle of squeezing the Italian fleet out of Taranto into the dangerous waters of the Ionian Sea had been applied all that March to the Government of Yugoslavia, and when the failure of the Mussolini offensive was clear that pressure was doubled. As early as March 13th the departure of the Yugoslav Premier and Foreign Minister to Germany was announced; but probably on account of pressure in a contrary direction by Soviet diplomacy this departure was postponed. Indeed, on March 16th Russia definitely advised the Yugoslav Government not to sign their adhesion to the Tripartite Pact. The Government would not listen, and on March 20th a Cabinet meeting was held at which it was agreed to accept the latest demands made by the Reich. These included the formal adhesion of Yugoslavia to the Tripartite Pact (with certain qualifications) and the granting of a free passage to German war material and hospital supplies over the railways north to south. As a result of this surrender four of the Serbian Ministers resigned from the Cabinet. Protests against the surrender poured in from all over Serbia, and the British Government sent one of those familiar warnings with promises of help. The Prince Regent Paul, Dr Cvetkovitch, and Mr Cinkar-Markovitch were not to be diverted from the course they had elected to follow, and on March 24th the Premier and the Foreign Minister left Belgrade for Vienna. Meanwhile, Mr Eden had flown from Cairo to Cyprus, where he was met by Mr Sarajoglou, the Turkish Foreign Minister. There was a transient hope that at last Mr Eden would succeed in achieving something concrete, but it faded almost at once. The autograph letter from Hitler to Ismet Inönü was not alluded to in public. Nor was the menacing situation in Yugoslavia. The usual perfect agreement about the past, present, and future was advertised to the world. And that was that.

On March 25th Independence Day was celebrated in Greece. In view of the latest blow dealt to the Italians in Albania and with the thought of what the country had achieved in five months of war against an adversary six times as strong in numbers and much more than six times as strong in material resources, there would have been some justification for making this Independence Day an occasion for exuberant rejoicing; but the dark thought of the German swarms in the north lay heavily upon the imagination of the Hellenic people, and the national festival was kept soberly and solemnly. On that day sacred to the liberty not only of Hellas but of all the Balkan States to which she had set the example of rising against the oppressor, Cvetkovitch and Cinkar-Markovitch, with the attendant tawdry display in which the vulgar German delights and by which he tries to allay his gnawing sense of inferiority, ceremoniously prostituted the Triune Kingdom to the Axis at the Belvedere Palace in Vienna.

The Prince Regent Paul sent a message of gratitude to Hitler and his good wishes for the future prosperity of the German people. The door of the political brothel closed behind Yugoslavia. She was inside with Rumania, Slovakia, Bulgaria, and Hungary to make the fifth of a quintet of serviceable strumpets. The Teuton bawd advertised her new attraction.

"Yugoslavia," she announced, "has not rejected any clause of the Tripartite Pact. She has signed this Pact and thereby accepted all the obligations and all the advantages which accrue from it. The Tripartite Pact is an instrument of peace and does not impose any military obligations upon small States.

"The obligation of military assistance envisaged by Article Three [1] concerns particularly the three principal partners in the Pact."

Belgrade was less exultant than Berlin. When Dr. Dragiska Cvetkovitch and Mr Cincar-Markovitch returned to Vienna on the evening of March 26th they found a dark railway station and only four journalists to greet them.

In the small hours of the morning, at 2.30 A.M. of March 27th, a *coup d'état* was effected by forty officers of the Yugoslav air force. The Prince Regent was deposed and young King Peter II declared of age. Cvetkovitch and Cincar-Markovitch were placed under arrest. General Dushan Simovitch, Chief of the Air Force, formed a new Government representative of all parties. The Prince Regent fled, with an odd lack of sensitiveness, to Athens.

Since Europe had been thrilled by the news of that other drama in the small hours of the morning when the Italian ultimatum was rejected by Greece this was the most inspiriting moment; and the devoted lover of Yugoslavia will not deny that it was above all the example set by Greece which made it impossible for Yugoslavia to accept the betrayal of her honour. That exhilaration of the mind is reflected in another letter from the anonymous Gunner quoted earlier in this chapter, for which this second extract provides a fitting close:

In Camp at Edessa

The little town above us is great fun. Narrow streets, evil smells, shabby cafés and ultra-modern barbers' shops . . . quite good shops selling German goods. . . . It is a very mixed population. Some of the villages were pure Bulgar, though the Bulgarian that they spoke was, I imagine, unrecognizable. When the news of the Jugo coup d'état

[1] Yugoslavia had not signed Article Three.

came through, half the population in their enthusiasm declared they were Serbs! We were warned that there was a good deal of espionage and fifth column work going on in Macedonia. We were even warned on no account to drink from mountain streams, because German agents had poisoned the rocks! I think we're getting a fifth column complex. . . . I doubt if there was very much anywhere except in Athens. Certainly I never came across anything but sincere friendliness from everyone I met. That fortnight was very peaceful. . . . Occasionally the sirens sounded and a plane would come over, very high, on reconnaissance. The Greeks always said they were Italian, from Albania, but they probably came over from Bulgaria. One German plane came down in March, but the Greeks kept it quiet. . . . You can imagine how thrilled we have been by our friends the Jugos. . . . Even here in Greece the excitement was intense. There must have been something primitive and frightening about those demonstrations. The Greek papers had long descriptions of the crowds, of the cheering and mobbing of the British and Greek ministers. . . . It is a privilege to fight this war with two peoples like the Greeks and the Jugoslavs. They have the fire and directness and simplicity which we, with our Anglo-Saxon diffidence and doubt and sophisticated cynicism, seem to have lost.

CHAPTER FOURTEEN

WE shall probably never know whether without that abrupt upset of all their plans in Yugoslavia the Germans would have taken the risk of not invading Greece, for no historian will be able to accept as evidence the word of a Nazi leader, and no other evidence is likely to be available. At the time, everybody was obsessed by the idea that the German desire to control Yugoslavia was in order to use the Serbian routes into Greece down the Axios (Vardar) valley and through the Monastir Gap. To this was added that British obsession by the idea that the only German objective was a pincer movement against Suez, and that the invasion of Greece was only the necessary preliminary to the achievement of this. Since June 22nd, 1941, we have been able to obtain a better perspective of the Balkan situation and, aware now that it was Hitler's Russian project which by this time was dictating Axis strategy and diplomacy in the Mediterranean and South-East Europe, we can realize the absolutely vital importance of controlling Yugoslavia. First of all it has to be grasped that the Yugoslav revolt was inspired by hopes pinned on Moscow not on London, and that at a long view it was a demonstration of pro-Russian sentiment not pro-British. There was a great warmth of good-will toward Britain and toward Greece among the people of Serbia; but the new Yugoslav Government still believed anxiously in the possibility of arranging some kind of pact with Germany. It was to be a pact which would exclude any kind of military use's being made of Yugoslavia by the Germans, the kind of pact that Hitler had made with Stalin in 1939. Moreover, the fact that the Germans were utterly surprised by the resurrection of Yugoslavia meant that for once they were not ready, and the time they needed to prepare a *blitzkrieg* against this maddening rebel snatched from death at the last moment aroused once more that fatal optimism which had laid low half Europe.

On Sunday March 30th, after the news from Belgrade, Mr Eden and General Dill flew to Athens where a solemn Te Deum of thanksgiving was sung in the Russian Orthodox Church, and from Athens General Dill flew on to consult with General Simovitch about cooperative measures. The Chief of the Imperial General Staff proposed a close military alliance and the coordination of the Allied forces; but the old story repeated itself, for the Yugoslav Government and the Yugoslav General Staff, still hopeful of staving off direct German action, were unwilling to do anything that might be held provocative. The Government was engaged in negotiating a five-year Treaty of Friendship and Non-Aggression with Russia, and this was signed in Moscow on April 5th, the day before the open city of Belgrade was almost obliterated by German bombers. A month later the Soviet Government in an attempt to placate Hitler would denounce this Pact and withdraw its recognition from Yugoslavia.

The people of Serbia themselves were under no illusion. They expected war with Germany. They were ready to face war with Germany. But they did not expect to be betrayed by Hungary, for the Pact of Eternal Friendship and Permanent Peace with Hungary had been renewed not much more than a month ago; and the noblest tribute to a noble people was paid when on April 3rd Count Teleki, the Hungarian Premier, shot himself rather than betray such a people by consenting to the treachery which was being demanded from a country that used to be proud before the Danube became the main sewer of Nazism.

The final miscalculation of the Yugoslav General Staff was the time that Hitler would require before he gave the order to move. They did not believe the assault could possibly be delivered before April 20th, and they were very far indeed from being ready for that assault when it was delivered a fortnight earlier.

From the moment that Yugoslavia snatched her soul free of the diabolic Pact there was nobody in Greece who believed that Hitler would or could avoid fateful action. If superstitiously he had hoped to avert that premonition of ultimate doom by not defiling Hellas with his Barbarians, hope vanished when Yugoslavia refused to be damned with him. One can fancy him even as late as that March still hoping that the problem of a direct German assault upon Greece will be solved for him. He had feared for a while that the British would be able to send enough reinforcements and material to make it necessary for him to strike; but, as the days went by and the inadequacy of the British help became apparent, the British threat was receding. The strength of Rommel's counter-offensive in Cyrenaica would prevent any more support's arriving, and the despatch of troops to Greece had in fact helped his plans because the escort of them had facilitated the safe passage of his own convoys to Tripoli. When we are inclined to blame the Yugoslav General Staff for believing that the Germans could not attack before April 20th, we should remember the Imperial General Staff believed that there was no possibility of a Germano-Italian counter-offensive in Libya before May.

With the adhesion of Yugoslavia to the Tripartite Pact on March 25th Hitler could hope that even the Italians might manage to reach Salonika down the Axios (Vardar) valley. The British, severely pressed in Cyrenaica, would be hard put to keep their own army supplied let alone the Greek army as well. Trouble for the British had been planned in Iraq. With the help of Vichy, Syria should be another threat. Turkey seemed safely acquiescent in whatever might betide. And then by May he would be ready to place upon his head the crown of his ambition and turn on Russia.

But Nemesis had marked Hitler for her own, and through the martyrdom of the Greeks and the Yugoslavs the implacable goddess would draw nearer to him, and not to him alone but to all that diseased nation out of whose cancerous stomach he was spewed upon the world.

It will have been noted that the extract given in the previous chapter from the letter of the British Gunner officer was headed 'In Camp at Edessa'. That address was the result of the abrupt change of strategic plan after the resurgence of Yugoslavia.

The original plan, debated at the beginning of March, had been to effect a drastic shortening of the Greek line in the gloomy conviction that complete cooperation between the Yugoslav Government and the Axis was only a matter of days. The British troops were to hold a line along the Haliakmon (Vistritza) river across to Kozani and Grevena; and the right flank of the Army of the Epirus, confronting the Italians between Pogradetz and southward as far as Boubessi, was to swing back to join up with the British. Thrace and Eastern Macedonia including Salonika itself were to be abandoned, though the forts along the frontier with reduced garrisons were to resist the German onrush as long as possible. The only part of this plan carried out was the evacuation of Thrace. There was always the obstinate hope that the Germans would not attack directly, and the Greek General Staff dreaded the effect on the morale of the troops if they were called upon voluntarily to abandon hard-won ground to the Italians. When the resurgence of Yugoslavia seemed to offer a good prospect that Yugoslav forces would be in a position to hold the Germans from entering Greece either by the Axios (Vardar) valley or the Monastir Gap, and in addition attack the rear of the Italian armies in Albania, the hope that Eastern Macedonia could be held revived. Troops were moved there to support the forts on the assumption that if the weight of the German attack through Bulgaria was too heavy those troops would have time to effect an orderly withdrawal to the high ground of the Axios valley where the British expected to establish their main line of defence, again on the assumption that the Yugoslav forces would be able to hold up the Germans long enough for a Greek withdrawal.

The position of the Greek forces at the time of the German attack was that fourteen divisions were holding twenty-eight Italian divisions in Albania, three and a half divisions were holding the Metaxas line on the Bulgarian frontier, and three divisions had been allotted to cooperation with the British forces.

From Khimara to the river Aoos (Viosa) stood the First Army Corps (2nd, 3rd, 4th, and 8th Divisions). From the Aoos to a point a little north of Boubessi was the Second Army Corps which had borne the brunt of the defence against the Mussolini offensive.

Between Boubessi and Pogradetz by Lake Ochrida the line had been held by the Third Army Corps (9th, 11th, and 13th Divisions) and the Fifth Army Corps (6th, 10th, and another Division). These four Army Corps made up the Army of the Epirus under the command of Lt.-Gen. J. Pitsikas. The Fourth and Fifth Army Corps figure from time to time as the Army of the North and the Army of Western Macedonia. The confusion of disaster has made it impossible to extract a clear order of battle from the fog of censorship in which the Greek dispositions were wrapped. After the news from Yugoslavia, the 14th Division of the Fourth Army Corps was sent to join the 7th and 15th Divisions which were holding the Metaxas Line. Half of another Division—probably the 17th—was also sent to Eastern Macedonia.

Three divisions were allotted to cooperate with the British and Imperial Expeditionary Force. These were the 12th Division composed of men who had been called up before the war but had not yet been in action; the 20th Division composed of reservists who had not yet been in action; and the 19th Motorized Division. The last was but a month old and was the only Greek motorized division, an improvised unit consisting of 8000 men equipped with every kind of vehicle from Italian lorries captured in Libya to Athenian taxicabs. It had also six Dutch and two Italian medium tanks, and a few of those worthless Italian light tanks acquired in the Albanian fighting. The 12th and the 20th Divisions had each a nominal strength of 15,000 men. These troops had Divisional Artillery but no anti-tank guns.

The 6th Australian Division and the New Zealand Division each had a strength of between 10,000 and 15,000 men, to which must be added Divisional Artillery of 25-pounder field-guns and 2-pounder anti-tank guns, and an Anti-tank Regiment. The New Zealand Division had also a Divisional Cavalry Regiment, *i.e.* a mechanical force equipped with Bren gun-carriers and tanks.

The British Armoured Brigade consisted of between 3000 and 4000 men with upwards of a hundred tanks, artillery, an anti-tank Regiment (Hampshire Yeomanry), and Royal Engineers.

The R.A.F. had six squadrons of bombers and four squadrons of fighters. And there was what was left of the recklessly valiant little Greek air force, most of which was on the Albanian front.

It should be noted that a German Armoured Division has 201 tanks, many of which were much heavier than the heaviest of those with which the British Armoured Brigade was equipped. In addition to these tanks each brigade has a motorized machine-gun battalion of armoured cars and motor-cyclists, a motor-cyclist battalion, and an infantry regiment moving in motor-lorries. Finally each division has an anti-tank battalion and an anti-aircraft battalion the 8·8 guns of which are equally effective against tanks. These guns were already being used in Spain in 1938, but did not impress themselves upon British military observers until Rommel used them with such effect in Libya.

At 5.30 A.M. on Sunday April 6th,[1] Prince Erbach-Schönburg, the German Minister in Athens, presented a Note which informed the Hellenic Government that Germany was at war with Greece. At the same moment German troops crossed the Bulgarian frontier. Weakness was displayed by the Hellenic Government in not im-

[1] Until the Greek calendar was synchronized after the last war, April 6th was the date (N.S.) for March 25th (O.S.)—Independence Day.

mediately expelling the Minister and every member of the German Legation from Greek soil, and the apparent failure of the British Government to insist upon that expulsion looked equally weak. In view of the consistent abuse of diplomatic privilege by the Axis, the disregard by Axis diplomacy of every convention of established procedure, and the military outrages to which Axis diplomatists have played either the midwife or the lackey, it is an insult to civilized opinion to pretend that they any longer possess a respectable status. A diplomat like Prince Erbach-Schönburg who had degraded an ancient and honourable name merited no consideration.

The announcement of the German aggression was made in a brief communiqué:

"At half-past five on the morning of April 6th German troops from Bulgaria launched an attack on our troops along the Greco-Bulgarian frontier. Our forces are defending the soil of their country."

At midnight a longer communiqué was issued:

"Powerful German forces furnished with the most modern means of warfare and supported by tanks, abundance of heavy artillery, and numerous aircraft have been delivering repeated attacks since morning on our positions, which are defended by small Greek forces only. Throughout the day desperate fighting has continued in the principal zones of the frontier region along Bulgaria, particularly round Mt. Beles and the Strymon (Struma) valley. Our forces disposed along this front have maintained with their limited means a very tough struggle with the aggressor. As much as could be spared from the front in Albania of the little Greek air force has devotedly helped the struggle of our troops. In spite of an intensive bombardment by artillery and aircraft our forts have kept up their resistance, with the exception of one which fell after an extremely strong attack by the enemy. Ten enemy tanks were destroyed by artillery and anti-tank methods. Five or six enemy aircraft were shot down by our fighters and anti-aircraft guns. We made some prisoners. Several districts of the national territory had been evacuated in good time by our troops for strategic reasons and to avoid useless sacrifices. The enemy, though making progress in certain directions, was held along the whole of the main front.

"On the Italian front in Albania there have been operations by patrols and artillery."

At midnight on April 7th the following communiqué was issued:

"The attack by powerful German forces was continued to-day, the second day of the Greco-German war, with the same violence and persistence in the valley of the Strymon (Struma) and upon the Nevrokopi plateau. The weak Hellenic forces fighting there still managed to hold the enemy at important points. In the Strymon valley the fortified positions of Istimbey and Kelkaya, after holding out until they were destroyed, have fallen. Fort Rupel and Fort Ussita sustained repeated assaults by tanks accompanied by an intensive bombardment from aircraft and artillery, but these were all completely repulsed. On the Nevrokopi plateau the enemy after tremendous efforts managed to penetrate Fort Perithori. After a fight down in the subterranean galleries of the fort the enemy troops which had penetrated were cut to pieces and the fort remained in our hands. Another enemy attempt with tanks against Fort Lesai was repulsed and several enemy tanks were destroyed by our artillery.

"In the same region the officer in command of a Greek detachment having received orders to destroy the bridge north of Nevrokopi allowed enemy tanks to reach the bridge and at the right moment blew up both the bridge and all the tanks.

"For strategic reasons and to avoid useless sacrifices Western Thrace was evacuated in good time by our weak covering troops. Our forts Echinos and Nymphaios in that region are resisting the enemy's attacks and offering opposition to the passage of heavy enemy material.

"On the Albanian front by a strong offensive action we occupied some of the enemy's fortified positions, taking 500 prisoners and a quantity of arms and ammunition."

At noon on April 8th the Greek High Command issued a special communiqué:

"The Yugoslav Army fighting in Southern Serbia by falling back has uncovered the left flank of our Army fighting heroically along our frontier line. In spite of this our Army is fighting with an incredible spirit of sacrifice, claiming every inch of the country's soil."

At midnight on April 8th the following communiqué was issued:

"The pressure of the German forces against the front of our positions were powerfully maintained to-day. It has not achieved any result. For three days weak Hellenic forces in a valiant struggle have held up every effort of the aggressors. In the Strymon valley the forts of Rupel, Ussita, Parliouriones, and Karatash cooperating with cross-fire put up a barrage which the enemy could not pass. Fort Rupel and Fort Ussita in particular steadfastly sustained for the third time the full force of the enemy's bombardment and tank attacks. Parachutists whom the enemy dropped behind our positions were annihilated, and the rest, amounting to nearly seventy, were taken prisoner. On the Nevrokopi plateau violent fighting developed in which both the forts and detachments outside the forts took part. Our forts resisted successfully. One of them, Fort Dassavli, was occupied by the enemy but immediately afterwards it was re-occupied by us in a strong counter-attack. Fort Lesai sustained again to-day a violent bombardment by the enemy's heavy artillery without falling. Sections outside the forts re-occupied in a counter-attack several positions in which the enemy had lodged themselves for the time being. On the left flank of our positions a German Motorized Division penetrating through Yugoslav territory succeeded yesterday evening in reaching the high land of the Greco-Yugoslav frontier and occupied Doiran. At dawn yesterday this division invaded our territory by the flat pass east of the Axios (Vardar). Very weak Hellenic light motorized forces put up an unequal fight with an enemy incomparably superior in weight and numbers. This attempt to delay the enemy's advance lasted several hours, but finally he succeeded in making a dangerous thrust toward Salonika and cutting the communications of our forces in Eastern Macedonia with the rest of the country.

"On the Albanian front an offensive operation gave us a new enemy position and nearly forty prisoners were taken, including a captain."

At midnight on April 9th the following communiqué was issued:

"German armoured forces infiltrating through the valley of the Axios (Vardar) which had been held up to yesterday night in the Kilkis region, continued their attack toward Salonika and have entered the town. In spite of the difficult position in which that has placed them, our troops in Eastern Macedonia have not relaxed their resistance along the frontier and have kept their lines unbroken according to all the information which could reach us up to yesterday afternoon."

At midnight on April 10th the following communiqué was issued:

"In Eastern Macedonia there is nothing more to report."

Official communiqués do not provide an ideal epic narrative; but the stark record of those heroic four days in the exact form in which it was given to the world possesses a potency of evocation beyond the reach of a descriptive pen corroded by the debased epithets of modern journalism. Homer could have sung of the men who died in defence of those little forts against myriads, for they were the peers of Achilles and Patroclus, of Ajax and Diomed and Philoctetes. The heroes endure, but lost is the simple eloquence with which they could be meetly celebrated.

Karvalles, Rupel, Lesai, Kelkaya, Papádon, Ussita, Istimbey, Karatash, Nymphaios, Echínos, Dassavli, Parliouriones, Volax, Malianga, Agios Eustathios, Papanestíou, Perithóri—they seem to take the beat of hexameters, the names of those little forts whose defenders, obedient to their task, surrendered only to death.

The famous epitaph of Simonides, written for the dead at Plataea, has endured through the centuries to serve again for the men who held those forts:

> εἰ τὸ καλῶς θνῄσκειν ἀρετῆς μέρος ἐστὶ μέγιστον
> ἡμῖν ἐκ πάντων τοῦτ' ἀπένειμε τύχη·
> Ἑλλάδι γὰρ σπεύσαντες ἐλευθερίαν περιθεῖναι
> κείμεθ' ἀγηράντῳ χρώμενοι εὐλογίᾳ.

> *If to give life away well be the greatest portion of virtue,*
> *Then, above all other men, Fortune assigned it to us:*
> *We who struggled to set the crown of freedom on Hellas,*
> *Now in our glory lie here, glory that never grows old.*

Ageless, indeed, is their glory. Not a fort yielded to an attack of greater weight than that which swept through the Maginot Line. The two advanced fortified positions of Istimbey and Kelkaya were destroyed on the first day and one fort was overwhelmed; but every other fort held. The Germans broke into Perithóri and Dassavli, but the defenders put them out again in hand-to-hand fighting. When the Germans surged through the valley of the Strumitza on the way to capture Salonika the forts did not surrender. The doomed garrisons continued to fight on for another four days and by their devotion enabled nearly half of the Greek forces cut off in Eastern Macedonia to be embarked and transported to Crete and the Anatolian islands. Stukas from aerodromes just across the frontier dived upon those forts from the skies. Heavy guns battered them. Heavy tanks charged them. Parachutists dropped behind them were annihilated or captured by the outposts. The order was to delay the German advance at all costs. The order was obeyed. The whole tale has not yet been told; but there can be very few of those defenders left alive to tell it, so completely, so sublimely was that order obeyed.

All but a month of a quarter of a century earlier Fort Rupel had once been handed over to the Bulgars in answer to a diplomatic Note. It was the shame of that surrender by the Government in power that May which kindled the spirit in which the Provisional Government of National Defence was formed in 1916. For years Fort Rupel was a name which made a Greek patriot wince at the memory it wakened. Henceforth Rupel will be a name which shall stand beside that of Thermopylae. The echo from the mountains of the last shot fired by the guns of Rupel shall echo and re-echo for ever from that Hellas of the future whose brows the defenders of those forts have crowned with freedom. God knows that the tale of courage in our time is world-wide during this agony of human nature, and presumptuous indeed would be that writer who should dare to make comparisons. It is in no such spirit that the reader is asked, with all the humility that the inadequacy of words imposes, to contemplate those little forts commanding the passes from Bulgaria through which the Germans must come. For every garrison it was death or surrender. There was not the faintest possibility of being relieved. They were as utterly cut off as if they were holding passes through the mountains of the moon. If they had surrendered, nobody would have ventured to criticize such a surrender against odds of at least a hundred to one, and those odds armed a hundred times as powerfully. Since March 1st the garrisons of those forts had been waiting for the might of the German divisions to be unloosed against them. They had spent the five weeks of winter's end up there with the knowledge that for them, when the snow melted, the mantle of spring would almost surely be their shroud. That they would capitulate immediately to the Barbarian hordes was not expected; but when that German Armoured Division swept down the Axios valley to take Salonika on the third day of their resistance, and when they heard that the General commanding in Eastern Macedonia had capitulated, although his army was ready to fight on, who would have dared to blame the garrisons of those little forts if they too had capitulated? But they held on. They held on, and by impeding the German advance they prevented the envelopment of that half of the Army of Eastern Macedonia which, disdaining to capitulate, was fighting its way to the Aegean beaches where all the caiques that could be mustered were standing off to take the soldiers aboard.   Again the Barbarians demanded the surrender of the forts.   Again their garrisons refused.   Dive-bombers, tanks, and heavy guns could not prevail upon those men who preferred to die that Hellas might live.

> Ἄσβεστον κλέως οἵδε φίλῃ περὶ πατρίδι θέντες
> ἀμφεβάλοντο νέφος κυάνεον θανάτου·
> οὐδὲ τεθνᾶσι θανόντες ἐπεί σφ᾽ ἀρετὴ καθύπερθε
> κυδαίνουσ᾽ ἀνάγει δώματος ἐξ Ἀΐδεω.

By wrapping round themselves the dusky cloud of death these men clothed their dear country with an unquenchable renown; they died, but they are not dead, for their own virtue leads them gloriously up again from the shades.

Shall we find for the Germans such an epitaph by Simonides when their hour of doom is at hand?   Have they who have never learnt from the Greeks how to live now been taught by them how to die?[1]

It will seem very improbable after reading an extract from an article in the *Zeit*[2] of that April 12th 1941, the writer of which had been recalling the enthusiasm at the Berlin Stadium during the Olympic Games of 1936 when the Runner arrived with the torch kindled at Olympia itself.   Then he adds:

"With characteristic German magnanimity everybody forebore to ask whether Germany was not the real old Nordic Hellas, the last European bulwark of Hellenic culture, although Germany is so conscious of her origin and mission.   Ancient Greece closely approximates to the Germans, who recognize themselves in the men that made Hellas great.   The Germans admire Leonidas and feel at one with the uncompromising simplicity of mind and honesty of Aristides.   The Greeks are no longer the representatives of Hellas.   The Germans have become the holders of the true Greco-Nordic spirit.   The German has taken over the inheritance of his Nordic tribal brethren in Greece.   He cannot

---

[1] Since that question was asked, Germans at Stalingrad have shown they knew how to die; but their death was made an excuse for those vicious clowns in Berlin to mouth and rant their vulgar threnodies into the microphone like cheapjacks crying crape by the yard in Petticoat Lane.   "Τίς ἀλκὴ τὸν θανόντ᾽ ἐπικτανεῖν;" Teiresias asked.   "What prowess is it to slay the dead twice?"

[2] Quoted by Lt.-Colonel Stanley Casson in *Greece Against the Axis*.

understand how it is that men who represent Greece's name to-day can have thoughts so different from the promise contained in that name."

And when that infuriating twaddle was published the forts on the frontier were still at bay.

CHAPTER FIFTEEN

ON the night of April 6th German bombers raided the Piraeus heavily and dropped mines in the harbour. At 3 A.M. one of these mines, or according to other reports a delayed-action bomb, blew up a 12,000-ton British ship laden with T.N.T. The explosion destroyed a number of other ships in the vicinity, shook every house in the Piraeus to its foundations, broke many windows in Athens, and was heard 150 miles away. Miss Clare Hollingworth asserts [1] that the work of unloading the ship had been suspended for the whole of Sunday, and that at a moment when a swift display of German terrorism might be considered inevitable. If this be true, her comment that "under these circumstances, it was an act of criminal negligence to have left the ship in port still largely unloaded" is more than justified. She adds, "Though we could ill afford to lose the cargoes, the moral effect of the explosion was perhaps even greater than the material loss. It suggested that fatal amateurishness which was coming to be associated with the management of the British war effort in the Balkans."

News of the Belgrade horror, which began to come through almost immediately afterwards, made the people of Athens ask if their city was to suffer a like fate. The German Radio was giving ghoulish figures about the destruction wrought by the Luftwaffe in countries foolish enough to put their faith in British promises of help. It was not before time when Mr Winston Churchill declared in a speech that if Athens or Cairo were bombed Rome would be mercilessly bombed in reprisal.

When a nation bears such a load of iniquity as the German nation now bears, it may seem hardly worth while to differentiate between one damnable atrocity and another; but the obliteration of the open city of Belgrade by the Luftwaffe is conspicuous even in a criminal achievement that might satiate Hell itself, and the extent of its heinousness can be measured by the reflection that the horror of Belgrade did undoubtedly affect the nerves of the Greek Cabinet and of the Greek High Command. Some of them did begin to

[1] *There's a German Just Behind Me*, p. 268.

174

apprehend a like fate for Athens, and the white flame of Hellenic ardour, still burning as steadily as ever at the base, began to flicker occasionally at the top. It is bitter to have to write those words, and that they should have to be written adds yet a heavier weight to the load of iniquity that Germany bears.

At the same time as the German forces moved from Bulgaria to attack Greece they moved from Austria, Hungary, Rumania, and Bulgaria to attack Yugoslavia, and the speed, vigour, and ruthlessness with which these moves were executed provided a model *blitzkrieg*. It is becoming an accepted belief that the first army to offer any effective resistance to a *blitzkrieg* has been the Red Army. So far the only army to resist a *blitzkrieg* effectively has been the Greek army, though it may be readily admitted that a *blitzkrieg* does not mean quite the same thing when translated into Italian. Nevertheless, if we compare the equipment and numbers of the Greek army with that of the Red Army some of the advantage enjoyed by fighting against the Italian army is lost. Let that pass. What must be stressed is that the German advance into Russia in June 1941 was just as swift, vigorous, and ruthless as the German advance into Yugoslavia in the previous April, and if Russia had been the size of Yugoslavia, Russia would have been overwhelmed just as quickly. Moreover, thanks first and foremost to Greece's defiance and defeat of Italy, and secondly to the refusal of Serbia to sell her soul to the powers of evil, Russia gained at least five or six weeks the value of which appears inestimable now, and when we are allowed to hear the inner history of them no doubt that value will appear even more inestimable.

Here is an official view [1] of the Yugoslav army as it was on April 6th:

"The Yugoslav army was not fully mobilized when the Germans attacked. Its forces were not disposed in the parts of the country best suited for defence. It was not mechanized. It was not mobile by modern standards. It had no effective anti-aircraft defences, no anti-tank weapons, and no tanks. The greater part of the Yugoslav army was in the north, and the new Simovitch Government had not had time to do more than despatch large reinforcements to the south. Tens of thousands of men

[1] *The Campaign in Greece and Crete*, issued from the War Office by the Ministry of Information.

175

were marching, carrying packs and rifles, with their baggage in ox-waggons which regulated the pace of the columns. The German air force caught them like that. The dive-bombers swooped out of the low cloud and the long winding column— 150 miles jammed with marching men and beasts crawling at a foot pace—were bombed and strafed and blasted. The German aircraft flew along emptying their machine-guns when they had used up their bombs on what must have seemed an almost stationary target. That was the end of the Yugoslav reinforcements which should have held the southern passes from Bulgaria."

It would be profitless to spend words on the discussion of what might have been. To paraphrase an old English proverb:

> "If ifs and ans were tanks and guns,
> There'd be no work for Wops and Huns."

And as Euripides said, Ἄρης στυγεῖ μέλλοντας, the God of War abhors procrastinators.

While one German division was being held in the Rupel Pass and while a German Mountain Division was striving to envelop the frontier forts by flank attacks over Mount Beles to the west and the Nevrokopi plateau to the east, another Armoured Division and another Mountain Division was moving rapidly up the valley of the Strumitza into Yugoslavia. The Strumitza is the chief tributary of the Strymon (Struma), which it enters at right angles seven miles north of the Rupel defile through which the Strymon flows southward to enter the sea midway between Salonika and Kavalla. It was eastward along the Strumitza valley that in September 1918 Greek and British troops moved in pursuit of the broken Bulgarian Second Army whose defeat at Doiran was the first decisive battle of the last World War, the achievement of which was so long delayed by that military obtuseness which was proverbial in ancient Hellas as στρατιωτικὴ ἀλογία. Now the position was reversed with a vengeance, for although the Germans could not yet let slip the Bulgar hyenas to prey upon Eastern Macedonia and Thrace, their fetid breath already tainted the winds of Rhodope.

The Yugoslav forces holding the Strumitza valley were so small in number and so poorly equipped that there was no possibility of their offering any real opposition to the invaders. The drive of the German Armoured Division was not held up for as long as an hour. The town of Strumitza fell the first day, and on April 7th the German

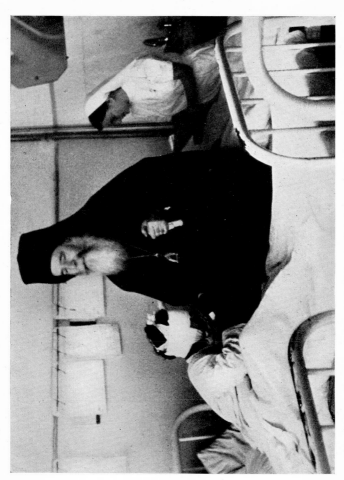

The Most Reverend the Archbishop of Athens, Monseigneur Chrysanthos

St Sophia, 1400-year-old Church in Salonika

Armoured Division and Mountain Division turned south to take Doiran, enter the Axios (Vardar) valley, and threaten Salonika with occupation within a matter of hours. By dark Lake Doiran under the snows of Beles are the graves of the thousands of British soldiers who gave their lives to prevent for evermore what was to happen in April 1941. They were not left to rest in peace even a quarter of a century.

Through the gap between Guegueli and Doiran the German divisions swept through into Greece. There were no forts there to hold up the Barbarians; the absence of them marked the confidence of Greece that Serbia would never be found in the ranks of her enemies. It was this entry into Greece on which the Germans had counted when they secured the adhesion of Yugoslavia to the Tripartite Pact, an adhesion on which the people of Serbia had operated with such spontaneous resolution on the night of March 26th–27th. It was by then too late for the Greeks to take any steps to establish a strong defensive line between Guegueli and Doiran. The pity of it was that neither the Greek nor the British Intelligence had been sufficiently well informed, or if well informed neither had been able to persuade those in command of the operations not to change the original disposition of the Greco-British line by attempting to hold Greek Macedonia in the expectation of the ability of the Yugoslav forces to resist in Serbian Macedonia. Nevertheless, in spite of the lack of preparation, part of the newly-formed 19th Greek Motorized Division with its tiny collection of inadequate tanks and its tragi-comic assortment of motor vehicles manœuvred and fought with such gallant determination that the German forces were held for several precious hours. This delayed the enemy's advance on Salonika long enough to enable Greek, British, and Australian Sappers to destroy oil reserves, installations, and stores, a work which was started as the last train left Salonika for Athens at three o'clock on the afternoon of April 8th. By that evening the Germans were on the outskirts of the city.

Among the communiqués printed in the previous chapter was a brief one issued at noon that day in Athens, in which in the baldest language it was announced that the Yugoslav army in Southern Serbia had fallen back and thus uncovered the left flank of the Greek army along the frontier line. It is permissible to doubt whether it was well advised to publish this communiqué twelve hours before the time when the usual communiqué of the Greek High Command was issued. The effect of such news upon Athens was worse than that stupendous explosion at the Piraeus on the night of April 6th. There was nothing to gain from anticipating the arrival of the train from Salonika. Athens itself was not in any immediate peril, and if Athenian opinion was to be prepared for the news of Salonika's fall this was certainly not the way to do it. Without knowing whether the blame rests with the soldiers or the politicians it would not be fair to cite this as another example of that proverbial 'stratiotic alogy' or military obtuseness; but it was a blunder. The military censorship, which in every country has been responsible for so many imbecile and unnecessary suppressions of the truth, can too often be relied upon when it decides on frankness to choose the least suitable moment for it, and the least suitable language with which to clothe such frankness.

The Press Bureau of the Greek Legation in London evidently felt uncomfortable about this communiqué. The statement that the Yugoslav forces had withdrawn and thus uncovered the flank of the Greek forces along the frontier was amplified into a withdrawal made with a view to consolidating its positions.

At midnight on April 9th the capture of Salonika was announced; but not of the little forts, all round which the forces of the Barbarians were now fiercely swirling. By midnight of April 10th there was nothing more to report from Eastern Macedonia. The line of those little forts was still unbroken when the last news of them came through. They were alone now with their glory.

The forcing of the Strumitza and Axios valleys, the capture of Salonika, and the isolation of the Greek Army of Eastern Macedonia were grave enough; but much more serious was the horrifying speed of the German advance farther north. By April 9th German armoured forces had already reached Uskub (Skoplje). Others were in Veles and Prilep next day, and converging at Monastir (Bitolj) were on the point of entering Greece through the fifteen-mile wide stretch of rolling downland known as the Monastir Gap. If they reached Florina they would have outflanked the line held by Greek and British forces along the high ground west of the Axios (Vardar) valley.

The line began where the Haliakmon flows into the sea, and this portion of it covered the coast road which runs south from Salonika to Ekaterini, on below Mount Olympus to the Vale of Tempe and

Larissa, to cross the plain of Thessaly and reach the heart of Greece. The New Zealand Division was entrusted with the defence of the coastal sector of the line. Westward the only passes through the mountains were the strong Servia Pass which led to Elassona where were the headquarters of General Sir Henry Maitland Wilson who commanded the British and Imperial forces, and the equally strong Verria Pass farther north. These were held by the Australian Division with the 12th and 20th Greek Divisions which had been added to General Maitland Wilson's command. The extreme left of this line was beyond Edessa on the Yugoslav frontier. The British Armoured Brigade and the 19th Greek Motorized Division, which as the reader has been told was nothing more than a heroic piece of improvisation, were out on the plain eastward, engaged in blowing up bridges and railway crossings.

It can be said that approximately the British and Imperial forces with the three Greek divisions (12th, 19th, and 20th) were holding a front of about sixty-five miles looking north-east and that the rest of the Greek forces were holding a front of about the same length between Pogradetz and Khimara looking north-west. Between the two flanks was the Monastir Gap held by 2000 Greek Frontier Guards armed only with rifles.

When on the evening of April 7th the news of the rapid German advance on Uskub (Skoplje) reached General Papagos, who was in supreme command of the Allied troops, he gave orders for a small reserve to be formed at Amintaion, some miles south of Florina. This force, commanded at first by a Brigadier, consisted of British artillery, a British anti-tank regiment, a New Zealand machine-gun battalion, a battalion each of New South Wales and Victoria infantry, and a battalion of London Territorials, the Rangers. At the same time the only Greek Cavalry Division, which had been moved from Albania, was sent north of Florina in the hope of protecting that vital railhead for supplies to the Greek forces in Albania. The British Armoured Brigade was ordered to withdraw from the low land west of Salonika to Edessa. The 19th Greek Motorized Division covered the front held by the New Zealand Division. The Greek and British commanders, who had by now given up hope of the Yugoslav army's being able to hold any of the passes into Serbia, could only hope that the bad weather and the R.A.F. would between them slow down the rapid advance of the German forces. The two hopes cancelled one another, for if the weather was to be bad enough to impede the German advance it would be bad enough to make operations by the R.A.F. impossible. As it fell out the weather did impede the R.A.F., but the advance of the German motorized columns was not slowed down by the state of the roads.

The prospect was grim. By April 8th one German Armoured Division and a German Mountain Division were already in Salonika, and at least one other German Armoured Division with another German Mountain Division must very shortly be in a position to join up with them and move forward against the right flank of the British and Imperial forces with an overwhelming superiority of tanks, mechanization, and men. Farther north and west two German Armoured Divisions were concentrating to enter Greece through the Monastir Gap, and beyond them again the Adolf Hitler S.S. (Black Guard) Regiment, enlarged to a division of motorized infantry, was also southward bound. It will be remembered that every German Armoured Division has 201 tanks, so that the enemy's superiority in tanks alone was nearly eight to one. The superiority of the Luftwaffe to the R.H.A.F. and the R.A.F. was round about sixteen to one. And just to add a final touch to the grimness of the prospect, news was coming in all the time of British reverses in Libya, with the certainty of no more reinforcements in consequence either by sea or air. In any case the Piraeus was no longer practicable as a port of disembarkation on account of enemy air superiority. The only spark of comfort was that the Yugoslavs might be able to launch an offensive in Albania and take the Italians in the rear. That spark was soon extinguished by the news on April 9th that the Adolf Hitler S.S. (Black Guard) Division and armoured forces had reached Struga on Lake Ochrida and joined up with the Italians.

On that day Major-General Iven Mackay, an Anzac veteran of Gallipoli, was given command of the reserve south-east of Florina with his headquarters at Amintaion, and the British Armoured Brigade took up a position behind the Australian Division on the left flank of the British and Imperial line. On April 10th mechanized machine-gun units of the Mackay Force made a dash thirty miles northward and reached Monastir in time to catch and shoot up German infantry as they were getting out of their transport. On the afternoon of the previous day New Zealand patrols had been in action for a while with German tanks scouting toward the Haliakmon.

The first communiqué from British G.H.Q. in Greece was issued on the afternoon of April 11th:

"German troops advancing into northern Greece came into contact with British and Imperial Forces on April 10th.

"The situation in Eastern Macedonia is obscure, but it is characterized by the magnificent resistance of the Greeks.

"Further west German forces have reached Monastir and Yannitsa.

"In southern Yugoslavia resistance to the German advance is stiffening."

The wisdom of adding that final paragraph may be questioned. British G.H.Q. had received no information from Yugoslavia which warranted such an assertion and it raised hopes which had not the slightest chance of being fulfilled.

At midnight on April 11th the Greek High Command announced:

"German motorized elements coming from the region of Monastir made contact with our troops in the Florina-Vevi region".

This referred to the desperate battle between the Greek Cavalry Division withdrawn from Albania and the Adolf Hitler S.S. (Black Guard) Motorized Division. A division of cavalry in Greece still meant what it used to mean. The Greek cavalry like the Polish cavalry were not motorized. The valour of the Greek horsemen was overweighted by metal. The sabre and the carbine could not withstand the fire-power of the enemy. Yet so courageous was the resistance offered by the Greek cavalry in hopeless conditions that this Adolf Hitler Division—the poisonous flower of Nazidom—was held back long enough to give the Greco-British line a breathing-space in which to swing round upon its easterly pivot with a view to meeting the ferocious German drive.

And once again Simonides, celebrating the Athenian vanguard at Tanagra, who were overcome by the superior forces of Spartan Nazis, provides the epitaph:

χαίρετ᾽ ἀριστῆες πολέμου μέγα κῦδος ἔχοντες
κουροὶ Ἀθαναίων ἔξοχοι ἱπποσύνᾳ.

Farewell, you princes of war, you glorious cavalry,
the flower of Athenian youth.

Florina fell, and with the fall of Florina the main road for supplying the Greek army on the northern sector of the Albanian front was cut. The only other available from the eastward lay through Amintaion by the Pass of Klisura (not to be confused with the Klisura at the entrance of the Tepelene Gorge) and Kastoria to Koritza. This was now the immediate objective of the German drive through the Monastir Gap. On the morning of April 11th in a heavy snowstorm the German Armoured Divisions advanced against the positions held by the Mackay Force round Amintaion. To quote Mr Tahu Hole:[1]

"Tall Adolf Hitler shock troops were the spearhead of the attack. They swirled out of the snow, wave after wave. Great grey Atlantic rollers rather than human formations, they looked. Avalanches of men, avalanches of shells; whirlwinds of machine-gun and tommy-gun bullets . . . in waves they came, and in waves our machine-gunners mowed them down."

The first attack was repulsed. They came forward again. The second attack was repulsed. They came forward again. The third attack was repulsed. Night fell. But next day the attacks were heavier, and it was realized that the Mackay Force must be over-whelmed by sheer quantity. It was outnumbered by ten to one, not to mention the 402 tanks of which the enemy disposed.

On April 12th General Papagos ordered the Allied line to swing back on its easterly pivot to establish a new line. This new line was to run from the coast round the base of Mount Olympus, north-west to the pass of Servia, south-west along the Haliakmon, the curve of which it was to follow north-west again to the high ground west of Kozani.

It may have been noted that nothing has been heard of much activity on the part of the Luftwaffe during the fighting in Western Macedonia. Their activity was on the whole confined to bomb-ing military objectives much farther south. The Piraeus suffered heavily. For this the weather between April 6th and April 12th was responsible. Any air activity above the mountains that there was came from the little Greek air force and a few squadrons of the R.A.F. A patrol of Hurricanes from 33 Squadron at Larissa found thirty Messerschmitt 109's near the Rupel Pass and shot down five without loss to themselves. Six Wellingtons of 70 Squadron bombed

[1] *Anzacs into Battle*, p. 108.

the railway station at Sofia, where an ammunition train blew up. Wellingtons of the same squadron destroyed the bridge over the Vardar at Veles. On April 10th Blenheims bombed enemy tanks and motor transport. Mostly, however, the tale of those six days was a tale of frustrated effort because the targets could not be found.

Soon the Luftwaffe, estimated to have at least a thousand machines, was able to bring the full force of its superiority to bear. The R.A.F. squadrons, which had had to abandon their aerodromes on the Thessalian plain and were now concentrated on the two aerodromes near Athens, became every day more vulnerable.

Of Italian activity during those six days only one fact can be traced in the record. On Holy Saturday in the Western calendar an Italian aircraft reacting to the traditional slaughter of a lamb for the Easter dinner flew low in a desolate part of the Western Peloponnese and machine-gunned a flock of sheep.

WHILE the shortening of the line was being carried out, the German threat to outflank the new Greco-British line had to be met and the withdrawal of the Mackay Force had to be covered. The task was entrusted to the British Armoured Brigade, which withdrew from Sotir just south of Amintaion to another position south of Ptolemais (Mesovouni). Here for two days a battalion of cruiser tanks, a Hussar squadron of light tanks, a regiment of Royal Horse Artillery, an anti-tank regiment of Hampshire Yeomanry, and a battalion of London Territorial Riflemen, stood in the way of the German advance. On April 13th Blenheims, probably from 30 Squadron at Larissa which had been bombing the enemy's motor transport, brought news of about 2000 German motor vehicles moving south-east from Vevi on Ptolemais. The first attack made by motor-cyclists and motorized infantry was engaged by the gunners of the Royal Horse Artillery over open sights and melted away. Attack after attack was repulsed; but the Germans brought up quantities of tanks, and dive-bombers also began to take part in the assault.

By April 14th the Greco-British forces were getting into position along their new line. The Mackay Force had taken up a position on the other side of the most southerly curve of the Haliakmon. The time had come for those units of the British Armoured Brigade standing at Ptolemais to abandon positions they could not hope to hold indefinitely. The last onrush of German tanks under cover of a smoke screen was checked by the gunners of the Royal Horse Artillery at point-blank range. Then the Armoured Brigade fell back on Grevena by way of Kozani to cover as far as it was possible the passes down into the plain of Thessaly and support the Greek 12th and 20th Divisions which were taking up positions along the rising ground west of Kozani.

The German advance by now presented itself as a trident. The prong on the left consisted of the German Second Armoured Division and the Mountain Division which had reached Salonika by Lake Doiran. To these two divisions was added one of the Mountain

Divisions which had entered Eastern Macedonia through the Rupel Pass. This prong was being thrust along the coast at the time held by the New Zealand Division from Ekaterini to Servia. The central prong consisted of the Ninth Armoured Division, with Motorized Infantry Divisions in support. This Division, driving southward through the Monastir Gap, had already reached the north bank of the Haliakmon and was facing the Servia Pass. The prong on the right consisted of yet another German Armoured Division which had thrust at the point where the Greek forces had joined the British and Imperial forces near the Pass of Macedonian Klisura. The thrust of this prong was blunted for a while by the desperate resistance of the Greek Mountain Guards; but a couple of thousand men armed only with rifles could not hold out against the weight of artillery and armour the Germans could bring to bear. And now with the improvement in the weather there was added to this the intensive bombing of the Stukas.

The central prong plunged deeper along the Kozani plateau until it came up against an Anzac Brigade holding the Servia Pass; but the full force of the German thrust was kept for the 12th and 20th Greek Divisions. The big 105 cm. guns, the heaviest tanks, the clouds of dive-bombers, and the apparently infinite resources of men and metal almost completely obliterated those two divisions. It was death or surrender, and they chose death. The broken remnants either took to the mountains or fell back southwards to Kalabaka where what was left by now of the British Armoured Brigade was hoping to bar the war to Trikkala and Larissa.

If it had not been clear before, it was clear enough at last that the Greek Army of the Epirus was threatened with an attack in its rear by German forces moving on Koritza from Florina.

At midnight on April 14th the following communiqué was issued by the Greek High Command:

"In Western Macedonia there was fighting with armoured units in the Ptolemais region. German forces pushed on toward Klisura, towards Kozani, and toward Siatista. On account of the occupation of Southern Yugoslavia by German forces and the consequent opening-up of passes which lead from Yugoslavia to its flank and rear, our army on the north Albanian front was ordered, for strategic reasons, to fall back and evacuate the region of Koritza. The enemy was unaware of this withdrawal until

24 hours after it had begun, and tried in vain to interfere with it by throwing forward motor-cyclists. We captured several dozens of these. Along the rest of the Albanian front the enemy undertook offensive actions at different points but was everywhere repulsed. We took nearly a hundred prisoners."

At midnight on April 15th the following communiqué was issued:

"On the Albanian front local Italian attacks were repulsed, the enemy sustaining serious losses. In Western Macedonia the orders given to our troops to take up new positions were carried out. Ten enemy aircraft were brought down by our anti-aircraft artillery and in aerial fights."

At midnight on April 16th the following communiqué was issued:

"In Western Macedonia German forces which penetrated to the upper valley of the Haliakmon are now operating in the region of Grevena trying a thrust toward Kalambaka. On the Kozani plateau they pushed on south of the Haliakmon. In the region south of Koritza the gorge Kiaffe Tiret Karits was occupied by the enemy."

At midnight on April 17th the following communiqué was issued:

"In Western Macedonia no important change has occurred in the situation. On the Albanian front several movements of withdrawal were carried out by our troops in good order. As a result of these movements Klisura [1] and Erseka were evacuated."

At midnight on April 18th the following communiqué was issued:

"In Western Macedonia all enemy pressure in the Grevena region, in the central valley of the Haliakmon, and in the region of Olympus was successfully kept under control. On the Albanian front our movements in Albanian territory were carried out without interference."

At midnight on April 19th the following communiqué was issued:

"Our troops in Albania continue their struggle in good order. Following upon operations against the Germans in Macedonia our troops in Albania successfully accomplished a manœuvre of withdrawal without being disturbed by the enemy. In every case in which the enemy did attempt to interfere our units turned and put him to flight, inflicting heavy losses. Two of our regiments par-

[1] This was Klisura in Albania.

186

ticularly distinguished themselves in these operations and their colours were mentioned in an Order of the Day. A German thrust southward has been repeated which affects the operations in Macedonia."

At midnight on April 20th the following communiqué was issued:

"In Albania great activity by enemy aircraft. The enemy attempted at two points to attack our troops, but he was repulsed with heavy loss to himself and was chased back beyond the lines from which he started. We took several prisoners. In Macedonia and Thessaly in spite of the intense activity of his air force the enemy has not succeeded in breaking at any point our line which has been taken up according to plan."

At midnight on April 21st the following communiqué was issued:

"Movements of withdrawal by our forces to their new defensive positions have been completed successfully."

At midnight on April 22nd the following communiqué was issued:

"The readjustment of our lines toward the rear was effected without serious interference by the enemy. Enemy air activity continues to be intense, but the enemy suffered serious losses from our air force and from our anti-aircraft artillery."

At midnight on April 23rd was issued the hundred and eighty-first and last communiqué of the Greek High Command:

"The unexpected dislocation of the Yugoslav front, the rapid advance of German forces over the Monastir plateau, and through that our separation from the Yugoslav army together with the threat to the rear of our troops in Albania, completely upset the line held by our forces and compelled us to make a hasty withdrawal on a large scale. The rapid thrust of German mechanized forces from the Monastir region toward the south and the consequent cutting of the principal route for the withdrawal of the left wing of our Albanian front compelled these troops which had no anti-tank defences to swerve round into mountainous country where the possibility of further retreat and supply had become problematical. The great bulk of our forces in the Epirus, who until the last moment victoriously confronted Italian forces twice their number, also took part in this general withdrawal. Their movements were effected in good order in spite of determined action by Italian forces which were counter-attacked several times and from which prisoners were made. Numbers of Axis aircraft

were able to attack our retreating troops at will without interference, and the state in their rear created difficult conditions for
the continuation of the unequal struggle of the Hellenic forces on
the Albanian front with the German and Italian forces. As a
result, on the evening of April 20th, our forces mentioned above
capitulated to the German forces. It is certified that at the
moment of the capitulation no Italian troops had succeeded in
entering Greek territory but were kept in Albanian territory."

Those ten communiqués may provide an ill-fitting, ungilded frame
for a nation's Calvary; but without that frame the picture would lose
some of its tragic significance, and therefore it is right that they
should be set out in full.

Those few bleak words in the first of them, which announced the
necessity to abandon Koritza, imposed a moral strain upon the spirit
of an army such as few armies have had to bear. To yield ground
to the Italians for the first time since those days at the beginning of
November when ground was yielded for a little while only to be
gloriously recaptured was bitter indeed. Moreover, the prospect by
now of recovering lost ground was as bad as it could be. Northward,
the soldiers of Yugoslavia were being swept into dissolution. They,
not through their own fault, had been too late. Eastward, the
soldiers of Britain and the Dominions were getting farther away all
the while. They also, not through their own fault, had been too
late. This abandonment of Koritza to Mussolini looked likely to
be for a very long time. The humiliation of it was intolerable.
And alas, even that abandonment was now too late.

Something of what these soldiers of Hellas were feeling was reflected in an Order of the Day made by H.M. King George of the
Hellenes on April 15th:

"From the Commander-in-Chief's reports I am fully ac-
quainted with the situation as it is developing. The honour and
interest of Greece and the fate of the Greek race preclude all
thoughts of capitulation, the moral calamity of which would be
incomparably greater than any other disaster. In view of this I
appeal to your patriotism as soldiers and as Greeks, enjoining you
to do your duty to the end in the above spirit. It must not be forgotten that the British army continues to fight in defence of
Greek soil."

Oh yes, the British army was continuing to fight; but it was fighting under conditions that seemed to offer no hope of achieving what it had come to Greece to do. Here is what an Australian correspondent was writing [1] of those days when the Greek army was being called upon to evacuate Koritza:

"For two days I have been bombed, machine-gunned, and shot at by all and sundry. German Stukas have blown two cars from under me and have strafed a third. . . . All day and all night there have been waves of Germans in the sky. Eighteen Messerschmitts strafed us on the road last evening. Bullets ripped the trucks, and one was destroyed, but nobody was hurt and nothing lost except the truck. Before that, the convoy I was in was attacked seven times in two hours, but not once was the convoy disorganized or broken up. The Germans are using a fantastic amount of aircraft: more than I ever saw in Norway under similar conditions of terrain. Goering must have a third of his air force operating here, and is bombing every nook and cranny, hamlet, village, and town in its path. . . ."

The Germans were pouring through the passes to the plains of Thessaly. The Haliakmon Line had been abandoned. The Germans were driving on along the coast southward. One New Zealand brigade was taking up a position at Tirnavo. Other small New Zealand forces were holding the eastern end of the Vale of Tempe where the great plane-trees were in bud by the rushing granite-grey waters of the Peneios, and the judas-trees were aglow with vivid carmine blossom, and the monk's-pepper was a pastel of rose and mauve. Two Australian battalions which had fought and marched southward from Verria for four days and nights had just arrived to support the New Zealanders. These Anzacs were covering the retreat of the British Imperial Forces a hundred miles further south to Thermopylae that they might escape encirclement. It was hardly surprising that in the deepening twilight of Athens rumours of disaster should gather noisy and multitudinous as starlings.

On April 17th Mr Papademas, the Minister for War, in a sombre broadcast, left everybody under the impression that further resistance was impossible. The Generals in Epirus were given discretion to take what steps they thought best; and on the same day a special Army Order released for two months' leave all those on the point of being called up for military service. The contents of this second

Order quickly became public property, as was to be expected, and it had a most discouraging effect on Athenian opinion.

By now the squadrons of the R.A.F. in Greece had been practically broken up by the overwhelming numbers of German aircraft and by the loss of all their aerodromes in Thessaly where many of their machines were destroyed on the ground. The aircraft that remained were all either on the Menidi or the Eleusis aerodromes.

On April 18th General Papagos reported gloomily to the Cabinet on the military situation. Apart from the ability of the British forces to hold even the comparatively short Thermopylae-Amphissa line at which they were aiming, the question was whether the Greek Armies of the Epirus and the North could extract themselves from the mountains and reach the Peloponnese.

Every road except one by which supplies could reach the Greek forces falling back in Albania was now in German hands. The one that remained forks with the road from Santi Quaranta some twenty-five miles above Jannina and then runs southward through Arta (with a branch to Preveza), Agrinion, and Missolonghi, to follow past Naupaktos the northerly shore of the Corinthian Gulf. This road west of the Pindus was now choked with traffic and was being bombed continuously by Italian and German aircraft. Trains of heavily-laden mules, ammunition carts drawn by oxen, guns dragged by horses, wounded men in litters, broken-down motor-cars, taxis, omnibuses used as ambulances, waggons, handcarts, barrows, refugees, soldiers . . . and over them the Savoias and Dorniers, and swooping down on them the C.R. 42's and the Messerschmitt 109's with their machine-guns. Once this road was cut by the Germans the Greek Armies of Epirus and the North were at the mercy of the mountains of which they had been the masters.

General Papagos had given orders for one of the divisions of the Army of the Epirus to make a forced march and attempt to hold the Pass of Metsovo in a supreme effort to prevent the Germans reaching Jannina. Along the ravines and the mountain tracks of the Pindus that 5th Division marched: it was one of those which had cracked the skull of the Italian ram in March. The road was impassable for rapid movement. Over the Pindus the 5th Division climbed and clambered without its heavy artillery. After an exhausting effort the Division reached Metsovo with its batteries of Danglis-Schneider mountain-guns in time to fight but not in time to entrench itself. The Germans pouring down from Grevena flung against it an armoured force supported by many Stukas. Presently two more Greek Divisions were struggling across the mountains to help their comrades of the 5th try to achieve the impossible.

So, down in Athens General Papagos was reporting gloomily to the Cabinet on the prospect. The Greek army in Albania looked unlikely to effect its withdrawal. The Olympus line had gone and the British forces might or might not be able to hold the short line from Thermopylae to Amphissa. Athens itself was in danger. The immediate question to be settled was whether the Government should leave the mainland and retire to Crete. The Cabinet, which included some of the strong men from the authoritarian Fourth of August régime, was creaking. The King, however, was absolutely determined to hold out in Athens to the last possible moment. The news that the Yugoslav armies had capitulated the day before did not mean that Greece was finished too.

Alexander Korizis was in the throes of a mental struggle. He like his King could not contemplate anything in the nature of the surrender at which some were already hinting; but he could not make up his mind to leave Athens. If the Government should move to Crete it might leave the way open for the admirers of Germany to seize power and by accepting the German terms hand over Greece to the ignoble condition to which the pride of France had bowed so meekly. The admirers of Germany were saying, as they had said from the first, that if Greece trusted Germany, Germany would protect Greece against Italy. Was Greece to surrender and leave to Poland the glory of being the only nation in Europe which in its agony had not produced one man willing to barter away its freedom either from the honourable motive of desiring to avert more misery for his country or from the less honourable motive of aspiring to gratify his own ambition?

Korizis could not make up his mind, and the meeting of the Cabinet broke up. The British Legation was anxious to know what course was to be followed. Was it or was it not proposed to change the seat of Government? Mr Ziphos, the Minister of Shipping, was charged to find out the Prime Minister's intentions. Korizis himself could not achieve a decision. If the Government should leave Athens and find itself replaced by another Government willing to accept German terms, that might mean the destruction or capitulation of the British forces in Greece. Mr Ziphos pressed for an answer. Korizis moved across to a door that led into an inner room. He turned before he passed through to say that his answer should be given in a minute. The door was closed behind him. There was the sound of shot. The Prime Minister of Greece had given his answer.

And up in the Pass of Metsovo simple soldiers of the immortal Fifth who had fallen in that desperate fight to hold off the German hordes from reaching Jannina accompanied Alexander Korizis on the long journey of death, he setting out tormented by indecision about his duty, they in the serenity of duty done, but both he and they having given their lives for their country.

Until a new Government could be formed Mr K. Kodzias, the Governor of Athens and Vice-President of the Council, acted as Premier. In the twenty-four hours of his holding office Mr Kodzias made a great effort to revive Athenian confidence which had naturally been much shaken not by rumour alone during the previous three days. There was a demonstration in front of the British Legation, when some of those young men about to be called up who had been given that two months' leave cried, "Give us rifles!"

Lt.-Colonel Stanley Casson had motored in to Athens from the latest G.H.Q. of the British Imperial Expeditionary Force situated in a grove of pines between Thebes and Chalkis. The previous headquarters for twenty-four hours had been near Pharsalos where Julius Caesar defeated Pompey and laid the foundations of the Roman Empire. Colonel Casson was seized with the happy idea of showing the people of Athens, for whom the spectacle of Italian prisoners had become banal, what German prisoners looked like. A hundred and fifty of them captured by the Anzacs that were holding the Servia Pass had just reached a prisoners' camp at Daphne, beside the Sacred Way to Eleusis. He packed them into ten lorries with Australian guards and took the convoy to Omonia (Concord) Square—the Piccadilly Circus of Athens—where he stopped long enough to give the crowd time to recognize what they were. Germans are not at their best when a crowd appears hostile, and a hostile Greek crowd is one of the most unpleasant to face. When spectators looked like passing from words to deeds, the convoy moved along up Stadium Street where another stop was made to give the Athenians an opportunity to view the menagerie. One final show was given in Constitution

Jannina Barracks

Eleutherios Venizelos

His Excellency E. Tsouderos
Prime Minister of Greece

Square, after which the *Herrenvolk* were deposited in the Greek prison-camp up the Kephissa road where so many Italians had been entertained.   Germans rarely possess either the natural dignity of the savage or the acquired dignity that comes from a long inheritance of civilization.   They are exposed as what they are by an ordeal like that, and nobody who has beheld frightened Germans can ever think of them again except as a lower breed.   As such the Athenian people recognized them on that April day.   As such the Athenian people regard them now.

On Sunday April 20th, the King temporarily assumed the Presidency of the Government with Vice-Admiral Sakellariou as Deputy Prime Minister.   This measure was resorted to after General Mazarakis had for two days considered an offer made to him to form a non-party government and had finally declined it. Mr Sophoulis, Mr Deliyannis and other political leaders had been approached without definite result.   Nobody felt able to shoulder the task, and time was urgent.   It is to the King's eternal renown that he took full responsibility into his own hands at that hour of crisis and saved the honour of the Hellenes.

The news from Albania and the Epirus was growing worse all the time.   That 5th Division which had tried to hold the Pass of Metsovo had been almost wiped out by the force of the German onset. The other two divisions despatched to reinforce it had not been able to reach Metsovo in time.   The Adolf Hitler Motorized Division had moved south and entered the smoking ruins of Jannina, which had been bombed to pieces by the Luftwaffe.   No building was spared. Even the hospitals were deliberately bombed from an altitude low enough to recognize the conspicuous Red Cross markings.   Six hundred wounded men, fifty nurses, and several doctors were buried under the ruins.   With the fall of Jannina the last supply road of the army in the Epirus was cut.

By command of the King Vice-Admiral Sakellariou, who was acting as Vice-President of the Government, addressed an Order to the fighting forces, an extract from which will give the heroic gist of it:

"I fully appreciate the situation from the standpoint of your communication to us.   But there is every need for us to continue the struggle.   This can be achieved by one final effort.   Consider the historic responsibility of this moment, and, in the reflection

193   O

that heroic decisions are called for, do even more than your duty. There is no dishonour in being taken prisoner if every effort, human or superhuman, has been exhausted, whereas the desertion of our allies would wipe out the capital that has always till now accrued to our country through the blood of our heroic dead."

A reference back to the Greek High Command's communiqué of that April 20th will not reveal any apparently deep anxiety about the immediate future of the army in the Epirus. There is a suggestion that the Italian hounds were venturing at last to attack the wounded stag, but the stag had turned to bay and they had fled yelping; and presumably the line in Thessaly, the unbroken line take up according to plan, was the British Imperial line at Thermopylae.

Nevertheless, the situation in the Epirus was already desperate. A withdrawal on such a scale even by superhuman effort was not imaginable. The capture of Jannina and the exposure of the only road southward to the full fury of the Luftwaffe and the Regia Aeronautica, now able to operate with occasional interference by what was left of the little Greek air force and without interference at all by what was left of the R.A.F. squadrons deprived of all except the two aerodromes near Athens, had destroyed any chance of obtaining further ammunition and supplies. The Greek armies in the Epirus had hardly enough ammunition left for two weeks if used sparingly. There was never a great store of it, because Greek guns were made for French ammunition, and of course there had been no supply of that available from the stocks when Italy attacked Greece. The Greek factories did their best, but they were not capable of supporting the strain upon their resources. No British nor any American munition factory was prepared to readjust its machinery to supply the Greek demands. That statement does not necessarily imply a reproach. It may not have been possible, when the demand was so heavy in Britain itself, to spare ammunition for Greece. Still, the lack of that ammunition must be remembered, and when we marvel at what the soldiers of Hellas accomplished, let that admiration be heightened by the reflection that from October 28th 1940 it had always been vital not to waste a single round. And what was true of the ammunition was equally true of all the rest of the Greek equipment. We have heard too often during this war the melancholy tale of the under-equipment of British troops compared with their antagonists; but the under-equipment of British troops at its worst would have seemed to Greek troops lavish. Even if the Greek forces in the Epirus should succeed in breaking out of the mountains in which they were almost surrounded by their enemies, it was obvious that they would never be able to reach and take up a position that would extend the line from Amphissa in the Gulf of Arta and thus prevent the enemy's reaching Attica or the Peloponnese.

And it was upon this Sunday, April 20th—Easter in the Orthodox calendar and by an obscene coincidence the birthday of that "blood-thirsty guttersnipe" of Berchtesgaden—that the preliminary negotiations for an armistice were undertaken by Greek Generals with the Germans at Jannina and at Larissa.

That Sunday, the last fifteen Hurricanes gathered at Eleusis from 33 Squadron which had been at Larissa, 80 Squadron which had been at Jannina, and 208 Squadron fought over Athens from dawn to dusk. Some of those fifteen Hurricanes would have been marked 'Unserviceable' in less desperate circumstances, but they all flew that day. In the afternoon a number of Stukas protected by Messer-schmitt 109's and 110's came over to bomb the Piraeus as they had been bombing it, first by night and since the almost complete destruction of the R.A.F. squadrons by day also, ever since April 6th. There were more than a hundred of them. Squadron Leader M. T. St. John Pattle, D.F.C., a young South African who had thirty enemy aircraft to his score, led those fifteen Hurricanes into that cloud-flecked azure which has canopied some of the supreme scenes of history. Three of the Barbarians he shot down, and then while he was shooting a 110 off the tail of another Hurricane his own was attacked by two 110's. His aircraft broke up in mid-air and he crashed down into the waters of the Bay of Eleusis; but both the 110's that shot him down were themselves shot down after him. What was mortal of Squadron Leader Pattle came to rest in waters consecrated to Liberty, and the Barbarians plunged down into waters where so many other Barbarians, they more civilized enemies of Liberty, had been plunged nearly two thousand five hundred years ago. Twenty-two of them were exterminated on Hitler's birthday, and of the fifteen Hurricanes eight were left to carry on the fight against at least eight hundred aircraft of the enemy.

Up in the Pindus while Generals were discussing the terms on which an armistice would be granted, Hellenic airmen were still fighting against even greater odds, and two days later they were still inflicting losses on the aircraft of the Barbarians and of the Fascist renegades from freedom.

To celebrate that birthday of Adolf Hitler a few young Nazis scaled Olympus and dared to plant the swastika on its summit. Such Ganymedes would have been more suitably employed serving their god in his Munich beer-cellar. The profanation of Mount Olympus by that black distorted cross demonstrated more perfectly than any of the gestures the Germans had hitherto made their insensitiveness to the great moral commonplaces of human behaviour and the great moral lessons of human history. That scarecrow flag flapping in the free wind of the mountain and the sea was an outburst of *hubris* for which the imagination demands retribution.[1]

On April 21st Mr Emmanuel Tsouderos, who had accepted his King's offer on the previous evening, took over the Premiership. Mr Tsouderos was a Cretan who had served under Venizelos with the Greek delegation at Versailles in 1918. He had been for some years a Cretan deputy and in 1924–25 had held for a short time the office of Minister of Finance. After that he had been in turn Deputy Governor and Governor of the National Bank of Greece from 1925 to 1939. When Mr Tsouderos agreed to accept the Premiership he performed an outstanding act of moral courage. It was a moment which might have made the most confident man quail before such a responsibility. He wasted not a moment in expressing his policy. On the very day on which he took over the Presidency of the Government, Mr Tsouderos sent this order to the Army of the Epirus through General Papagos, the Commander-in-Chief:

"I am informed that Lt.-General Tsolakoglou has taken the initiative in negotiating a capitulation. It must be understood by everyone that the country's highest interests forbid this. I appeal to the patriotism of all. The Army must struggle on to the extreme limit of its powers. Replace Tsolakoglou immediately."

[1] The principal sanctuary of Nemesis in ancient Hellas was at Rhamnos, a rocky promontory some miles north of Marathon. The older temple was probably destroyed by the Persians, and a second one was built in which was a statue of the goddess wrought, according to tradition, by Pheidias, from a block of Parian marble which the Persians had brought with them as material for a monument of their victory. This statue has vanished, but a colossal statue of Themis was discovered in the original temple. Themis, who dwelt on Olympus, is the personification of that established law and order which the 'philosophy' of Nazidom seeks to destroy, and the violation of which brings Nemesis to exact retribution. Strangely, the modern Greek name for Rhamnos is Ouriokastro, a corruption of Ebraiokastro or *Jewish* castle.

It would be presumptuous for one who is not a Hellene to venture a judgment of those negotiations, but this can be said: if it *was* possible for that encircled army to fight on, it was not because the soldiers of Hellas were unwilling to fight on but because some of the officers, and particularly the general officers, lost heart. Yet they cannot be judged except by their countrymen. Lt.-General George Tsolakoglou, who took the lead in those negotiations on that Easter Sunday which so miserably coincided with the birthday of Adolf Hitler, was later to form a Government in Athens to work with the Germans and the Italians. He must face one day the judgment of the Hellenes when Hellas is free. If he can convince his countrymen that what he did was done because he believed it would help them, he will receive their charity. If he shall fail to convince them of the purity of his motives, it were better for him that he had never been born. In the matter of the armistice it may provisionally be urged in his defence, first of all that he and the officers associated with him were only taking the advice given to them by Mr Papademas, the Minister for War, on April 17th, and secondly, that the terms offered by the Germans were generous enough to suggest that even they, with all their long black record of perjury, insolence, barbarity, and insensitiveness, were capable of feeling a certain shame over the vileness of their latest exploit, and that these maniacs of self-esteem were momentarily awed by a nobility to which they themselves, half-baked in the mighty oven of civilization, could not aspire. The armistice was signed in the name of Hitler by General Jodl, who had been specially flown to Salonika *aus dem Führerhauptquartier* (from the Führer's headquarters), and a communiqué from those headquarters of April 23rd proclaimed to the world that, as a result of the attacks carried out by German forces on the flank of the Greek Army of the North (*i.e.* the Army of Western Macedonia), in spite of the courage with which the Greeks had fought, proposals for an armistice had been made to the Twelfth German Army on April 20th at Larissa and Jannina. The terms agreed upon were that the Greek victory over the Italians should be recognized; that the Greek forces should withdraw from Albania over the Greek frontier; that the Germans would prevent any attempt by the Italians to cross that frontier; that all Greek officers should retain their side-arms and equipment; and that the soldiers after surrendering their arms should be free to return to their homes. If there was a clause providing that the actual capitulation should be offered to the commander of the Eleventh Italian Army, that was presumably exacted as a sop to the pride of Mussolini; but it should have made General Tsolakoglou pause and ask himself whether, if such a sop was necessary, an excuse would not soon be found to sacrifice Greece completely to Mussolini's vainglory.

It is exasperating and yet at the same time a kind of relief, like the verbose capers of a Shakespearean clown that relax for a while the tension of developing tragedy, to turn from the glory of Greece, not less glorious in disaster than in triumph, to the grandiose balderdash of Rome.

The rest of the world had been mildly astonished when the Duce's impudence egged him on to boast that it was the intervention of the Italian army which had decided the fate of France; but on the authority of the President of the United States, Italy had stabbed France in the back, which did suggest a certain amount of violent action, even if it was cowardly and treacherous action. Presently, it transpired that the only action taken by Italy was to kick in the back a France already prostrate. Yet even that repulsive piece of self-assertiveness could be claimed as an ignominious sort of victory because France submitted to the treatment.

But when, after the capitulation of the Greek army in the Epirus as a result of being assailed by Germany from behind at a moment when the enemy confronting it was afraid to attack, Mussolini in his capacity as Supreme Head of the Fascist Army dared in a special Order of the Day issued from General Headquarters to congratulate his troops on a victory, the world gasped for a moment, and then across the surface of our globe rolled a tidal wave of derisive laughter.

"The victory has lighted up your colours with fresh glory. The Country is prouder of you than ever," the Duce declared in an outburst of lyrical mendacity. Hitler chose well when he chose a General called Jodl to represent him at the signature of the armistice. Victory! *Per Bacco*, if Fascism last another year Caporetto will have become an Italian Austerlitz. It will not require a more difficult flight of fancy than the manufacture of a victory out of those twenty-five weeks, which cannot be called ignoble only because for every one of them five thousand simple Italian soldiers became casualties, 125,000 in all: as many Italian casualties as the total number of the defenders of Hellas on the Albanian front. The manufacture of that victory went forward rapidly. Within a week or two the seizure of Jannina by the Adolf Hitler Motorized Division had become a gigantic Italian manœuvre which had brought about the crumbling to pieces of the Greek front in Albania. It had been the 'superb dash' of the Italian infantry and Alpini which had broken the Greek line at the strategically vital spot.

On April 6th the Germans launched their invasion of Greece and Yugoslavia. By April 8th they were on the outskirts of Salonika, having broken through the Yugoslav defences in the Strumitza valley and the weak Greek defences between Guegueli and Doiran. On that evening the communiqué of the Italian High Command announced that on the Greek front their troops had repulsed local attacks in the sector of the Ninth Army, that is the northerly sector facing the Greek Army of Western Macedonia from which divisions were already being withdrawn to meet the fearful threat to the Monastir Gap. On April 11th the communiqué of the Italian High Command was so jejune as in the shattering circumstances to achieve a kind of inverted sensationalism: "*On the Greek front nothing to report*". Yet on that very day German forces driving down through Southern Yugoslavia had established contact with the left flank of the Italian Ninth Army at Struga at the north-west point of Lake Ochrida. On the Greek front nothing to report! Yet the German Armoured Divisions were already menacing the left flank of the Greco-British line, and the very next morning General Papagos would order a withdrawal to the Haliakmon Line. A reference to the Greek High Command communiqué of April 14th will show that the Greek forces had already evacuated Koritza of their own volition and that the withdrawal had been executed so skilfully and in such good order that the Italians had known nothing about it for twenty-four hours, when motor-cyclists had been hastily sent forward, presumably to give the impression of pursuit, several dozens of whom had been taken prisoner.

It may be said by some in criticism of the strategy of General Papagos that he should have taken advantage of the Italians' unwillingness to attack, until they were perfectly sure that they had enough Germans within reach of their cries for help, to evacuate Koritza the moment that news came to him of the Germans having reached Skoplje (Uskub); but it can certainly never be said that the evacuation of Koritza was hastened by even the shadow of a coming

Italian assault upon it. Yet these day-dreams of the adolescent which is the limit of Fascist development managed to transmute that evacuation of Koritza they did not discover for twenty-four hours into a battle! The journalists of the Fascist Press agreed with the unanimity of Tweedledum and Tweedledee to have a battle, and the battle of Koritza was duly invented: "The hour having struck, our Ninth Army was given the task of dealing the first mortal blow at the defensive system of the enemy".

There were twenty-four hours which had to strike before the Ninth Army ventured to advance against an empty town. 'Timeo Danaos et dona ferentes', they observed, and sniffed suspiciously at the Wooden Horse that evacuated Koritza was seeming.

In order to exalt the valour of the Italian troops in this terrific imaginary battle of Koritza the Fascist journalists went so far as to pay a belated tribute to the courage and fighting spirit of the Greeks: "We have deliberately drawn attention to this aspect of the battle," wrote a war correspondent of Mussolini's own paper, "because we should not like it to be supposed that our troops are advancing against an army in flight. On the contrary, our troops are moving forward impetuously and fighting all the way, and that enormously enhances the valour of their irresistible advance."

Virginio Gayda, whose task it always was to make a tune out of the trumpet blown by the Duce's wind, improved on this. He discovered that the Greeks were not withdrawing at all, but that at the very moment when the Italians moved forward to attack the Greeks were on the point of moving forward themselves to attack. According to this well-worn disc of His Master's Voice, the Greek High Command was not in the least disturbed by the German threat to the right flank of the Greek line. They were leaving the Germans to the British and had kept 22 divisions up to full strength on the Albanian front. Therefore the Italians had broken the Greek front when it was at the height of its offensive power.

That the Ninth Italian Army, rendered secure through the German elimination of all danger of its being attacked by the Yugoslavs on its left flank between Lake Ochrida and Lake Presba or in its rear from farther north, and doubly secure by the comparative proximity of the German armoured forces which threatened the rear of the Greeks, was able to advance over ground evacuated by the Greeks is undoubtedly true. Yet it is to be noted that in seven full days it was unable to reach the Greek frontier. Two miles a day forward, with only isolated detachments fighting rearguard actions to detain it, compares badly with the records of speed established over the same country when moving backward.

However, if the Italian Ninth Army moved forward like a tortoise, the Italian Eleventh Army had no heart to advance even at the pace of a snail. True, it had been from the Eleventh Army that Mussolini had exacted that disastrous offensive only a month ago, and therefore its cautiousness can be appreciated. With the evacuation of Klisura by the Greeks on April 16th, the snail emerged from the shell and set out. On April 18th the withdrawal of that incomparable Greek Army of the Epirus allowed the Italian Eleventh Army to reoccupy Argyrokastro, and a fanfaronade in the Fascist Press proclaimed that Porto Edda was already in sight. The prospect of recovering the harbour he had named after his favourite daughter went to the philoprogenitive Duce's head. There was no verbal extravagance he did not allow to his young war correspondents of the *Popolo d' Italia.* On April 19th one of them wrote that the war machine of the Italian armies, so patiently prepared and equipped, had gone into action with formidable blows from a battering-ram and that nothing could stop it any longer. Nothing was indeed the word. There was nothing now to stop that battering-ram, because the Greek Army of the Epirus had abandoned all its hard-won gains in a last desperate effort to fall back southward and establish a new line from the Gulf of Arta to join up with the British line from Thermopylae to Amphissa. Hard-won gains! "Our divisions are occupying in a few days, often literally in a few hours, ground which the Greeks took weeks and months of bloody fighting to conquer." Thus neighed one of the newspaper hacks from Mussolini's own Augean stable of excremental journalism. The recapture of Santi Quaranta (Porto Edda) when it had been abandoned by its captors roused fresh exuberance. The hacks began to curvet and caracol. The Italian infantry were hailed facetiously as lads with such a devil in them as began to embarrass poor journalists who, famous for their own speed, were not used to being outrun.

Whether the formal capitulation of the Greek Army of the Epirus to the commander of that Eleventh Army which had been transformed into a very Pegasus of snails by the absence of opposition was dictated by the Germans, or whether it was handed to him by General

Tsolakoglou's orders to forestall an Italian crossing of the Greek frontier, is not clear.　Be the reason what it may, the soldiers of that Eleventh Army, whose task, according to a correspondent of that once reputable journal, *La Stampa*, could not be daunted even by the mud, did not succeed in gratifying their "ardent desire to get back as quickly as possible to the positions they had conquered at the end of the previous October".

It is a bitter reflection on the moral degradation which Fascism can impose upon its victims that those Italian soldiers, who after all had fought hard and suffered greatly in Albania, should allow themselves to be presented to the world as so many zanies mimicking the chief clown of the Roman circus.

Naturally the capitulation of the Greek army was claimed by the Fascists as the result of Italian pressure, and two days later six divisions were mentioned as being already on Greek territory when the capitulation was made.　It was solemnly affirmed in the Greek communiqué of April 23rd, which announced that the curtain had fallen upon the tragedy, that not a single Italian soldier had set foot upon the soil of Hellas when what was left of the two glorious Armies of the Epirus and Western Macedonia laid down their arms; and inasmuch as not even Fascist myth-mongers have been able to name one single locality in Hellas on which those six divisions set their muddy feet, posterity is not likely to buy the tale.

Whether willing or unwilling, whether stalwarts or poltroons, whether betrayed by incompetence or deceived by lies, the Italian soldiers who fought against the Hellenes will be celebrated through the ages as the most ignoble military expedition in history, despicable in its conception, despicable in its execution, and despicable in its end.

"The victory has lighted up your colours with fresh glory.　The Country is prouder of you than ever."

Even the Germans had laughed.　It was said in Berlin that the French had put up a signboard on the frontier between France and Italy:

NOTICE

TO THE GREEKS

FRENCH TERRITORY BEGINS HERE

CHAPTER SEVENTEEN

ON the evening of April 21st, before the news of the armistice had reached Athens, Mr Tsouderos, the new President of the Council, broadcast to the Army and the people of Hellas:

"Brave soldiers and citizens of Greece, the Government with whose Premiership the King has entrusted me to-day undertakes the administration of the country without hesitation. With the support of the King and people, we are sure that we shall serve the interests of the nation, carrying on the country's fight to a victorious finish. In this we are guided solely by a sense of duty transmitted to us by the traditions of past generations.

"The Government, representing a united nation, considers that its first duty is to pay a tribute of respect and gratitude to the glorious dead, whose example might serve for any people determined not to become slaves, nor to allow country, Church, and family to be profaned by tyrants.

"Our fight is a Godly fight, for Hellenic civilization includes the Christian faith, and the sacrifice of self in such a cause is its own reward.

"The glory of the dead will remain for ever present in the minds of future generations, and the mountains of Albania and Macedonia will be the noblest monument with which they could be honoured.

"We must now turn from the dead to salute our gallant men of all services and all ranks, and to send them a message of admiration and gratitude on the part of the whole Greek race for their magnificent bravery in defending the country. The history we are making to-day is worthy of any that has been written by enlightened people who have in the past fought for freedom and the rights of man.

"The need for liberty, which proceeds from a sense of human dignity, is indigenous to our land. Men who are conscious of their dignity are masters of their own thoughts, acts, and life, and so will not allow others to decide their fate for them as though they were but sheep. The Greek people have always fought throughout their history for the right to decide freely as to their destinies. They have always been supported by a sense of collective order and social responsibility.

"This determination is to-day upheld by a feeling that they are also fighting for the liberation of friendly and even of enemy

people. The leaders of our enemies have set over the free will
of the peoples they govern, over Christian civilization and order a
régime of violence and outrage contrary to all rights and feeling,
human and divine.

"The whole nation will continue the struggle until Greece and
the Balkans and Europe are cleared of the invaders and until those
who have led them in this infamous aggression are utterly crushed.
You all know that struggles are never fought on paths strewn with
flowers. Let us hope that the present path, which is strewn with
thorns, will be but a short one. We shall perhaps have hard times
to go through, but we shall not give in until we have reached the
end of our journey as conquerors.

"Greece will ever remain faithful to her friendships and agreements and will be grateful to the great and noble British people
who, with splendid self-sacrifice, now offer the highest service of
humanity ever offered and whose sons have come to our land of
their own initiative and of their own free will to fight for us in the
cause of justice. Behind Great Britain stand the United States
of America holding up the unquenchable torch of liberty, from
which light and strength go forth to sustain every noble effort of
humanity.

"Through America the peoples of the world will in due time
be inspired for the organization of their mutual solidarity against
the rape of their freedom and tranquillity by mediaeval criminals.
With such Allies and friends and with the force of our own purpose
we may be sure that right will prevail. Greece takes courage.

"Look what has befallen those people who lost heart and gave
up the struggle midway. Let no one in Greece be found lacking
in spirit. I call to you all to believe in victory and to remain calm
in the face of any dangers or calamities. These ills are nothing
in comparison with those which would come upon us if we yielded
to the flatteries of the enemy.

"I conclude with the words of our gallant Sovereign: 'Let us
stand firm in this hour of national resurrection. Let us stand with
reverence before Almighty God and the Blessed Virgin who protect us and before the immortal legions of the heroes of so many
generations of Greece: before those who defend with their bodies
the honour and glory of eternal Hellas. Let all our thoughts go
out to the mountains where the epic fight in defence of the sacred
soil of our country is being fought in splendour and beauty.'

"Long live the nation! Long live the Army! Long live the
King!"

Earlier on that April 21st the Greek Government, recognizing
that the Greek army could give no more help to the British and

Imperial troops, had released the British Government from its obligations, and it was decided to evacuate the Expeditionary Force. No doubt the German Command was expecting such a decision, for the Adolf Hitler Motorized Division drove on southward from Jannina in an attempt to reach Missolonghi and Naupaktos in time to get across to the Peloponnese and, by seizing the bridge over the Corinth Canal, to cut off the British retreat. At Antirrhion, hard by the Bay of Naupaktos, the Corinthian Gulf is hardly more than a mile wide. If the specially selected blonds that composed Hitler's *élite* troops had been able to drive down unopposed, few would have been the British and Imperial troops evacuated. That they failed was due to the Hellenic forces which held up a portion of the Adolf Hitler Division at Preveza, where the Greeks were cut to pieces before the Germans could break through. That Greek troops after the capitulation were able to fight this action is enough to expose the myth launched by the Fascists about the victory of the Italian Eleventh Army. Thanks to the gallantry and devotion of that Greek force, the Adolf Hitler Motorized Division did not reach Patras until April 26th, that is six days after it had entered Jannina.

On April 23rd, St George's Day, King George II of the Hellenes broadcast to his people his decision to go to Crete and there fight on to the end. The Germans took advantage of this proud declaration to maintain that it broke the terms of the armistice. Considering that the Greek Generals had taken matters into their own hands and that the German Command had treated with them over the head of the Greek Government, nothing that the King said could affect the armistice terms. Mr Tsouderos had sent orders through the Commander-in-Chief, General Papagos, to forbid any attempt to treat with the Germans and to replace the leader of the parley, Lt.-General Tsolakoglou. However, although the King's broadcast was made the excuse for revoking the clause which allowed the soldiers to return home and for now declaring them prisoners of war, this revocation was never acted upon. There was in the black German heart a much fouler breach of faith in contemplation, which was the partitioning of Greece between Italy and Bulgaria, after the Germans themselves had plundered the Hellenes to their own satisfaction first. It should have been obvious that the armistice signed by General Jodl on behalf of Hitler would be treated as waste paper when it had served its purpose. The Germans despise honour and call it realism:

they debase truth and call it diplomacy: they spurn pity and call it strength: they exalt insolence and call it pride: they worship complexion and call it race. Yet these supermen when beaten cringe like curs. We heard them whine for twenty years about Versailles, and Hellas will hear them whine again when Nemesis shall choose her ineluctable hour.

The Greek Premier proclaimed the certain advent of that hour in his message to the nation before he went with his King to Crete:

"In this tragic but great moment, when I am leaving for Crete with the heroic King of the country—a worthy symbol of the great struggle that the nation is pursuing—I feel the need to say that I am truly proud of this political and national move, which illustrates in the fullest manner possible the unconquerable soul of Greece, and proclaims the firm determination of us all not to give in to the invader.

"We are defending ourselves against an unjust aggression of unprecedented baseness. To save a cowardly partner that we had vanquished, an empire of 100,000,000 souls has struck us in the back.

"From these trials, which a hard struggle has imposed on our race, and which all free peoples of the earth look upon with disgust, we shall emerge victorious—a glorified and greater nation.

"Moreover, the moral strength of our country has never in the past reached the heights attained to-day.

"The military armistice signed with Germany without any authorization appears to be a precipitate act which may be put down to fatigue, brought about by six months' unequal but victorious struggle, and which is the result of overwhelming pressure brought to bear by the enemy on our valorous army.

"Our struggle has been filled with military catastrophes and cowardly blows showered on non-combatants. But material losses do not intimidate the brave. They can be repaired and they will be made good.

"All Greeks will share these losses with those who have suffered them. This is a sacred and irrevocable obligation.

"Hold firm. By so doing we shall increase the moral gains of the country, through which a new and great Greece will arise.

"Nations that keep their honour and respect their undertakings toward their friends will acquire the right to have their interests safeguarded. Our own rights are written in blood and bear witness to our sacrifices and supreme heroism. We must venerate and defend them.

"Be assured that the dawn of a brilliant day for the nation will not fail to break, and that day will be the greatest of Greek civilization."

A study of the various accounts published of the evacuation of the British and Imperial Expeditionary Force from Greece leaves the reader in a state of bewilderment over the failure of the German High Command to prevent some 45,000 out of 58,000 troops from being taken off. We have noted the hold-up of part of the Adolf Hitler S.S. Division by Greek forces near Preveza and the length of time it took that division to reach the Corinthian Gulf and join up with parachute troops dropped at Corinth to seize the bridge over the canal, the numbers of which vary in the estimates of their strength from two thousand to a couple of hundred. But why were those parachute troops so late in arriving on the scene and so unenterprising when they did arrive? Why did they wait to attack that vital bridge until the great majority of the British Imperial troops were safely in the Peloponnese? Why was the attempt to outflank the Thermopylae line by landing at Euboea delayed until April 25th? By that time the British forces had fallen back beyond Thebes, where on April 26th a New Zealand brigade was still fighting a rearguard action to cover the withdrawal. And above all, why did not the overwhelmingly strong armoured forces of the Germans press on with more resolution across the Thessalian plain while the earlier British withdrawal from the Olympus line was in progress?

A clue may perhaps be found in Hitler's obviously personal anxiety to avoid many casualties in the Greek campaign. The figures he gave of German casualties in the speech he made in Berlin on May 4th claimed that of the army and S.S. troops 70 officers and 1414 men were killed or missing, 181 officers and 3571 men wounded; and that of the Luftwaffe 150 officers and 42 men were killed or missing. He further claimed that the German troops engaged consisted of not more than two Armoured Divisions, one Mountain Division, and the Adolf Hitler S.S. Motorized Division. These figures were derided at the time; but it is difficult to believe that Hitler could afford to tell a factual lie too remote from the truth to obtain credence even from the Germany he held like a hypnotized fowl with its beak on the chalk-line he had drawn for it. Wild assertions were made by correspondents that the lowest figure at which the German casualties could be estimated was 40,000 to

50,000 killed, wounded, and missing, that is to say, eight to ten times as many as Hitler was prepared to admit. In one British book about the campaign it is claimed that 20,000 Germans were killed in a single day when on April 11th the Mackay Force met the onrush of the Adolf Hitler Division supported by one of the Armoured Divisions.

In the same speech Hitler claimed 9000 prisoners and put the figure of the British Imperial troops in Greece at from 60,000 to 70,000. Allowing that 45,000 were evacuated and that the figure of 9000 prisoners is approximately correct, which it seems to be, we reach a figure of 4000 casualties in the field for the British and Imperial Forces, besides those wounded among the prisoners. If Hitler's casualties are trebled we may be near the truth.

The evidence of those with first-hand knowledge of the campaign always testifies that the Germans were looking for a way round and that when at all badly hit at any point by the defence they took time to recover. In fact they did their utmost to avoid casualties. Hence probably their failure to prevent the evacuation. Like the giant stingaree or sea-bat, the German army loves to envelop its victim: the mountains and the sea of Hellas did not favour such tactics.

In the final issue it can be asserted that the Germans relied upon the Luftwaffe to accomplish the task of driving the British Imperial forces out of Greece, which could most improbably have been accomplished even by armoured forces twice as powerful as they were able to employ.

Strong defensive positions were numerous in Greece; but the weakness of a strong defensive position in such country is the difficulty of supply along the necessarily narrow and mountainous roads that lead to it. Such roads offered the perfect objective for the disorganizing powers of a hostile air force which had obtained the mastery of the air. That mastery the Luftwaffe possessed.

But besides the ability to dominate during daylight the roads, the Luftwaffe was able to strike more fundamentally at supply by the havoc it could wreak upon the ports. The Piraeus was put out of use within a week. The Saronic Gulf was sown with mines. Volo was smashed to pieces. The Luftwaffe was ruthless. Even five hospital ships were bombed and sunk, and that deliberately from so low an altitude that the survivors struggling in the water were machine-gunned. Apart from all problems of supply no Expeditionary Force which had come to the aid of a hard-pressed ally would have been justified in remaining in the country, every town of which was at the mercy of that dominant air force.

Kozani, Kastoria, Servia, Elassona, Grevena, Larissa, Jannina, Kalabaka, Trikkala, Arta, Preveza, Patras, Corfu, Khalkis, Nauplia, Lamia, Thebes, Corinth, Argos, Sparta, Piraeus—these are but some of the places either utterly destroyed or heavily damaged by the Luftwaffe. In Trikkala 3000 out of its 18,000 inhabitants were killed. How far the mastery achieved by the Luftwaffe was due to lack of Allied aircraft from November 1940 onward, how far to lack of aerodromes, how far to lack of foresight in failing to set to work at once to provide both them and the fighters that were wanted most of all, how far to Greek opposition to such enterprise for fear of provoking Germany, how far to lack of coordination between the three British fighting services in providing for contingencies in Greece, how far to lack of good staff work by the R.A.F. command in Greece itself, provide an amalgam of questions which certainly cannot be analysed at present. This only can be said now with perfect confidence: nothing was lacking in the men who flew what aircraft there were. And it was the knowledge of what those young airmen gave of themselves for Greece added to the knowledge of what the officers and men of the British and Imperial Expeditionary Force gave too with equal recklessness of self which won from the heart of the Hellenic people a warmth of gratitude, a tenderness of comprehension, and a dignity of regret beyond the power of one who did not earn it himself to express in words.

"It was with thumbs up and shouts of 'Nike! Nike!' (Victory) that they said their last farewell to their departing Allies", wrote the Special Correspondent of *The Times*.

And of waiting at Nauplia for the transports Lt.-Colonel Casson writes: [1]

"I have never seen any hospitality to compare with what these women and children of Nauplia gave to us. They knew that it was only a matter of time before the bombs that were destined to fall on us would fall on them too. The mere use of their port for our evacuation implied that their homes would be bombed and ruined, and yet without hesitation they gave us all they had."

Of the retreat itself that Gunner officer whose account of the Expeditionary Force's arrival was printed in an earlier chapter writes:

[1] *Greece Against the Axis*, p. 185.

As we drove south the roads were littered with all the depressing junk of a retreating army—charred lorries, abandoned guns and harness and packs, dumps of petrol and ammunition and rations, some burning, some intact and left to the enemy, dead horses, broken-down vehicles—for miles and miles on end. One night we drove for 12 hours and covered 15 miles. The traffic blocks were heartbreaking. An endless stream of Greeks, on horseback and on foot, plodded patiently on—not a trace of bitterness when we had to refuse them lifts on our guns, for we had to be ready to drop into action at any moment. Their lorries broke down one after another—poor old crocks requisitioned from every town in Greece from Patras to Kavalla, with five months' hard war service behind them. Many of them I helped to push over the cliff, to clear the road for us. And many Italian lorries and guns and superb mobile workshops and ambulances and tractors were left behind for their lawful masters to recover. And to add to the desolation we blew up the bridges and mountainsides and blocked the roads wherever we went. But it didn't seem to stop those amazing German tanks.

The first port from which the men were taken off was Megara, where in spite of the mines in the Saronic Gulf 5500 men were embarked by H.M.S. *Coventry*, an A.A. cruiser, with some destroyers and a merchant ship. That was on April 24th. On the afternoon of the same day H.M.S. *Calcutta*, another A.A. cruiser, with one transport went to Porto Rhaphti on the south-east coast of Attica and took off 5700 men. Porto Rhaphti is a good natural harbour divided into two basins by a tongue of land. From the southernmost of these the State trireme of Athens used to sail each year with the sacrificial embassies to Delos. Two other transports were sent to Nauplia escorted by destroyers. One of the transports went aground and was bombed so heavily that she became a wreck. The other transport and the escorting destroyers took aboard 7800 men. So on April 24th–25th a total of 19,000 men were evacuated.

On April 25th, when Anzac troops were being taken from Megara and Porto Rhaphti and Nauplia to Suda Bay in Crete, German troops landing from Samothrace attacked Kastro in the island of Lemnos. Their landing was resisted by some forty Greek gendarmes, the whole garrison of Lemnos, but without avail. It was before dawn on April 25th, 1915, that Anzac troops sailed from the great harbour of Mudros on the other side of the island to that immortal landing in Anzac Cove. Surely it is not extravagant to discern looming in a future not very far away the figure of Rhamnusian

Nemesis calling Anzacs to land again upon that time-hallowed Attic shore where they were preserved to carry on the fight for liberty.

On April 26th the *Calcutta* came back with a convoy of transports, three of which with the *Calcutta* herself went on to Nauplia. The others escorted by destroyers made for Porto Rhaphti and Rhaphina. The latter diminutive fishing haven lies a few miles north of Porto Rhaphti, and its beach of shingle used to be a favourite spot for moonlight bathers from Athens.

The *Calcutta*'s convoy was attacked by eighteen Ju. 87's and 88's. One of her transports was disabled and another damaged; but she reached Nauplia with two of them. That day the Germans seized the aerodrome at Argos only a few miles away from Nauplia; and the weather which had been calm changed that night, with a strong wind and a rough sea which made boat work extremely difficult. Bombers were over from seven in the morning of April 27th until ten. One transport was hit and began to sink. The destroyer *Diamond* went alongside to take off troops and was joined later by the destroyer *Wryneck*. The destroyers *Vampire* and *Voyager* joined the *Calcutta* in the fight against the enemy bombers. Later both the *Diamond* with 600 men and the *Wryneck* with 100 men from the sunk transport were themselves sunk by bombs. Only fifty survivors were picked up, and these were machine-gunned by German aircraft while they were in the water.

That night other transports protected by the cruiser *Phoebe* took off 8000 men from Kalamata, and altogether 16,000 men of the British and Imperial forces were taken off that night. 35,000 were evacuated by now.

On the night of April 27th–28th some 4200 men were taken off between Marathon and Porto Rhaphti, bringing up the total of troops evacuated to 39,200. Some of those had previously been waiting at Eleusis hidden all through the daylight of April 26th, after which they had driven through the darkened streets of Athens to the east coast of Attica. Miss Clare Hollingworth met the last British officer to leave Athens on that night before the Germans entered it. "He told me of the friendliness of the people to the very last and their warm appreciation of the British effort."

A vivid picture of that last day of freedom in Athens is given by an American, Mr Ralph Kent,[1] a member of the Staff of Athens

[1] *The Nation*, August 16th, 1941.

College. The troops who had fought that rearguard action by Erythrae to cover the evacuation were on the way now to the sea themselves:

"On Saturday morning the first of the dusty British lorries began to pour in, and having begun, they seemed never to stop. They dripped with tin-hatted men, guns, and a great many things snatched up in a hurry. Their progress through the streets was oddly like a victory parade, for everyone cheered and 'thumbed up', and the flower-sellers took roses from their stalls and threw them into the trucks. To the eye, the Australians and New Zealanders seemed as happy as boys just let out of school.

"All day long there were intermittent explosions as the demolition squads went their rounds. As darkness fell, barricades were thrown across the main roads. We were told they were put there only as a precautionary measure, in case the Germans arrived too soon.

"When I went to bed there were machine-guns at fifty-foot intervals along the road outside my gate. The ditches at the side of the road were full of New Zealanders. Until three in the morning field guns, light tanks, and lorries went by. After that there was an unfamiliar and rather awesome silence."

On the night of April 28th–29th about 8000 troops and a number of Yugoslav refugees were hoping to be rescued from Kalamata; but the Adolf Hitler Division had at last penetrated deep into the Peloponnese, and Kalamata was in the hands of the enemy when the ships arrived. In spite of that, 500 men were rescued. That was the night when Sergeant Hinton, V.C., a New Zealander, charged with two grenades a German 6-inch gun and destroyed the crew of it, when followed by other New Zealanders he drove the Germans at the point of the bayonet to take shelter in two houses in which they were bayoneted, when he and his New Zealanders held the German guns until overwhelming armoured forces arrived, and when he fell with a bullet in the lower abdomen and was taken prisoner, he and about 7000 others. Nevertheless on that same night 3750 British Imperial troops were evacuated from Monemvasia, whence came the strong sweet wine the English in the Middle Ages called malmsey and of which they used to drink so much before they discovered port. On that same night from the island of Kythera 750 R.A.F. personnel were evacuated. The total number of troops evacuated was now 44,200.

On the following night, April 29th–30th, British destroyers

searched in the neighbourhood of Kalamata, but only 33 officers and men were found.

The final search of the Kalamata area was made on the night of April 30th–May 1st when 202 officers and men were rescued. That was the last night on which a rescue was feasible. The grand total of troops evacuated by the Royal Navy was 44,435. Besides these a good many more were rescued by air, and there were also those rescued by the Royal Hellenic Navy, which played its part intrepidly and suffered heavy losses. From remote beaches in the Peloponnese and on the islands Allied troops were picked up by ships of the Greek navy. Caiques and small coasting steamers were dauntless in their rescue work. It was a time of Odysseys innumerable. Of the Royal Hellenic Navy the venerable cruiser *Averoff*, which is acquiring the marine majesty of Poseidon himself, seven out of the ten destroyers, two out of the thirteen torpedo-boats, and five out of the six submarines reached Alexandria. They are still fighting the enemy with the Royal Navy.

A young Greek naval officer told the writer how when his ship was sunk by dive-bombers he swam ashore on the little isle of Antikythera which lies where the Ionian and the Aegean mingle their waters, and there spent one of those exquisite days at April's end in a profound serenity of mind which put him in such accord with the natural scene that the Junkers and the Dorniers and the Messerschmitts appeared to his mood a part of it and as harmless as the gulls. Antikythera had been emptied of its people, and that young Greek naval officer made himself comfortable in a beautiful house the doors and windows of which had been left wide open when the owners fled. At night he was rescued, and since then he has been serving in the long battle which Hellas is still waging against the enemy.

In the channel between Kythera and Antikythera divers working at the beginning of this century upon an ancient wreck brought to the surface many marbles and bronzes. Some of these are in the Athens Museum, among them the statue of a wrestler who has fallen to his knees and is eyeing his adversary, unbeaten. Like a wrestler fallen upon his knees stood Hellas upon that April day, and her will to rise was expressed by the profound serenity of that young naval officer alone on Antikythera.

And now to bring this tale of the evacuation to a close here is a last extract from the letters of that Gunner officer:

On the Beaches (April 27th)

"This is a disastrous affair. But how inevitable, when one looks back on it. Three divisions against thirty, with the Greek army worn out by 5 months of Albania, and pitifully thin on the ground. But I still believe Dill was right to send us. We had to come. . . . The complete lack of liaison with the Jugoslavs gave Hitler just that chance to smash across Serbia and down the Florina Gap. And he succeeded brilliantly. I admire the Greeks more than ever. We saw their pitiful broken army in retreat. There was much panic and confusion, but they stood up to the ceaseless bombing and machine-gunning better than the French or Belgians. I was in Athens the morning the public was told that the King and the Government were in Crete. The shops closed down, the police turned out, and huge silent crowds filled the streets. But not a trace of bitterness against us, though it was obvious we were leaving. And the leaders in the morning papers were thrilling in their tone of proud defiance. Even now they are helping us: ten miles up the road behind us I met a dozen Greeks this morning with two machine-guns, gloriously drunk, resolved to fight it out. In spite of all their mistakes and strategic follies, I take my hat off to the Greeks."

But the chapter cannot be thus concluded, for as those words are being transcribed comes news from Egypt:

"A feature of yesterday's operations was the ground-strafing mission undertaken at their special request by a squadron of the Royal Hellenic Air Force in honour of the anniversary of the date on which Greece, treacherously attacked by the Italians, took her place among the Allied nations. The target chosen was Italian Headquarters, and the attack was carried out to the complete satisfaction of the Greeks. Hundreds of rounds were poured into tents, and vehicles and lorries were seen to go up in flames. One Greek aircraft crashed inside our lines, but the pilot was unhurt."[1]

Submarines and destroyers of the Royal Hellenic Navy have been helping to destroy the enemy's supplies coming from Italy to North Africa; and a Greek brigade, now indeed fully equipped, is taking part in the great battle for the Mediterranean which has begun. The blue and white colour shot through by bullets in Albania waves again. The war-cry of the Evzones, "Aera! Aera!", is heard once more. The wind, the wind, the swift, the swerveless, the incontestable wind of freedom sweeps on. "Aera! Aera!"

The wrestler has risen from his knees.

[1] *The Times*, October 29th, 1942.

CHAPTER EIGHTEEN

ON Sunday April 27th, at 9.45 A.M., the vanguard of the German troops consisting of motor-cyclists, armoured cars, and tanks entered Athens, and the swastika defiled the Acropolis. It was not until the following day that an entry in full force was made. Mr Ralph Kent [1] has recorded the scene:

"For some hours it was impossible to cross certain roads because they were clogged with every conceivable sort of mechanized vehicle. One's first impression of these was that they were shoddy and *ersatz*, that they had been through a good bit of hell and had just managed to do it. But the drivers, the mechanics, the operators were anything but *ersatz*, despite the fact that their uniforms were shabby, their faces dirty, and the look in their eyes that of drug addicts. In cold fact they frightened me. Strong faces these, intelligent faces, but inhuman like characters in a Wellsian fantasy.

"By Wednesday (April 30th) the occupation was virtually complete. Every house where the English had lived had been broken into. Every house that enjoyed a strategic position or struck the fancy of the army had been requisitioned. The owners might be left a servant's room or two, or they might be ordered out altogether. When houses otherwise suitable did not have furniture to the taste of the occupants, it was 'borrowed' from other houses."

On that Wednesday April 30th, Lt.-General George Tsolakoglou agreed to form a Government to cooperate with the Germans. Archbishop Chrysanthos, the Metropolitan of Athens, was called upon to administer the Oath of State to the new Government. He refused, denying that it was a Government which represented the will of the Hellenic people. The Archbishop was deposed and interned.

Compared with the Germans, the Harpies and the Stymphalian birds were ascetic monsters. Mr Laird Archer, the Director of the Near East Foundation in Greece, has recorded: [2]

"The Nazis perfected in Greece their vacuum-cleaning process which they invented as a part of their enfeebling system months

[1] *The Nation*, August 16th, 1941.　　　[2] *Greece Fights On*, pp. 15, 16.

215

before. It has six major suction pipes. The first one came down upon us the day following that tragic Sunday, April 27th, when myriads of motorized equipment streamed like ugly black beetles into the white city of Athens. Seventy-five thousand Nazi soldiers were each given the equivalent of 50 dollars in buying power—100 freshly printed Marks—and were sent into the shops of Athens to 'buy' everything they could parcel-post out of the country, especially clothing and medical supplies. The second suction pipe struck when agents of German industries arrived and gathered up all lines of manufactured equipment from electrical goods to Diesel engines for which they paid the same kind of printing-press Marks and which proved to be non-negotiable outside of Greece when the merchants went to the importers to replenish their stocks.

"The third sucked up motor transportation which automatically cut off supplies from the countryside to the teaming cities, the fourth took control of the industries of Greece which then were set at canning vegetables and producing cotton and woollen goods for Germany, and the fifth cleaned out metal of all kinds. In this fifth process, a new building at 6 America Street where the Near East Foundation formerly had its offices was stripped even of light fixtures and the taps from the wash-basins to get metal for Hitler, as were all buildings and private houses occupied by the Nazis before they left for the Russian campaign.

"By far the worst was the pipe which sucked up food reserves. Greece already was short by 700,000 tons in her bread stocks for 1941–42. This seizure cut the average working man from his three-pound oka loaf per day, his principal food, down to four ounces: hod-carriers fainting under their loads were a common sight even when I left Athens about August 1st. The country had been able to bring in only 44,465 tons of its annual 75,000-ton requirement of sugar in 1940, this year practically nothing, and the Nazis took what was left. With the annual import of 10,000 tons of milk shut off and 200,000 tons of local production reduced to less than half by slaughtering, infant mortality has tripled. When the heads of the tuberculosis sanatorium and the foundlings' institution petitioned the Nazi High Command for milk for their patients, they were told: 'Sorry, our soldiers are so used to having milk for their coffee!' "

On Friday May 2nd, the German Command published an announcement in the evening papers that from 5 A.M. until noon of the following day no vehicles of any kind were to circulate in the streets of Athens or about the immediate outskirts of the city. Furthermore, no person was to appear in the streets or even on balconies and terraces overlooking the streets, and every window was to be closed. The reason for this was that the Germans were to make their official entry into the city, profane the tomb of the Unknown Warrior with a wreath, and ceremoniously hoist the swastika on the Acropolis.

Then in Berlin on Sunday May 4th Hitler reviewed the Balkan campaign in a speech at the Kroll Opera House. The Italian Ambassador was the only one of the Diplomatic Corps who did not occupy his box, and therefore he was unable either to wink or to blink when Hitler had the effrontery to declare solemnly that the Germans had not gone into Greece to help their allies.

That the onslaught on Greece was still fretting the superstitious fears of Hitler was discernible behind what sounded like a whimpering appeal to be judged mercifully by the Hellenic people:

"Even to-day I feel that I must, as I believe in the interests of historical accuracy, distinguish between the Greek people and that thin top layer of corrupt leaders who, inspired by a King who had no idea of the duties of true leadership, preferred instead to further the aims of British war politicians. . . . I must stress categorically that this action was not directed against Greece. . . . Nothing is impossible for the German soldier. Historical accuracy, however, obliges me to say that of the opponents who have taken arms against us, the Greek soldiers have most particularly fought with the greatest courage and contempt for death."

Yet it was not only superstitious fear which prompted this attempt to propitiate the Greeks. The wheedling note of the gutter-cheat was there too. Hitler was hoping that Greece would be amenable because, with his plan to attack Russia at the earliest possible moment, he could not afford to maintain in Greece the number of German troops necessary to hold the population down, and by this time he must have had the gravest doubts whether the Italians would be able to do so without German help. Unless he could win the Greeks over he must make a desperate effort as soon as possible to overwhelm Crete, because if Crete with British help remained in Greek hands there would certainly be no possibility of the Italians being able to hold the mainland. This meant more delay. Rudolf Hess was to depart within a few days on his mad mission to secure British cooperation against Russia, but it seems most unlikely that Hitler himself believed in the faintest possibility of its success. Indeed, it is probable that he really was unaware of Hess's project. Hitler may have been worrying about the interference presented by a hostile Crete to schemes for occupying Syria to strike at Suez or Iraq; but Crete was also a menace to the Russian plan, because it was a menace to Salonika and the Dardanelles. Turkey had been kept neutral up to now, but nothing must be left undone which would help to keep her neutral.

The answer Hellas gave to the corrupt flattery of Hitler was given in ways innumerable; but the most crushing reply would be given by the women of Crete. Seventeen of those heroines, wearing their bandoliers, were taken prisoner and brought to Athens. The German commander informed them that the Führer, instead of having them shot as civilians helping the enemy, intended to honour them as prisoners of war. Then spoke their wounded leader, the wife of a former Deputy: "It is impossible for Hitler to honour the Cretan women."

It sounds like a line from one of the tragic poets; and she who spoke it died of her wounds in the prison hospital at Ampelokepi.

Ignorant that women of so much nobler breed than themselves existed, the shoddy Berlin crowds stood agape in the drizzling rain of that Sunday in May while their god ranted at them through loud-speakers.

Dr. Homer W. Davis, the President of Athens College, in the course of an address to the Pan-Hellenic Congress at Cincinnati on August 18th, 1941, said: [1]

"Three weeks after the invasion, the Germans entered and raised the foul and sinister swastika over the Acropolis.

"The work of our Committee was almost at an end for, as was to be expected, the Germans made it clear that American organizations, regarded as instruments of Democratic propaganda, were not wanted and would not be tolerated. We had a short time to help meet tragic needs. Greek wounded harried out of hospitals, sometimes actually put in the street, were in a pitiable plight. Every hospital ship had been sunk, every ambulance seized. Greek soldiers filled the streets, seeking food and shelter and a means of getting to their homes. . . . Ruined homes, looted villages and towns, young men maimed for life, farms without their farm animals, demobilized soldiers with no jobs and often no homes to go back to, food almost unobtainable, Germans quartered in

[1] *Greece Fights On*, pp. 31, 32, 33, 34.

thousands of private homes; in short—a plague of locusts devouring everything. . . .

"Is there, therefore, a feeling of regret among Greeks that they stood up against the greatest military machine the world has ever seen? Many people here have asked me this question. I can say that I have never heard anyone in Greece express such a sentiment. As I went about the country visiting bombed areas in behalf of the American Relief Committee during the weeks when the German threat was becoming a very real one, I found that the spirit of resistance, everywhere strong, was strongest in places that had suffered most. People of all classes would say, 'We'll fight the Germans, too, if necessary. Let them come if they must. We will risk destruction and keep our honour. We may be beaten, but in the end we shall be victorious with Britain and America.'

"Other countries may try to justify submission without fighting by the excuse of the helplessness of small nations. To Greeks such an attitude was unthinkable. They have saved their honour. That is all-important to them.

"This is why the people of Greece are enduring their suffering with courage, patience, and dignity. Though active resistance is impossible now, the spirit of resistance is as strong as ever. In spite of hunger, in spite of the realization that conditions will get worse, they have confidence in the outcome of the struggle in which they have so good reason to be proud of their part. In spite of hunger, they display a sense of humour which helps them to bear, with amazing cheerfulness, hardships which they believe cannot be of long duration. They have no guns, but they, too, have a secret weapon—the Greek spirit which cannot be broken— which cannot be broken even by mechanized Attila.

"They also have the inimitable Greek gift for ridicule . . . and they are exercising that gift. Perhaps this explains the precautions adopted by the Germans and Italians on the occasion of their victory parade which, much to the amusement of Athenians, no one was allowed to see as the streets were cleared for two blocks on either side. Italian soldiers are rarely seen in the street except in twos and threes, for even small boys think of subtle ways of making them appear and feel ridiculous. The Germans admit that they are made to feel more uncomfortable in Greece than in any other occupied country. The stolid Teutons are up against a people who have no difficulty in outwitting their conquerors in most embarrassing and, to them, amusing ways.

"Perhaps the most telling form of passive resistance, however, is the instinctive coldness of Greeks toward invaders, who added to the natural hatred felt for them by adopting the pose of liberators.

One day the heavy tread of German boots on an apartment house stairway caused a dog on his mistress' leash to crouch against the wall with averted head. Seeing it, one of the soldiers observed, 'Even the dogs!'

"It is true—even dogs.

"When the Italians took possession of Cephallonia, a huge picture of Mussolini was promptly placed over the Demarcheion of Argostoli. The next morning, finding it mutilated and defaced, the military commander imposed a fine of 10 drachmas per head on the inhabitants of the town. When to his surprise he found that everybody had paid 20 drachmas, he asked for an explanation, which perhaps surprised him still more. 'That's for to-morrow's picture,' he was told.

"You all know what pride Greeks and especially Athenians take in their knowledge of languages, and how, with their famed hospitality, they eagerly come to the assistance of less fortunate foreigners who do not know Greek. The Germans may perhaps have a different impression. One day on a bus in Athens, I noticed a German officer struggling in vain to get some information from a conductor. Finally the conductor appealed to the crowded bus: 'Is there anyone here who knows German?' Complete silence. 'Is there anyone here who knows French?' Again complete silence. Then following the conductor's 'Ti Na Kano?' a voice came from the back seat, 'We speak English, here.'

"They speak English. They enjoy speaking it more than ever before. They are uncompromisingly loyal to their British allies. When the English bombers come at night no one begrudges the loss of sleep. House-tops are crowded with hopeful crowds who the next morning go about their business, with a smile and with flowers in their buttonholes. As yet, there is no law against wearing flowers. That, too, may come, for an official announcement of the Germans published in the Press naïvely threatened that continued demonstrations of sympathy for the British in public were forbidden and would be severely punished."

And here is testimony from Miss Ruth Parmelee and Miss Emilie Willms, the Director and the Chief of the Nursing Division of the American Women's Hospitals in Greece:

"Our patients, who had made such splendid recovery, soon became listless, hollow-cheeked and heavy-eyed, and their wounds reopened. Daily, some commodity was dropped from the diet list —milk, butter, cheese, macaroni, olives, bread rationed to less than seven ounces (one quarter of the normal amount per person), lemons, oranges, tomatoes, sugar, coffee, etc. etc. When the

Mayor remonstrated with the German authorities for taking all the rice and begged them to leave some for the sick and infants, the reply was, 'You Greeks are in Paradise. No one is falling in the streets from hunger. In Poland, one and a half million people starved to death.' And this was in the first weeks of the occupation!

"This ever-increasing scarcity in food commodities was due to the systematic seizure by the Germans of all kinds of supplies for the use of their army and to ship home by aeroplane. Each soldier was permitted to send packages up to fifty kilos, containing food, clothing, etc. They confiscated truckloads en route from the farms into town, or emptied the shops before the eyes of housewives standing in line to purchase vegetables for their families. Often a woman went to market at dawn, to return home hours later with but a bit of parsley. We found only shoe-strings for sale at the fish market and on the grocery shelves, pickles and mustard as the sole display.

"Produce was taken right from the ground—the potatoes as they were dug, the grapes as they were gathered. Tomatoes were canned and shipped, potatoes were fried before sending. In a few weeks it was a serious problem to find anything to eat, let alone meat, eggs, cheese, oil, butter, or coffee of which there was none to be had. . . . One of the hardest sights to which we had to accustom ourselves was that of the German soldiers strutting the streets in English khaki uniforms, and the Italians in their chic blue-grays and plumes, while the Greek convalescent soldiers had to discard their uniforms on pain of death, and, since most of them came from the provinces and islands, roamed the streets of Athens in pajamas. . . . It was a common sight, long after the German occupation had taken place, to see stray lone soldiers arriving from the front, care-worn and foot-sore. While in the business district of Athens one day with a Greek friend, we noticed such a figure, still in the forbidden uniform. His toes were out of his shoes, uniform torn and shabby, as if it hadn't been off his back for days, face swollen and unshaved, lips parched, eyes bleary. We accosted him gently as he appeared dazed, offered him help, food, and to take him to his destination. Gradually and with great effort he succeeded in straightening himself to a soldierly height and spoke in a barely audible voice, saying, 'No, thank you. You have your laws and we have ours.' For a moment we were at a loss to understand his meaning. Then it dawned on us that we were taken for German women. Our Greek friend explained that we were Americans and wanted to help him. The scene that followed was pathetic. It was hard for him to realize that Americans were still in Greece.   Finally, he accepted some help, but refused food and walked away mumbling, 'God bless America!' "

On the night of May 30th the swastika was pulled down from the Acropolis and after being torn up was used in the only serviceable way in which that Yahoo flag could be used.

On the following day the German Command in Athens issued this Order:

> "Because German military flags have been pulled down and torn from public buildings, because the Greek people are hoarding foodstuffs and preventing their reaching German soldiers, because of the Greek population's sympathy with British prisoners, and because the Greek press refuses to conform to the new order, the German authorities in Greece have decided that in future those found guilty of the above-mentioned offences will be shot."

To this threat was added the immediate imposition of a curfew at 10 P.M., and the shedding of a few crocodile tears by the German Military Command.

The German Command in Athens, it moaned, had until then been doing all it could to show its good-will toward the people of Greece; but now with deep regret it must take whatever steps it considered necessary to end the situation.

In other words, Hitler's attempt to propitiate Hellas had been flung back at him.

λαβὲ λαβὲ λαβὲ λαβέ, φράζου.
Seize him!   Seize him!   Seize him!
Seize him!   Mark him down!

The Furies were awake.   Nor shall they sleep until they sleep sound in their ancient Athenian sanctuary, their task accomplished.

CHAPTER NINETEEN

TO the people of Great Britain and the Dominions the failure of the British and Imperial Expeditionary Force to save Greece was a most profound mortification; and the Vote of Confidence accorded so unanimously to the Government at the end of a two-days debate on May 7th was accorded not because the House of Commons with such unanimity thought that the Balkan situation had been skilfully handled, but because the motion had been drafted in such a way as to obtain the House's approval of the decision to aid Greece and the determination to prosecute the operations in the 'Middle East' with the utmost vigour. There was nobody who would not have preferred to leave even a Government of congenital idiots in power rather than seem to grudge the attempt to help Greece. As for prosecuting the operations in the 'Middle East' with the utmost vigour, who even in that ductile and senescent Parliament did not desire that?

There had been a good deal of disquiet over the ease with which the Germans and Italians had been able to occupy the islands of the Aegean one after another. Thasos, Samothrace, Lemnos, Mytilene, and Chios had been taken by the Germans, though Thasos and Samothrace were to be handed over to the Bulgarians soon. The Italians made themselves responsible for the occupation of Samos and the Cyclades. An uncomfortable feeling that Turkey was being directly threatened, the outbreak of the Rashid Ali revolt in Iraq, the complicity of Vichy in attempts by the Germans to send arms and aircraft to help him, and the establishment of diplomatic relations with Rashid Ali by the Soviet Government seemed to portend a German move against the real Middle East. When Mr Eden attributed our difficulties in the Mediterranean first and foremost to the collapse of France he was obviously right, and when like the deserted Oenone he seemed to exclaim, 'Faithless Paris, cruel Paris!' the House sympathized. What was worrying the House, however, was not Oenone but the holy mount of Cretan Ida on which the poor deserted was now standing, and it was with a volume of cheers that the members welcomed Mr Churchill's declaration that the island would be defended to the end. The country was reassured. If there was any doubt in the minds of the High Command about British ability to defend Crete, none of that doubt was communicated to the public. It was generally supposed that an island which had been occupied since November 1940 by a garrison of British troops and the R.A.F., not to mention the use that was being made of the great harbour of Suda Bay by the Royal Navy, would in six months have been made impregnable. A well-played and well-conducted chorale of defence was expected from the organist, not the improvisation which comes from letting the fingers wander idly over the noisy keys. The country was reassured; but the failure in Greece had made it extremely ill at ease, and it was in no mood to be consoled by any more lost chords, however eloquent an expression of what might have been.

In the event it was to transpire that there had been neither the men nor the material to spare for the achievement of impregnability when the island was occupied and that for the security of both Crete and Cyprus more reliance had been placed on the distaste of the Italian armed forces for adventurous action than upon a constructive plan of defence.

It would seem that Crete did not become an urgent problem until after the evacuation of the British and Imperial troops. An effort was then made to reinforce the island with men and material; but that effort was too late to make up for the time wasted or lost during the previous six months in building up the defences against an enemy who had had ten years during every moment of which he had been building up his offensive power. Indeed longer, for as far back as 1926 the French were already worried about the number of civil aeroplanes that were being built in Germany with the design of converting them into troop-carriers; and troop-carriers played a very prominent part in the attack on Crete. The debatable point on which the military historian of the future will have to express an opinion is whether those six months were wasted because the British High Command, lacking in foresight and not fully aware of Crete's importance, failed to achieve the coordination between the three arms of the Fighting Services necessary to put each of them to the best use or whether those six months were lost only because, whatever the strategic importance of Crete, the means to recognize that importance did not exist.

The island of Crete (3336 square miles) is the largest island in the

His Hellenic Majesty King George II

Suda Bay

Mediterranean after Sicily and Sardinia, with a length of 160 miles and a breadth of from 20 to 35 miles. Throughout its entire length runs a limestone mountain range with peaks as high as 8000 feet. Two-thirds of the island can be called a savage, barren, and rocky waste, and from one end of the south coast to the other there is not a single harbour except for the very smallest craft. Along much of it the mountains run sheer down to the sea. On the north coast the harbours of Canea, Rethymno, and Herakleion (Candia) had to be artificially deepened even in antiquity, and, except Herakleion, which can berth a destroyer, they are not available for warships. A little way east of Canea, however, is the great harbour of Suda Bay which is capable of holding a large fleet, though the water is too deep for the ideal anchorage. There were three aerodromes—one at Maleme in the extreme west of the island about 10 miles south-west of Canea, the capital; the second at Rethymno, 29 miles east of Canea; and the third at Herakleion, 41 miles east of Rethymno. Of these the Maleme aerodrome was much the largest; the Rethymno aerodrome was hardly more than a field. What was left of the fighter squadrons from Greece, five Hurricanes in all, with some Blenheims, Gladiators, and Brewster Buffaloes, shared these three aerodromes. In Suda Bay were a few Fulmars of the Fleet Air Arm. Many of the pilots had never flown single-engined fighters, but they all helped to keep those five Hurricanes flying as long as they could. It was not long, for the three Cretan aerodromes were exposed to constant attacks from enemy aerodromes at Sparta, Argos, and Melos, besides those in the Dodecanese. There was no possibility of protecting the aircraft, and as soon as the main attack began they were all withdrawn. Such a withdrawal meant that the R.A.F. had to work from aerodromes in North Africa 400 miles away and therefore beyond the range of fighters. An experiment was made of fitting extra petrol tanks on Hurricanes, but it was not successful. Bombers could not operate by daylight without fighter escort, and although a certain amount of damage to German air bases on the Greek mainland was done in night raids it was very far from exercising the slightest influence on the struggle for Crete.

The original British garrison of the island had consisted of the 14th Infantry Brigade (2nd Black Watch, 1st Welch Regiment, and 2nd York and Lancaster Regiment) together with about 2000 Royal Marines of the Marine Naval Base Defence Organization. These were highly trained specialists responsible for anti-aircraft and coastal defence artillery, searchlights, and maintenance; but they were equally competent as infantry, and it was as such that when their weapons were put out of action by the enemy's aircraft they fought their last action. Besides the British garrison there were some Hellenic infantry training battalions composed almost entirely of young recruits. At the end of April, with a few additions from those units of the divisions in Eastern Macedonia which had been evacuated, these battalions numbered in all about 10,000 men. There were also 2800 of the armed Cretan gendarmerie, 300 (Euelpidae) cadets of the Hellenic Military Academy, and 800 (Ikaroi) cadets of the Royal Hellenic Air Force Academy.

It was intended to reinforce the 14th Infantry Brigade with the 16th Infantry Brigade; but the only battalion that arrived before the storm broke on May 20th was the 2nd Leicesters. During the desperate fight for Crete another battalion, the 2nd Argyll and Sutherland Highlanders, was landed, but the ship carrying the third battalion of the 16th Brigade and Brigade H.Q. was damaged by enemy bombers and had to put back to Alexandria. Two Commandos also were landed in the middle of the struggle, and they took part in the rear-guard actions, most of them having to be left behind. Besides a certain amount of supplies and munitions, eighteen anti-aircraft guns, four 3·7 howitzers, six 'I' tanks, and sixteen light tanks with the gun and tank crews were landed before May 20th.

The main reinforcements consisted of weary men of the two Anzac divisions who had fought through three punishing weeks in Greece and were waiting in Crete for transhipment to Alexandria. To quote *The Campaign in Greece and Crete*: [1]

"The forces already in the island had been joined by the tired and more or less disorganized men from Greece (the survivors of the 4th and 5th New Zealand Infantry Brigades and of the 6th Australian Division) who had to be formed into new units. Thus the Australians and New Zealanders were sorted out at reception camps and re-formed. Composite infantry units were formed out of gunners who had lost their guns, sappers who had lost their tools, and R.A.S.C. drivers who had lost their cars. A staff to run the battle had to be improvised by calling in regimental officers, few of whom had had any staff training. Trenches, gun emplacements, wire obstacles, and demolitions had to be prepared, and such

[1] Issued for the War Office by the Ministry of Information.

was the lack, even of spades, that men used their steel helmets to scoop out slit trenches. British officers were attached to the Greek battalions which had had little training, and no equipment beyond rifles and twenty rounds a rifle."

It is impossible with the amount of information available at present to give accurately the numbers of troops at the disposal of Major-General B. Freyberg, V.C., who after commanding the New Zealand Division which had fought in Greece, took over after the evacuation the command of Crete from Major-General E. C. Weston, R.M. Mr Tahu Hole, who has published the fullest account [1] of the operations in Crete at the time of writing, says that there were just under 13,000 British troops, 7100 New Zealand troops, about 6500 Australian troops, and a few more than 1000 lines-of-communication Cypriot and Palestinian troops. If to these we add 10,000 young Greek troops, 1100 Greek cadets, and 2800 armed police, we have a total of 41,500. The account published for the War Office by the Ministry of Information gives the names of the various units, but does not give the numbers. It may be prudent to reduce the figures estimated above. In any case General Freyberg's problem was not numbers; it was equipment, transport, communications, arms, ammunition, and bigger than the problem offered by all these put together, the insoluble puzzle of how to defeat an airborne invasion without the help of aircraft.

The appearance of parachute troops in Greece had made their use against Crete a strong probability; but it may be doubted whether the use of troop-carriers on the scale employed was anticipated. The orders given to the Royal Navy suggest an expectation that the main force of the enemy would be seaborne. It was reasonable to suppose that, if the three aerodromes at Maleme, Rethymno, and Herakleion could be defended against parachute troops and if the seaborne invasion could be stopped by the ships of the Royal Navy, there was not much danger to Crete apart from the damage that could be wrought by persistent and savage bombing. The obvious way to hold the island seemed to be by the establishment of strong garrisons at the key-points along the north coast, that is to say the Maleme aerodrome, Canea, Suda Bay, Rethymno, and Herakleion. But here arose another problem, which was the impossibility of handling a mobile reserve. There was only one road, and that full of hairpin

[1] *Anzacs into Battle.*

bends, running along the north coast of the island, while the three roads fit for motor traffic across the island north to south led nowhere from the point of view of supplies and reinforcements because there was nothing except diminutive fishing-havens all the length of that savage south coast of Crete. In any case those roads were easy to cut, and in fact two of them were cut in the course of the battle. The road to Sphakia stopped in the hills seven miles short of the beach.

All through May Crete had been raided steadily by enemy air-craft. At eight in the morning of Tuesday May 20th a particularly heavy attack was made on the Maleme aerodrome. At a quarter to nine enemy aircraft appeared flying low, towing behind them groups of gliders. These crash-landed and disgorged between them about 600 men, who took cover in the pits made by the bombers earlier. Simultaneously in four different areas round the aerodrome troop-carriers coming down to 300 feet released numbers of para-chutists. By the afternoon there were about 3500 of the enemy in action over a stretch of country ten miles by three, and before dusk the A.A. guns on the aerodrome were out of action. Worse still, the 22nd New Zealand Battalion had been driven back from its posi-tion round the aerodrome. Eastward the 21st and 23rd New Zea-land Battalions had exterminated four-fifths of the parachutists while they were coming down.

At Rethymno parachutists succeeded in capturing the aerodrome, but they did not live long to enjoy their triumph. A counter-attack by young Greek troops in action for the first time and by troops be-longing to the 19th Australian Infantry Brigade annihilated them.

At the Herakleion aerodrome which was defended by battalions of British troops not a single German reached it alive. Many of the troop-carriers were hit by A.A. fire and as they came crashing down in flames released in a display of ghastly pyrotechnics numerous parachutists all ablaze. Other troop-carriers driven by the A.A. fire out of their course ran into flocks of parachutists released from other carriers and flew away decked with the mangled remains as though with ribbons and streamers. Beyond the perimeter defences a few groups of parachutists were able to land and cut communications for a while with G.H.Q. at Suda Bay: but they were soon disposed of by Hellenic troops.

On that Tuesday night, May 20th, in spite of the fact that the enemy had managed to established himself in some force in the Maleme area, there seemed good reason to suppose that he could be successfully thrown out.

One of the first objectives of the parachutists early on that May morning had been the villa in which the King of the Hellenes was living after he and his Government left Athens in order to preserve both the reality and the symbol of the nation's sovereignty. That such a decision was the right decision is indisputable. It is unnecessary to look beyond the confusion of authority created after the British and American landing in Morocco and Algeria by the negotiations with Admiral Darlan to appreciate what problems can be created by the least ambiguity of status.

The Germans regarded King George as their chief enemy in Greece. He was nominated as such by Hitler in the speech he made on May 4th in Berlin, and a personal denunciation by that infernal talking-machine may be accounted the highest order of chivalry a Royal Personage can receive to-day. The King's withdrawal to Crete on April 23rd was regarded by the Germans as the primary cause of their failure to obtain from the Hellenic people as a whole what they had obtained from that tiny minority of Greek soldiers and politicians from which their cooperators were collected. There is no doubt that the German invaders of Crete had orders either to kill or capture the King of the Hellenes.

On the night before the assault Mr Tsouderos, the Prime Minister, "urged by a strong premonition", in his own words, begged the King to remain in the house where he was himself staying instead of going back to his own villa which was more exposed to a hostile attack. The King accepted the clairvoyance of his Prime Minister, and the next morning was able to watch the beginning of an operation never attempted in warfare until that Tuesday in May. His own villa was heavily bombed and later occupied by parachutists; but for the moment he was safe where he was. With the King was his cousin Prince Peter and Colonel J. S. Blunt, the British Military Attaché in Greece, besides the Prime Minister, the Governor of the National Bank, and two or three Court officials. Colonel Blunt saw by the scale and ubiquity of the attack that it would be impossible to guarantee either the safety or the life of the King and advised an attempt to reach the other side of the island by taking to the hills at the back of the house. A party of parachutists dropped scarcely half a mile away, but fortunately they turned down the valley instead of in the direction of the house. It was high time that the Royal party set out on the adventurous attempt to cross the island.

Here is how Mr Tsouderos himself has described that journey:

"Our guard consisted of two score of men, Greeks and New Zealanders, who performed their task loyally and unflinchingly. After indescribable difficulties and tribulations, which would have told on the strongest nerves, we succeeded, thanks to the admirable heroism and exemplary sangfroid of the King, in foiling the enemy's plans. We slipped through his fingers by the narrowest of margins.

"The King, our national symbol, so far from falling into German hands, maybe as a hostage, remains unharmed and well. He is ready to strike, in his turn, when the time comes. For three whole days and nights the King, Prince Peter, and myself, with a handful of others, marched through the high mountains of Crete where human foot rarely treads and the eagle soars majestically. In almost unbearable heat by day and in bitter cold at night, we struggled on almost without pause or rest, sometimes where there were no footpaths, only steep ravines.[1]

"Enemy aircraft frequently passed overhead. But we had ceased to be afraid or care about them. During the whole of this fatiguing and heartbreaking march the King did not for a moment lose his smile. With a majestic simplicity he shared with us all dangers, all privations, all hardships. He slept for a few hours on the cold ground, and shared with us the scanty food and snow which the peasants used to bring to us to sustain us and to quench our thirst in the absence of water. One night we slept on a peak of the White Mountains at an altitude of 6000 feet. We found some shepherds with their flocks. They milked the goats and brought us milk and cheese.

"That night the King slept in the open air. As for myself, I crept into a small hut which was barely two feet high and not large enough for one man to sleep in. The devotion which the Cretans showed to us throughout our march was a great moral tonic to us. On our way elderly Cretans, whose classical features used to remind us of the ancient statues of Zeus—who, according to legend, grew and was brought up on the Cretan mountains—used to surround the King in order to kiss his hand in loyalty and reverence."

At last the sea was reached at a desolate spot on that savage south

[1] Some of those ravines, called 'pharangs', are so narrow and deep that the bottom of them is in perpetual twilight.

coast of Crete called Saint Roumeli where the Royal party was joined
by General Heywood, the former head of the British Military
Mission, and Sir Michael Palairet, the British Minister, who had
made their way round the west of the island. They had tried to get
in touch with the King by telephone at his own villa and later had
been told of the direction the Royal party had taken. That they
contrived to meet was providential. Now came the question whether
the attempt to give a British warship a rendezvous by this remote
beach had been successful.

That it had been successful can be told in the words of Mr
Tsouderos:

> "Our meeting with the British warship which was to take us
> from Crete was likewise dramatic. We could not be sure that
> she would find us at the appointed hour in that deserted corner of
> Cretan soil called Saint Roumeli.
>
> "But even there God came to our aid. Well after midnight,
> thanks to primitive signals we made from the coast by means of a
> small pocket torch, we were sighted by the warship. We went
> on board with the help of a Cretan peasant boat which was pro-
> pelled by a small motor. It took us about an hour to reach the
> warship from the coast."

With the Royal party went the bodyguard of New Zealanders
who had fought their way down through Greece to this romantic
last duty. The Greek bodyguard and the Cretan guides turned back
to carry on the fight in Crete.

> "Dawn found us in the midst of a powerful British Mediter-
> ranean Fleet," Mr Tsouderos has written, "which was also on its
> way back after the glorious Battle of Crete, in which, in accordance
> with time-hallowed tradition, it had carried out its orders, despite
> grievous loss of men and ships—*the enemy must not make a sea-
> borne landing*'. . . . During our voyage we were subjected to air
> attacks and submarines were also signalled. During lunch we
> were dropping depth charges to deal with lurking U-boats. We
> escaped damage in all these attempts and finally the enemy aban-
> doned his efforts. . . . At midnight between May 28th and 29th
> we reached Egyptian waters safe and sound. In Egypt we laid
> the foundation of the reorganization of our national forces."

Thirty-six years earlier in those same White Mountains Eleutherios Venizelos had hoisted the standard of Cretan revolt from the
administration of Prince George of Greece, demanding absolute

union with Greece. Prince Peter was the son of that Prince with whom Venizelos had contended. Five years earlier Venizelos had put himself at the head of the republican revolt in Crete against the return of King George II. It is difficult not to feel that the spirit of the great Cretan, rejoicing in such ardour, was with King George and Prince Peter as they struggled across those White Mountains to carry on the fight for the Hellenes: indeed, it may have been that spirit who warned his successor Mr Tsouderos of the King's danger. And it is certain that Venizelos would have smiled his magical smile of approval when his successor called King George II the 'national Symbol'.

Rarely is a King accorded by Almighty God the privilege of displaying in his personal experience a microcosm of the national experience. King George II of the Hellenes returned after a long exile, determined to heal the political dissension of two decades. He insisted upon an amnesty for those who had opposed his return, and if he was not successful in securing fair treatment for all republicans and Venizelists, none of the critics of the injustice and intolerance of the Fourth of August régime has suggested that he was responsible for the injustice or the intolerance. His support of that régime effected by the *coup d'état* of John Metaxas was necessary at the time, and it is admitted even by those who voted against his return to Greece that a drastic cure had to be faced if the country was ever to recover internal tranquillity. Hellas was blessed in not having to endure the destructive effects of authoritarianism protracted beyond the point when the stimulant becomes a poison, and twice blessed in being able to emerge from it in response to the impelling call of patriotic devotion. There is no likelihood of imposing a domestic tyranny upon Hellas when the foreign tyrant has been driven out.

In the moment of crisis John Metaxas rose above his political theories and confounded the two dictators who had counted upon his subservience because he had copied some of their methods. He was granted the boon of death at the moment when one enemy had been humiliated and the other enemy had not been faced except in imagination. The King lived on; and if to John Metaxas be accorded the honour in history of that 'No' given to the Italian ultimatum, to the King must be accorded the equal honour of having been able to show forth in himself the determination of the Hellenes to defy the tremendous might of Germany. If King George had wavered, it is difficult to believe that the small minority in favour of coming to terms with Germany would not have had their way. It is easier to give an abrupt negative than to sustain a prolonged negative over a period of anxiety under pressure from without and within. If King George represented the will of the Hellenes when he challenged Germany by encouraging the British attempt to give aid—and who that has experienced in his soul the catharsis of the great Greek tragedy slowly being played before a mundane audience will deny that he did represent the will of the Hellenes?—such a King, when the *deus ex machina* determines the conclusion of that tragedy, will indeed be the symbol of his nation. And having made his choice, as he believed for the honour, the glory, and the ultimate salvation of his country, King George accepted all the consequences. When resistance upon the mainland was impossible he went to Crete. He was in Crete when the assault was delivered. He escaped by his own courage under God; and in Africa, in America, and in Great Britain he has been the living evidence of that unconquerable spirit of the Hellenes of whom he is the King.

The Germans have accused King George of sacrificing his country to his own Anglophile prejudice. This is what Mr David Walker wrote [1] in the course of a profoundly moving plea for the starving population of Greece:

"A curious sidelight on the psychology of the German troops is that they are made savage not by impudence or insubordination, but by suffering. To one of my informants (in Lisbon) a group of German officers angrily demanded that the Greek authorities should themselves shoot the legless Greek soldiers who still crawl about the pavements selling matches: another was twice an eye-witness of German privates brutally thrashing Greek youths who had fallen in the street from faintness or hunger. . . . It is almost impossible to write on the subject of Greece without being accused of sensationalism. . . . I am not objective on the subject, for the simple reason that I was given the privilege of being allowed in the Greek front line during the vile winter of 1940–41, and I shared with Greek privates whatever frozen black bread and olives might be available. But at least I was an eyewitness of heroism. I lived with an army that fought for Greece and for Our Lady. I found a spirit greater even than the spirit of Britain. I can still see the Greek private whom we found dying in the snow, his blue, swollen

[1] *The Tablet.* June 6th, 1942.

feet bursting through his boots, who tried to struggle to his feet crying, 'Let me salute an Englishman, and then I can die.'

"I think that for him and his people an occasional shipload of wheat is insufficient recompense."

Did that Greek private belong to what Hitler dared to call the "thin top layer of corrupt leaders who, inspired by a King who had no idea of the duties of true leadership, preferred instead to further the aims of British war politicians"?

And now it is time to leave the King, Prince Peter, and Mr Tsouderos in the small boat on their way across the dark water to the British warship and turn back with his Greek bodyguard to the battle for Crete, where things had been going not too well for the defenders.

Throughout that Wednesday, May 21st, while the Royal party were arduously struggling across the White Mountains, the Germans were sending over troop-carriers to make crash-landings all round Maleme. It was estimated that more than six hundred came over, and before dusk fell there were ten times as many of the enemy in position as there had been the evening before. To-morrow there would be as many again landing from those troop-carriers, and it was decided that a counter-attack must be delivered that night in the hope of loosening the grip the enemy had secured of the western extremity of the island. The counter-attack was entrusted to the 20th and 28th Battalions of the 5th New Zealand Infantry Brigade supported by a few tanks, and while the darkness lasted it made good progress; but unfortunately it was two hours late in starting, and with the light the casualties became heavy. The dive-bombing was incessant. The line fell back, and the stream of troop-carriers started again.

There seems little doubt that the British High Command did not grasp what could be done in the way of landing troops by carriers, provided the enemy was ready to face heavy losses, which in this case when the speed of the operation was essential to its success he was ready to face. Otherwise it is difficult to understand why orders were given to the Royal Navy that the enemy must not make a seaborne landing. The Royal Navy did not require any enhancement of its prestige, and the capture of Crete did not depend upon a seaborne landing. The Royal Navy destroyed on that night of May 21st one invasion fleet, and on the following day dispersed another; but the casualties inflicted were not worth the price paid in ships and lives.

CHAPTER NINETEEN

If 5000 casualties were inflicted upon the enemy, and that is by a good deal much the highest estimate, twice that number had already been landed by air during the previous two days. The dispersal of the invasion fleet cost the Royal Navy two cruisers and four destroyers, and before the evacuation of Crete was complete another cruiser and two more destroyers were lost, with many other ships damaged. The skill and heroism displayed in carrying out the order make criticism too distasteful a task to pursue; and, after all, what will endure for the people of Hellas and Britain is the glorious memory of that effort to do all that could be done without counting the cost. Caution could not have bequeathed that.

"There was equal heroism displayed in the task of supplying our own army as in that of attempting to deny supplies to the enemy. For the first six days of the battle, naval vessels and not less gallant merchant ships managed to nose their way into Soudha port through the curtain of bombs. Some were hit and lost; others had to be beached and their supplies laboriously extracted by stevedore units improvised from every sort of material from staff officers to Cypriot pioneers. Quite a few managed to unload their cargoes almost normally, take on board casualties and steam out again. Nobody either on the ships or on the shore stopped trying to keep the stream of supplies flowing. The bells in the little church occasionally tinkled out in a primitive kind of air-raid siren, but after a very short time nobody on shore took any notice of anything except actual bombs; and the sailors never took any notice of the more grisly air-raid warnings of beached and blazing ships." [1]

By Friday May 23rd the situation in the Maleme area was very grave. The enemy had been able to reinforce his troops almost continuously and, what was more, show menacing signs of an ability to pass from the defensive to the offensive when the 5th New Zealand Infantry Brigade was withdrawing eastward to link up with the 7th New Zealand Infantry Brigade. By Monday May 26th, in spite of gallant actions by Greek and New Zealand troops, the last hope of recovering the Maleme area had gone. A small detachment of Royal Marines which had held Canea for six days had to fall back to the slopes of Suda just east of the town and on the left another small detachment of Royal Marines was holding on west of Stilos. The rest of the defending forces had fallen back on a line from Suda to

[1] *The Campaign in Greece and Crete.*

235

Stilos. The enemy now had the freedom of the Maleme aerodrome and was bringing in his reinforcements by air with no more interference than planes arriving on a civil aerodrome in peace-time. On Tuesday May 27th the decision to evacuate Crete was taken.

This decision came as a surprise to the garrison holding Herakleion, where Greek and British troops helped by the Cretan men and women formed into a militia had beaten off every attack and felt confident of holding out indefinitely. What the garrison of Herakleion did not know was that Italian troops from the Dodecanese were landing from boats in Sitia Bay on the east of the island and that it was only a matter of time before Herakleion would be completely surrounded and cut off. On the night of May 28th–29th the garrison was evacuated by British destroyers.

Simultaneously with the order to evacuate Herakleion an order was sent to the garrison of Greeks and Australians holding Rethymno that they were to withdraw southward across the mountains to the coast. This order could not be sent by land because communication between Rethymno and Suda had been cut by the enemy who had established himself in improvised blockhouses on either side of the road. So the order was sent by an aeroplane; but the aeroplane was shot down, and the Rethymno garrison never received it. Attack after attack was launched against the Greeks and Australians during these four days when the rest of the troops who had been defending Crete were fighting a rear-guard action across the mountains to the south coast, and every attack was beaten off. On May 31st an onslaught was made with the support of tanks, and except for a few small parties that managed to break through and escape to the mountains (where they are still fighting eighteen months later), the rest of the garrison, with inadequate weapons and insufficient ammunition, were killed or taken prisoner.

The retreat across the island from Suda to Sphakia, which lies some twelve miles east of Saint Roumeli where the Royal party was taken off, consisted of a series of heavy rear-guard actions in which troops of Vasey's 19th Australian Infantry Brigade and the Royal Marines covered the withdrawal of the 4th and 5th New Zealand Infantry Brigades, the leading units of which reached the hills above Sphakia at dusk on Wednesday May 28th.

For three days the troops were lying hidden in caves and among the scrub, and for three nights they were being taken off in small boats to the destroyers and other light craft which came in so near to the shore that their keels almost grounded.

No German bombers attempted to attack the beach or the hills above it; but on the afternoon of Saturday May 31st some enemy troops did reach the ridge above Sphakia. They were disposed of by the Royal Marines who were covering the final embarkation. Major-General E. C. Weston, their commander, received this message from General Wavell on that May 31st:

"You know the heroic effort the Navy has made to rescue you. I hope you will be able to get away most of those who remain, but this is the last night the Navy can come. Please tell those that have to be left that the fight put up against such odds has won the admiration of us all and every effort to bring them back is being made. General Freyberg has told me how magnificently your Marines have fought and of your own grand work. I have heard also of the heroic fighting of young Greek soldiers. I send you my grateful thanks."

Only two or three hundred of Weston's Marines were able to get away. Fourteen hundred of them were still standing on guard while the last ship the Navy could send steamed away southward toward Egypt in the darkness. These men were gunners, searchlight technicians, and coastal defence experts, but they turned themselves into infantry and added a page glorious even in the glorious records of the Royal Marines. It can be said that they were the last help the Navy gave, and that their loss was the loss of one more ship on top of the three cruisers and six destroyers already lost first in trying to prevent a seaborne landing and then in evacuating some 16,000 troops, Anzac, British, and a few Greek. That final message of General Wavell in which he couples with those Marines of long service the heroic young soldiers of Hellas may serve as the epilogue of this story of the valour, discipline, devotion, and self-sacrifice which Britain and Hellas could achieve when fighting side by side; but it must be read also as the prologue to a story of peaceful cooperation in the victorious future not less admirable.

Youth was the chief characteristic of those Greek soldiers who fought in Crete. Many of them were no more than seventeen years old. They were in training battalions for recruits, and with them were three hundred Euelpidae (military cadets) and eight hundred Ikaroi (air force cadets). It is so strange a coincidence as almost to

seem worthy of being granted a mystical portentousness that Crete
should have been chosen by fate as the place which will go down in
history as the first example of an offensive operation by parachutists
and airborne troops on a large scale. The earliest myth of man's
attempt to conquer the air was a myth of Crete. It was there that
Daedalus got the better of the Minoan ships by making wings for
himself and his son Icarus and was thus able to escape by air to Italy.
Icarus was less successful; he flew too near the sun. The wax with
which his wings were fastened to him melted, and falling he was
drowned in the sea which still bears his name. And now after how
many thousands of years Ikaros was again in Crete. Many of those
Ikaroi gave their lives to crown their country with freedom. Some
of them flying over Egypt and Libya since they left Crete have died
like the first Ikaros. We may hope, indeed we may feel sure, that
some of those Ikaroi will one day not far hence land from the air in
Italy like Daedalus. Crete deserves so rich a completion of that
coincidence, Crete the cradle of our Europe.

Of what happened to Crete itself we may read in the words of the
Memorandum submitted by the Prime Minister of Greece to the
Inter-Allied Conference at St. James's Palace on January 13th, 1942:

"... The ferocity of the invaders to the civilian population of
that heroic island was unprecedented in deliberate wantonness.
The three principal towns, Canea, Herakleion, Rethymno, were
bombed time and again from north to south, and from east to west,
with mathematical precision until not a wall was left standing,
not one stone upon another.

"The wretched inhabitants, as they struggled to escape from
their primitive shelters, were mercilessly butchered by the machine-
guns of aircraft flying at low level, and the agony of the mutilated
women and helpless little children left these raging beasts unmoved.
Here, too, hospitals were smashed, wounded men were finished off,
and the orgy of destruction was complete. Canea, which was an
open town, after being subjected to incessant raids of this nature,
was bombed and machine-gunned for ten consecutive hours on
Saturday May 24th, in a final display of Nazi heroism.

"Nevertheless, the Cretans—men, women, and children—in
the face of this brutal assault were unsubdued. Enraged by the
savagery of their enemies, they formed an extemporized militia
which was attached to the troops, and fought gallantly at their side.
Legality of such a body is provided in International Law by the
annex to the Hague Convention of 1907, concerning the Laws of

Land Warfare (articles 1 and 2). But the Germans, who like all bullies are insensible and unmoved by true courage in their enemies, proceeded to a campaign of vengeance which they waged against the civil population of Crete for months, because they had exercised their legal and natural right of defending their native soil."

The Germans tried to palliate their own atrocities in Crete, of which other horrible examples will be given later, by accusing the Cretans of having mutilated the German dead and trapped German soldiers into ambushes by wearing their uniforms and carrying their Yahoo flag. In point of fact they accused first the British troops of committing these mutilations and donning their own uniforms. The accusation against the Cretans was substituted later. It is just possible that there were a few isolated instances of mutilation. The mountaineers of Crete had been almost continuously fighting for their liberty against ruthless enemies for over two thousand years. They defied the power of the Macedonian monarchs and fought as the allies of Mithridates against Rome. This brought them the enmity of Rome; but it took Quintus Metellus three years before he could make a Roman province out of Crete and earn the surname Creticus. From Rome the island passed to Byzantium. It was conquered by the Saracens early in the ninth century and reconquered by Byzantium in 960. When the Byzantine Empire was partitioned among the Fourth Crusaders, the Marquis of Montferrat drew Crete as his share, and he sold the island to Venice which held it for four hundred years. The Cretans themselves remained always in revolt. There were fourteen major insurrections between 1207 and 1365. In 1645 the Turks began their attempt to conquer the island, but it took a quarter of a century before they achieved it. Herakleion (Candia) withstood a siege of twenty-one years, the longest in recorded history. Revolts went on under Turkish rule, and when in 1821 Hellas rose, the Cretans, headed by the men of Sphakia, rose too. The Turks and Mussulman inhabitants were kept penned in the three fortified cities for three years, and then after being heavily reinforced the Turkish commander reduced the island to temporary submission. In 1830 Greece was declared independent, but owing to the mutual jealousies of Britain, France, and Russia the annexation of Crete was not allowed. To pacify the Cretans by some kind of change they persuaded the Sultan of Turkey to cede the island to Egypt. In 1840 Crete was taken away from Egypt and restored to

Turkey. Insurrections went on at short intervals throughout the rest of the nineteenth century. In 1897, when war broke out between Greece and Turkey, a Greek Expeditionary force landed, but the Great Powers intervened with warships to prevent effective action. From then on until it was achieved Crete was fighting for union with Greece. At last, in October 1912, Greece defied the Great Powers by admitting the Cretan deputies to the Chamber, and on October 18th war was declared on Turkey. It need hardly be added that when Venizelos decided to set up the Provisional Government of National Defence in 1916 it was to Canea he went from Athens.

Upon this island whose inhabitants for sixty generations and more had fought and suffered for their liberty descended on May 20th, 1941, a phantasmagoria of bloody horror. Children, women, and old men were massacred as the oppressors of Crete had massacred them so often in the past. Ancestral voices called to the Cretans. Memories of battles long ago burned within them. The men and the women took up arms. Some of those arms were rusty old muskets dating back to insurrections against the Turks a century since. Were they going to deny themselves the tommy-gun of the parachutist if they could kill him and take it? Bombs bursting among the orange groves, bombs in the olive yards, bombs upon their houses, their churches, their hospitals. Children and women and old men torn by bombs and machine-gun bullets. Cretans taken prisoner shot by their captors as civilians with arms. Those islanders who had been fighting for their freedom (and among themselves) almost continuously for two thousand years did not recognize one another as civilians. It is not admitted that the Cretans, between two of whom the writer if sorely pressed would sooner find himself than between any other pair of fighting men in the world, did mutilate dead Germans; but if just rage roused any of them thus to express their detestation, why, it is not incomprehensible. How were they to distinguish those Germans from their barbaric oppressors of an agelong past? But one is suspicious of an accusation which is made first against British troops, and when that cannot be sustained, against Cretan militia, and one becomes doubly suspicious when such an accusation is made in order to justify the aggressor's own outrages against the code of civilized warfare. That the Cretans were likely to be stern warriors the Germans knew. So did the Italians, who

His Excellency S. M. Dimitrakakis, the Greek Minister for War, decorating Major-General B. C. Freyberg

German Parachutists nearing the Ground during the
Invasion of Crete

prudently did not start landing from the Dodecanese until they had good hope of finding the fighting all over. The Germans adopted a policy of terrorization deliberately as what they believed was the only method to use with such warriors. If any of them paid in death for such a policy, it was the fault of their own mutilated minds: even if some of their bodies *were* mutilated, the civilized world will find it as difficult to shudder as that young hero of one of their own popular fairy-tales.

The air invasion of Crete was a deep disappointment to Hitler as a military operation. The German High Command expected to master the defences on the first day. Crete was presented to the public as an impregnable fortress in order to justify the loss of life its capture entailed; but the German High Command was perhaps better aware than the British High Command of its vulnerability. Apart from the number of them exterminated, the crack Parachute Corps suffered a blow to its morale from which it has not recovered eighteen months later. The men of the Parachute Corps, mostly volunteers, were drawn from the pick of German youth and they felt themselves superior to any other troops. If the operation against Crete had fulfilled what was expected of it, there is little doubt that it would have been followed up by further similar demonstrations of offensive power. Cyprus might well have been tackled, and if that had been successful there might have been serious interference with the British plan to secure Syria. There might have been a grand attempt to overwhelm Malta. Crete dispelled many German dreams; and it also dispelled some British dreams. The price paid by both Commands for the mental disinfectant was a heavy one. To call the Battle of Crete a revolution in offensive tactics is to mistake novelty for change, and those military critics who perceived in it a dress-rehearsal for an invasion of Britain might with equal perspicacity have perceived in it a dress-rehearsal for an invasion of the moon. The operation was undertaken because the Germans were convinced that without air protection the Royal Navy, after the losses it had received during the evacuation of the British and Imperial Expeditionary Force from Greece, would keep away from the waters round Crete, and that without air protection the garrison holding the island would succumb long before it did. In the result the Germans lost at least 6000 killed and drowned and 11,000 wounded of their best troops besides numerous aircraft with their crews, and they were unable to prevent the evacuation of some 16,000 of that garrison.

It is idle to discuss whether Crete could have been held if a more determined attempt had been made to strengthen its defences earlier. There is no point in reflecting bitterly that with a few more guns at Maleme the aerodrome might not have been taken, or even in bemoaning the failure of the British High Command to grasp long before the war began what a decisive part mastery of the air would play. The imaginative failure lay much deeper than that. It was the failure of Britain to grasp that if she intended to prevent the domination of Europe by a continental power the control of the Mediterranean must rest with her and could not be entrusted to another power with whom she was merely hoping to remain in an effectively defensive alliance. The possibility of France's collapse should have been inherent in the Mediterranean policy of Britain. An alliance with Turkey was not enough. It demanded a close triple alliance with Greece and Turkey, and the energy to make that alliance a formidable threat to any attack upon the Mediterranean from whatever direction it came.

If that policy had been followed there would have been no 3 A.M. ultimatum by Italy to Greece, no ambiguity about Greco-German relations due to the economic desertion of Greece by Britain, no lack of aerodromes and aircraft on the mainland and islands of Greece, no Monastir Gap, no uncertain Yugoslavia, no doubt about the Dardanelles, and no inadequately defended Crete. Much glory would have been lost, but deep suffering would have been averted and many lives would have been saved.

If after final victory Crete is remembered and rewarded not as the island which provided a nine-days wonder of novelty warfare but as the island on which a noble breed of men and women was sacrificed to the lazy optimism of a quarter of a century, Crete will not have suffered for nothing, and those who died in its defence will not have died in vain.

CHAPTER TWENTY

WHEN darkness fell upon May 31st, 1941, and mercifully hid from the German bombers the ships bearing to Alexandria the last soldiers that the Royal Navy could evacuate from Crete, the Hellenic people entered that dark night of the soul which for nations and individuals alike is the Divine test of their spiritual life.

Greek Macedonia and Thrace were given to the Bulgars together with the islands of Thasos and Samothrace. In the rivalry for evil pre-eminence between the Germans and the Japanese a moral plague-spot like Bulgaria is apt to be overlooked on account of its relatively small size. Yet within the range of their power for evil the Bulgars have wrought the maximum amount, and their treatment of the Greek population handed over to them as a reward for letting their country be used as the German army's gut was bestial. The Bulgars believed that they were going to be able to retain Greek Macedonia and Thrace permanently, and under this belief they deliberately set about the expulsion and the expropriation of the Greek inhabitants, and the extermination of those they did not succeed in expelling and expropriating.

An extract from a Memorandum submitted by Mr Emmanuel Tsouderos, Prime Minister of Greece, at the Inter-Allied Conference at St. James's Palace, on January 13th, 1942, will give a faint idea of what the Bulgars perpetrated, and at the moment of writing are still perpetrating, in the country they have seized. There is not the paper available to be blackened with the full record of their abominations:

"The North-Eastern Provinces of Greece, Western Thrace, and Eastern Macedonia up to the river Strymon (Struma), including the islands of Thasos and Samothrace, have been handed over by the Germans to the Bulgarians. The fate of these provinces has been the most tragic of all Greek lands. No criminal record has been more complete and more deliberate than that of Bulgaria in these areas. Nowhere have 'the lives of persons', 'family honour and rights', 'religious conviction and practice', and 'private property' been more entirely disregarded. As soon as the Bulgars entered these purely Greek regions the most ruthless methods of forcible denationalisation and extermination of the population were applied. All Greek cultural life immediately ceased. Schools and churches were closed in order to make place for Bulgarian institutions. Priests, teachers, lawyers, doctors, and all cultural agents were expelled.

"All the merchants and craftsmen were forced to hand over their shops or their workshops to newly-arrived Bulgarians, within a time limit fixed by the authorities of occupation. At Cavalla, the prosperous tobacco market town, seven hundred concerns of all kinds were forcibly expropriated, and Bulgarians brought over from Sofia established themselves in the seized properties.

"As the taxes of 1941 had not been paid until the 31st December, because of the ruin caused by the war, property, both movable and immovable, is now being seized and sold by auction, while only Bulgarians have access to these sales. The Greeks who have left during the war are not allowed to return. Their properties, including articles of personal clothing, are confiscated. The population suffers such daily vexations from the Bulgarian police that they are forced to leave their homes and try to seek refuge in parts of Greece not occupied by Bulgarians.

"The above are comparatively minor evils. As the emigration of the population, the extermination of which is what the Bulgarians are aiming at, was not proceeding as quickly as they wished, massacres were systematically planned and carried out. The Greek Government has information, which will be published in due course, showing that the massacres have been premeditated by the Bulgarian authorities, and that the leaders of comitadji bands had been collaborating with them at least a month previously. The first massacre began in the Drama-Cavalla district on September 29th. On the 28th Bulgarian motor-cyclists and other Bulgarian agents were going round the villages of the district spreading the rumour that a revolution had broken out in Bulgaria, and exhorting the inhabitants to rise in arms. The villagers had no arms, and consequently the Bulgarian provocations, wherever they were believed, could only bring forth rather harmless manifestations. On the 29th extensive massacres began in the towns of Cavalla, Drama, Doxato, Prosotsani, Photoloivos, and in the villages of Nea Zihni, Aghion Pnevma, Alistrati, Sylindri, Kalos Agros, Kormitza, Angisti, Minaret. Mass executions took place in Cavalla, Drama, and other localities. Then Bulgarian aircraft bombed and destroyed Doxato, Alistrati, Photoloivos, and Prosotsani. Other villages were shelled. Minaret, Kalos, Agros, Sylindri, Alistrati, Prosotsani, Nikiforos, Adriani, Ravika, and Horiani were set on fire. Fleeing inhabitants were machine-gunned by Bulgarian troops posted at the entrance of towns and villages. It is not yet known how many thousands have perished in these massacres. The last figures that reached the Greek Government mention 3800 in Prosotsani alone, more than 2000 in Doxato, and similar numbers in the other villages. Following these massacres more than 100,000 Greeks from the Bulgarian occupied provinces took refuge in other parts of Greece, where the most appalling famine prevails. The persecutions did not stop here. Hostages are still being taken by the hundred from practically every town in Eastern Macedonia and Western Thrace, and shooting at random is carried out everywhere. The inhabitants of the Bulgarian-occupied territories are often witnesses to a horrible spectacle illustrating the ferocity of the Bulgars. The River Strymon is carrying bodies of Greeks tightly tied together. This way of killing is well known as a favourite one with the Bulgars from the past.

"A few weeks after the massacres of the Drama district, the Bulgarians slaughtered the inhabitants of two other Macedonian villages, Ano and Kato Parois, which were both wiped out in a similar way. The Bulgars accused both villages of giving shelter to 'bands of irregulars'. The so-called 'irregulars' were merely the survivors of villages previously destroyed."

And here from that same Memorandum is a brief summary of a little of what the Germans and Italians have done. It should be noted that what is said about the starvation of Greece under the Axis is but the merest wraith of the heartrending reality:

"The food conditions under Axis rule are appalling beyond words. Four hundred and fifty people are perishing daily of hunger in the Athens-Piraeus area. Five hundred thousand inhabitants in this area have to rely on public assistance for the very barest meal. The Italians view this situation with satisfaction as the resistance of a starving population is greatly reduced. Whenever an Axis ship happens to be sunk in the proximity of Greek waters, the occupation authorities deliberately suspend the distribution of the bread ration for three days, falsely alleging that the ship sunk was bringing food to Greece from the Axis Powers.

"The technique of pressure by means of hostages is ruthlessly applied. Throughout Greece innocent people are arrested as hostages either as a preventive measure or as a sanction. Thus on May 17th six hostages were executed at Mallaoi. In the first two weeks which followed the German attack on Russia, 750 so-called Communists were arrested in Athens by the Italians. These are kept in a concentration camp near Larissa, and they are not allowed to have any contact with their families. In Salonika on June 23rd, a day after their attack upon Russia, the Germans arrested some two hundred lawyers, journalists, and professors; and on July 11th they made a raid on the factories of the Salonika district and rounded up about seven thousand workmen. The fate of these unhappy people is not known.

"In the province of Thesprotia, in Epirus, Albanian begs, nominated by the Italians as village headmen, carry on a systematic campaign of fanatical persecution against the Greek Orthodox population; the same policy has been followed in Northern Epirus, and it aims at exterminating the Greeks and any other inhabitants of the towns and districts of Argyrocastro, Premeti, Chimara, and Korytsa, who are suspected of sympathizing with the Greek cause.

"In the district of Macedonia occupied by the Germans the situation is even worse. Proclamations have been posted up which warn the population that for every offence against the army of occupation punishment will be inflicted collectively on the inhabitants, and the whole district in which the offence occurs. The German military authorities have been instructed to arrest leading citizens and hold them as hostages in any district in which the slightest suspicion arises that disorders may break out. Should a clash occur the hostages are shot. Towards the middle of October a slight disturbance occurred in the village of Mesovouni in the district of Ptolemais, and German troops were sent there to 'restore order'. They set aside the women and the children under sixteen years of age, and then proceeded to execute the whole male population, about 200 in number, after which they burnt the village to the ground. Early in November the village of Stavros, in the province of Chalcidice, was subjected to the same fate. This village also was destroyed and 150 of its inhabitants were murdered. The pretext given in both cases was that of 'harbouring terrorists'. On October 31st thirteen hostages were hanged in the village of Lahana, near Salonika, after two German transport drivers had been found dead near the town."

And then there was the bloody epilogue of the battle for Crete, when vengeance was taken upon a people who have the right, if ever a people had such a right, to call themselves the sons and daughters of liberty. It is not without significance that Mr Winston Churchill, rolling upon his tongue the first sweet of victory, should in his speech at the Guildhall on November 10th, 1942, call upon a Cretan to testify that Britain always won the last battle. And from his tomb in Crete we seemed to hear the echo of that magical voice as the spirit of Venizelos confirmed the Prime Minister's testimony.

Here is a cable received on October 7th, 1941, by the Greek Government in London, from the Greek Minister of War in Cairo:

"After the capture of Crete the German army burned to the ground the villages of Skine, Prasse, and Kandanos. Their sites are now marked by posters bearing the inscription, 'Here once stood Skine, Prasse, and Kandanos'. The Germans looted every single house and store in towns and in villages, leaving them empty of every single object. They proceeded to innumerable murders of people flying for safety in the open country, of children and old people asleep in their homes, and to collective executions after summary parodies of trial. The condemned people were forced to dig their common grave before the execution.

"At Kystomadon three men, wounded during the execution, were buried while still alive. Their families were forced to offer a dinner to the murderers of their own husbands, fathers, and brothers, and to suffer the mocking jests of the feasting Germans. The Rev. Koukourakis, curate of the church at Roumaton, as well as the Abbot and Monks of the Monastery of Aghia Gonia, were put to death. The fate of the Bishop of Kissamos and Selines, Mgr. Evdokimos Singelakis, is not known. The altar of the church of Manolio was turned into a public lavatory by the Germans.

"The surviving inhabitants of Skine were driven away to Argyroupolis and Margarites. Eight hundred women and children from Lower Cydonia were seen being marched through Canea after being expelled from their homes. In the village of Vrises, in the Rethymno district, Police Sergeant Ipaitozakis was tortured to death, his limbs being wrenched off one by one with the object of forcing him to denounce the holders of German rifles.

"At Perivolia and Sellia, in the Rethymno district, people were executed one by one in the presence of others also condemned to death and of their relatives, after having been forced to dig their own graves.

"At Heraklion the prefect was executed, and Colonel Tsatsaronakis met the same fate because he tried to help the persecuted to escape. In the same place five more Greeks were executed because they failed to declare that they knew German. According to the first available information, the number of executions in Canea amounts to 506, in Rethymno 130, and Heraklion 50. The male population of the island, especially in western Crete, has taken to the mountains in arms.

"If anything," Mr Tsouderos adds, "the above description is

an understatement. When Logothetopoulos, one of the Athens Quislings, in obedience to the orders of his German masters, visited Crete last September (1941), he was told on the 9th of that month by General Andre, the German Military Governor of Crete, that between June 1st and August 30th, 890 Cretans had been shot after being sentenced by German courts-martial. The General did not, however, say how many had been murdered without recourse to this parody of justice."

But these and many and many another atrocity that could be cited were only a part of the sufferings of Hellas. The sharpest pang of all came from the withdrawal of the German forces, required on the Russian front, to give way for occupation of Greece by Italian forces. It may well be that the Italians committed fewer acts of brutality than the Germans; but when on June 25th, 1941, the Italian army formally took possession of Hellas, the affront to Hellenic pride was harder to endure than German or Bulgar brutality. The sight of these Italian soldiers prancing into Athens eight months after they had been chased out of Greece like intruding puppy-dogs was a mortification beyond adequate expression for one who writes in English. The despatch by Mussolini of a thousand cases of milk for the starving babies of Greece may have been a spontaneous gesture of compassion, or alas, more probably, it may have been an expedient attempt to gild the bitter pill of the Italian occupation, which, it must be remembered, the Fascists hoped would lead in due course to Greece's becoming a province of the new Roman Empire. The Greeks were not impressed, and when the Germans 'borrowed' nine hundred and ninety of those cases for themselves, with the promise to send as many from Switzerland in two months' time, the Greeks resented that much less, even when the promise was broken, than what to them seemed either a gesture of condescending charity or an ignoble bribe. Indeed, the worst behaviour of the Germans in Hellas was easier to suffer than the best behaviour of the Italians, for the wounds of the soul are more dolorous than the wounds of the body, and the treacherous Italian poignard had dealt a deadlier stab at the proud heart of Hellas than the butcher's blow with which the German cleaver had battered her head.

On one occasion a squad of British prisoners of war with iron bedsprings on their shoulders was being marched through the streets of Athens. The Athenians cheered them, and the prisoners answered the sympathy of the crowd with the gesture of 'thumbs up'. The German officer commanding the guard disliked this expression of popular feeling and drawing his pistol he fired it into the air. The crowd cheered more loudly. The German sent a shot over the heads of the bystanders; but nobody paid any attention. Then a little *loustros* (shoeblack) stepped up to that German officer and pulling open his shirt presented his bare breast. "If you want to shoot, shoot here," he challenged.

It is an agreeable novelty to be able to conclude this story by relating that the German officer put his pistol back into the holster and shook hands with the boy. The method the Athenian shoeblacks took with Italian officers when they were summoned to perform their task upon the Italian boots was to spit on them and then run away. These approaches to the two enemies illustrate the difference in the effect that each of them had. Unfortunately, the unarmed people of a country cannot spit upon the boots of nineteen divisions.

So the dark night of the Hellenic soul wore on.

In the mountains of the Epirus and the Peloponnese, among the remote crags of Macedonia and in the fierce ravines of Crete, there were bands of dauntless and happy warriors who for month after month assailed the enemy whenever and wherever they could, and are still assailing him as these words are written; but for the great majority of the Hellenes the struggle could not be maintained against a tangible foe. For them the fight was with famine and disease. Thucydides himself, whose lot it was to write of an Athens and Piraeus stricken by plague, might have found even his mastery over words fail him in narrating the ordeal of that Athens of close on twenty-four centuries later. Then Greek was fighting Greek, but much of what Sparta stood for then was what Nazism and Fascism stand for now. The taunts that Sparta and her laconizers flung at Athens and her atticizers were not so dissimilar from those which the Axis flings at the pluto-democracies to-day; and it is possible to discern behind all the superficial social and economic contrasts the evidence of two conflicting trends of human thought which were as irreconcilable then as now and were in essence the same irreconcilables.

All over Greece penury, starvation, and disease preyed upon the people. The very graves were robbed to find clothes for the living. The corpses of those who died were kept in the houses without notifying the civic authority so that they who still lived might add minutely to their sustenance by using the ration-cards of the dead. Young and old raked about for food in the garbage of their captors. Children fell dead of hunger in the streets as lightly as dead leaves fall in autumn from the trees. Legless and armless men who had succumbed in Albania not to the bullet of the enemy but to the gangrene of frost were wheeled about in barrows, selling matches, yes, and giving even those matches when they saw British prisoners of war who needed them. The sick and wounded were turned out of hospitals to make way for German patients, and many wandered about the streets clad in dressing-gowns or pyjamas.

Such men were the survivors of that glorious army thanks to whose devotion the words of Pericles uttered long ago in praise of dead Athenians can be applied with a passionate reiteration to the Hellenes of October 28th, 1940:

"They confided to hope the still clouded prospect of success, but with a grim faith in themselves they confided to action the clear vision before their eyes. And when the hour of battle was at hand, thinking it a finer thing to defend themselves and die than to yield and lose, they fled from the word dishonour, but held fast to the noble deed. Thus in that so brief moment granted them by fate, in that supreme moment of renown not recreancy, they passed from us."

But these legless and armless soldiers of Hellas, hawking matches about the streets of Athens, had not passed from the eyes of the living. They were still there. They are still there now, those of them who have not starved to death. And in moments of despair when hunger gnawed and help seemed to be receding ever farther and farther away there must have been a few Greeks who asked themselves whether the price paid had been worth the pain. Of what avail the 'No' Metaxas gave in the small hours of that October night? Of what avail the superhuman effort of the women and children and old men of the Pindus hill-villages who dragged the supplies and ammunition to the high ridges from which the Evzones charged to rout the Iulia? Of what avail Koritza and Klisura, Khimara and Argyrokastro? Of what avail the gift of life or limb to Hellas, of all that valour and endurance in the snow? Of what avail the 'no surrender' of the forts cut off and encompassed on the north-east frontier? Had it been for this that the bells of Athens had rung, for this that rich and poor had worked as one family, for this that dissension had been knit and faction forgotten? Had it been for this that maidens had given their trousseaux and wives their wedding-rings? Was this the guerdon of a nation's exultation, this the reward of a country's pride, this the premium of courage and the bonus on liberty? And to these questions the vast majority of the Hellenes buried in that dark night of the soul gave a 'Yes' as resolute and as vibrant as the 'No' of John Metaxas. We who stand beyond the shadow of that night can but pray humbly, if we be Hellenes, that we may prove worthy of such fellow-countrymen; if we be British, that we may prove worthy of such allies.

To that agony of mind and body suffered by the people of Greece, of which the merest shadow of a simulacrum can be expressed by facts of violence and figures of death, must be added loneliness. The Soviet Government in an effort to appease Germany had withdrawn its recognition of Yugoslavia on May 8th, and this was followed on June 3rd by the withdrawal of recognition from Greece. The proposal to erase from the map of Europe the two countries in the Balkans which with utter spontaneity and without the least regard for their immediate material interests had refused to bend the knee was apparently to be accepted by Russia. Worse was to come. On June 18th a Turco-German Treaty of Friendship, valid for ten years and coming into force on the day of signature, was signed in Ankara. Hitler and the Turkish President sent each other telegrams of congratulation, and on January 4th the Turkish Prime Minister declared in the National Assembly that Turkey valued the friendship and the words of Germany and respected its esteemed place in world civilization. The people of Hellas, amid the ruins of twenty-three of their cities, faced with the prospect of starvation and with the partitioning of their land between Italy and Bulgaria, might have been excused for turning at this late hour in the hope of material help to accord as sincere a recognition of German power behind as insincere a recognition of German civilization; but they were not prepared to truckle to Germany, even if by doing so they might have avoided an Italian occupation. This is not speculating about an improbable contingency. After the evacuation of the British and Imperial Expeditionary Force and the formation of the Tsolakoglou Government, the German Press had announced complacently that Greece had turned away from the criminal policies of the old Government under the King and seemed willing to join the New Order in

Europe. No more than a few days were necessary to prove even to German obtuseness that Greece was not willing to do anything of the kind, and that the very exiguous, the almost infinitesimal minority, from whom the exponents of cooperation had been recruited were less representative of Greece than a pound of her currants. It would do an injustice to Greek generosity to suggest that the signature of the friendship pact between Turkey and Germany roused the least bitterness. There was none. Greece understood the difficult position of Turkey and recognized that such a direct challenge to her pride as Italy had offered Greece on October 28th, 1940, had not been offered to Turkey. To some extent Greece herself had used similar tactics with Germany during the winter of 1940–41, and no Greek would have been so unrealistic as to pretend that if the circumstances had been reversed Greece would have chivalrously taken the risk of ruining herself to help a friend. In any case when the Turkish Prime Minister protested how much Turkey valued Germany's words it meant no more than telling a counterfeiter with a loaded pistol how much his coins were valued. After all, the Tass Agency of Russia had been assuring the world that Germany's note of hand was good for any amount only nine days before the attack on the Soviets was launched on June 22nd, 1941.

By that November Hellas had the right to claim that besides saving her own soul she had gained the world for freedom.

The full measure of the consequences that depended upon the rejection of the Italian ultimatum followed by the ejection of the Italian armies from Greece cannot even yet be gauged; but, with every week of this war that passes, the decisive influence upon the course of events cast by Greece's defiance of Italy becomes more apparent in the immense design.

The claim which writers and orators are growing into the habit of making that the British Empire confronted the Axis alone from June 22nd, 1940, until June 22nd, 1941, excellent though it may be as rhetoric, is not so accurate as even rhetoric should be if it is to preserve its texture and vitality when the emotion that inspired it is spent. The British Empire stood alone from June 22nd, 1940, until 3 A.M. on October 28th, 1940. A few minutes later, beside the British Empire stood Greece. It is true that only Italy was defied at first, but when the moment came Germany was defied with equal firmness.

Turkey did not march to the aid of either of her allies, of Britain or of Greece: it was intelligible and easily forgivable; but she did not march. Russia did not move to the aid of Yugoslavia. Greece and Yugoslavia had both been overwhelmed already when Russia was attacked, as later the United States was to be attacked, without an ultimatum.

The situation of Britain was not so precarious in October 1940 as it had been three months earlier; but it was precarious enough. The menace of invasion had not been completely dispelled with the defeat of the Luftwaffe by the fighter pilots of the Empire with all the help martyred Poland could give them. Yet the position was excessively grave, particularly in the Mediterranean where the strategic plan to which the security of the Empire had been pinned was torn to pieces when Marshal Pétain who had stood at Verdun knelt at Compiègne and signed an armistice with the enemy. There was a moment when it was hoped that the French Empire would refuse what France had accepted; but in the vital portions like Algeria, Morocco, Tunis, Syria, Indo-China, and Madagascar the forces of life were not strong enough to outweigh the forces of death, and after the lamentable naval action at Oran and the fiasco at Dakar the vital portions of the French Empire had to be counted out. The Polish Brigade in Syria turned right about and marched across the frontier into Palestine: they were the first reinforcements to reach General Wavell. When Mussolini flung down his stake upon the prostrate body of France and played for the Mediterranean he and his phrase-drunk Fascists were convinced that every card was in his hand.

And certainly a good many of them were. A million and a half men under arms, 2000 first-line aircraft, and a very powerful navy should be enough to take the Mediterranean while Great Britain itself was being taken by Germany. Weak British forces evacuated Somaliland. Italian troops pushed a little way into Kenya. A large and well-equipped Italian army under Marshal Graziani moved very slowly in the direction of Egypt. By September 13th it had reached Sidi Barrani, where it stopped to wait hopefully for the news that Great Britain was finished. In those anxious days when invasion seemed imminent and when practically all the available military equipment of the country amassed by the martial figureheads of the National Government over several years had been left behind in France, Mr Churchill had not called back the men and the munitions

on their way to Egypt and had even sent more from the sparse reserves. That was the very genius of resolution and courage. Mussolini and his military collaborators, a little less sure about the course
of events in Britain after Britain's incomprehensible failure in June
to acknowledge she was beaten, began to wonder if it would not
be as well to make assurance doubly sure in the Mediterranean by
occupying Greece before giving battle in Egypt. The manufacture
of pretexts for aggression began, culminating in the outrage at Tenos
on August 15th. Presumably Hitler warned Mussolini that the
time was not ripe to disturb the peace of the Balkans and advised his
accomplice to get on with the job of invading Egypt. By October
4th, when the pair met on the Brenner, the hope of invading Britain
had faded and Mussolini's project to occupy Greece became an
integral part of the grand strategic plan to drive the British out of the
Mediterranean as an alternative. This as originally conceived was
to be an attack by way of Spain and Sicily on Gibraltar and Malta,
with landings in North Africa coinciding with an attack from Libya
by Graziani and a heavy air offensive against Egypt from Crete and
the Aegean. Vichy was to be kept quiet by guaranteeing Pétain
French North Africa, a guarantee which could always be dishonoured
when Britain was out of the way. In any case Venice could once
again hold the gorgeous East in fee by seizing Constantinople and
recovering the Aegean and the Levant. Then Cyprus could be
mastered and, invading Palestine by way of Syria, Mussolini would
have the pipe-lines of the Mesopotamian oil.

Japan, which had signed the Tripartite Pact on September 27th,
would be able to support the Italian attack on Suez from the Indian
Ocean side. Iraq would revolt: Iran would join the Axis. By
May Hitler would have his preparations ready for the grand attack
on Russia. Japan would simultaneously strike at India. Turkey,
completely encircled, would agree to whatever Hitler and Mussolini
required of her. It is extremely unlikely that the question whether
Greece would resist occupation was ever asked. Perhaps the *Helle*
outrage had been a test to ascertain Greek reaction rather than a
precipitate attempt by Mussolini to wed the Aegean before Hitler
forbade the banns.

The whole world was their oyster on that October day, and they
swallowed it with the gusto of the Walrus and the Carpenter. The
indigestible pearl that was Britain itself they put on the side of the

plate to be pulverized later; but as a token of 'Axis solidarity' Mussolini sent a special squadron of the Regia Aeronautica to put new heart into the Luftwaffe's attack on the island. Brief as Julius Caesar's message had been to Rome, 'Veni, vidi, vici', one word was sufficient for the Regia Aeronautica. It was 'victi'. The pearl in the oyster that was Hellas the two dictators swallowed: they did not suppose it would be so indigestible.

After the oyster-feast on the Brenner Hitler gave Mussolini time to make his final preparations for the attack on Greece, and then on October 23rd he travelled as far as the Hispano-French frontier for a conversation with General Franco intended to secure cooperation by Spain in the projected expulsion of the British from the Mediterranean. Whatever else General Franco may have said on that occasion, we can feel fairly sure that if Spanish action was hinted at it was made dependent upon the success of Italian action. General Franco may have felt less sanguine than Hitler about the potentiality of the Italian army. He had had the chance of seeing the Italian army run in Spain. On October 24th Hitler met Marshal Pétain at Montoire, and no doubt the Marshal was no more encouraging than General Franco to any proposal that German armed forces should use Vichy France and Spain to seal the Mediterranean and prevent the British from escaping when they were crushed by the tremendous war-machine of Fascist Italy. Probably Hitler offered to guarantee Marshal Pétain against any enrichment of Italy at the expense of the French Empire in return for the use of the French fleet and the French bases in North Africa, and certainly Marshal Pétain refused the offer.

What was said at Florence when Hitler met Mussolini again on October 28th is guess-work; but it is not extravagant to guess that Hitler, however much disappointed he may have been by his conversations with General Franco and Marshal Pétain, was braced by Mussolini's exuberant optimism. If the Western Mediterranean was not yet theirs, the Eastern Mediterranean was as good as in their hands. Perhaps they discussed the glories of a Constantinople guarding a Black Sea cleansed of Bolshevik scum. Perhaps they discussed an Empire of Ethiopia which should extend as far south as old German East Africa, where of course the proposed German absorption of all South Africa would begin. It is most improbable that the Greek rejection of the ultimatum delivered in the small hours of that

October 28th raised the lightest cat's-paw of apprehension to ripple the placid surface of the Arno. By the middle of November at latest all would be running so smoothly that the Italian troops destined for the liquidation of the British on the Asiatic side of Suez would be concentrating in Greece, and Graziani would strike a week or two later. It seems certain that Mussolini offered to assume the full burden of responsibility for the Mediterranean so that Hitler could devote himself to the immense preparation, military and diplomatic, needed for the attack on Russia in May; and not the least of the blunders history may note against Hitler will be his susceptibility to the optimism of that 'genial man' Mussolini. Readers of Dickens will remember David Copperfield's devotion to the dazzling Steerforth. Hitler's devotion to Mussolini was not unlike it. After all, it was Mussolini who taught him how to look more like a dictator and less like a lavatory-attendant in a second-rate hotel. Most of us remember with gratitude those who helped us to present the face we wanted to present to the world, and there are enough human characteristics in Hitler to warrant us in supposing that he could not be immune from so natural an effusion of sentimental good-will. On top of that the epicene in Hitler would respond to the exuberant virility of the Italian, and indeed one discerns all through their earlier relationship a kind of grim parody of wedlock.

The world those two dreamers were building beside the Arno may seem to us even a mere two years later as remote as Dante's dreams beside the Arno; but the Inferno they were concocting was not nearly so remote when Metaxas, answering for the soul of Greece, rejected the ultimatum handed him by Signor Grazzi. No philhellene expected any other reply; but the most passionate philhellene was to be forgiven for feeling a dread for the fate of Hellas clutch at his heart. When the news that Italian troops had crossed the frontier from Albania was announced at one o'clock by the B.B.C. and the music of the Greek national anthem followed, there was one philhellene who turned upon his side on a sick-bed and wept tears, of pride for Hellas, of shame for the wrong a country he also loved had wrought her, of mortification for the little he felt his own country could do to help. It was indeed little enough, but it was the utmost Britain could give at that moment, and the very fact that it was so little is a proof of the desperate situation. How desperate it was Greece was completely aware when obeying the command of freedom she stood across the path of Mussolini and treated the lictor's rods like faggots. Her action was a tonic to the world. Even if the Italian troops had reached Athens within a fortnight in spite of all the Greeks could do to bar the way, the decision Greece took would still have exerted a moral influence the benefit of which would have lasted the length of the war. There were never any people in Britain who believed Britain would be beaten. That is a fantasy beyond even the imagination of a people which shares with Greece the greatest body of poetry in the world. The Greeks themselves noticed that the Germans were fond of asking who they thought would win the war, whereas not even British prisoners ever bothered to ask what would have seemed to them so silly and superfluous a question. Nevertheless, the course the war had taken had made the British a little ashamed of the extent to which their pre-war laziness had left them unable to give the help they would have liked to give to small nations at the mercy of the Axis. Greece's refusal to yield to Italian demands did not restore Britain's confidence in herself— that had never been seriously shaken, and any faint tremor of anxiety had always been immediately allayed by Mr Churchill's invigorating confidence both in himself and in his country—but it did restore Britain's confidence in her ability to be recognized as what she wished to be recognized as, the guardian and champion of liberty. It was the tonic effect of the moral courage that Greece showed which set the example to Yugoslavia, and Yugoslavia gloriously and recklessly emulated it.

But when in addition to defying the enemy Greece proceeded to punish him the moral exhilaration was more than tonic: it was life-giving. On the night of November 9th–10th, 1940, the three regiments of Evzones who routed the Iulia within ten miles of Metsovo destroyed the last chance the Axis had of winning the war. The scythe of Time, on whose help Britain was counting, would have been turned against her if the Iulia had reached Metsovo that November day and opened a road for the Italian armies to pour through into the plains of Thessaly.

Let us count the beads in the chaplet of events that were strung on the Greek decision to resist and the success of that resistance.

If Greece had accepted the ultimatum, there would have been no attack by Swordfish aircraft of the Fleet Air Arm on the Italian fleet in Taranto on the night of November 11th. The Italian fleet would not have had to move to ports too far from Africa for any kind of effective naval action against the British fleet in the Eastern Mediterranean. Crete would have become an Italian air base at a time when it would have menaced the British position in North Africa much more seriously than it was able to do nine months later. If Greece had succumbed to the Italian attack instead of revealing to the world by her sublime resistance the top-heaviness of the Italian war machine, the Italian General Staff would not have been in a condition of deliquescence at the very moment when General Wavell anticipated Marshal Graziani's offensive by striking first, and it is at least conceivable that the *débâcle* might have been less complete in Libya.

In any case, it detracts nothing from the fullest appreciation of that marvellous victory to suggest that the confidence of the Italian troops in their commanders cannot have been strengthened by the wretched leadership of their brothers in Albania. That four months later the Italians were able to recover a large part of Cyrenaica was not so much due to the weakening of General Wavell's forces by the despatch of the British and Imperial Expeditionary Force to Greece as to the German help which, beginning with the Luftwaffe in January 1941, had ended in Libya's becoming a German second-front rather than an Italian first-front. And it was the necessity of getting his accomplice out of a bad mess that upset the whole of Hitler's grand strategic plan.

In spite of the delay imposed upon his project by the resistance of Greece and the resurgence of Yugoslavia, Hitler persisted in the attack on Russia; but by starting it at least five weeks too late he failed to reach his objective. And if Greece's resistance secured five precious weeks for Russia, it secured six months of inestimable value for Great Britain's productive effort, and for that matter it can be added for that of the United States, apart from the moral impression the inspired fight for freedom Greece put up made upon American opinion.

And when we praise that defiance of Italy by Greece, fraught with such consequences for the future of humanity, let us bear in mind that it was given with the deep moral conviction, whatever hope against hope might be cherished, that such a defiance must mean sooner or later that Germany would have to be defied also. With a knowledge of the extremes of ruthlessness to which the Germans were prepared to go in order to achieve their purpose and with the spectacle of what had happened afterwards to countries which had dared to impede the march of the Third Reich toward the domination of the world, the people of Greece could not have been reproached if, after five months of victorious resistance to a nation six times as large as themselves, they had felt incapable of resisting on top of that the attack of a nation twelve times as large. It must not be supposed that there was any illusion in Greece about the strength of the aid Great Britain could give. There was none; and the noblest proof of this was the complete absence of any recrimination when that aid was shown to be as inadequate as it was expected to be. The people of Greece recognized that Great Britain had done all she could do. That is why no Greek has betrayed a British soldier for gold, or even for food, and why many Greeks have chosen death rather than not repay to the best of their ability with their own aid that aid which Britain gave.

At the same time, the British reader is entreated to clear his brain of the notion that the people of Greece defied Germany because they were convinced that Great Britain would be the ultimate victors of this war. They defied Germany first and foremost because they were resolved that no terms with Italy should be forced upon them by the blackmailing mediation of her accomplice and they accepted British help because they felt that British help was offered by free men to free men. If there was a minority which favoured an arrangement with Germany, that was the fault of Britain. During the First World War Greece was split in two because a cautious minority, which prevented a fervid majority for three years from taking up arms on the side of the Three Powers to whom the country believed it owed its freedom, provoked a revolution before that influence was dammed, and the soldiers of Hellas were able to play so great a part in that battle of Doiran which was the first decisive victory won by the Allies. Thanks to the imagination of Mr Lloyd George, the claims of Greece under the leadership of Venizelos were amply recognized at Versailles; but Mr Lloyd George was got rid of at a moment when Greece with British encouragement was confronting the formidable Turkey created by Kemal Atatürk with the help of France and Italy. Conservative politicians tumbled over one another to disown Greece. Newspaper proprietors deliberately corrupted decent British opinion. Greece was abandoned by Britain,

and Nemesis has exacted how much British blood and treasure as
the penalty of that abandonment. And it was not only a political
abandonment: it was to be a commercial abandonment as well. Imperial preference and mass-production between them could reduce
the export of Greek currants to Britain to practically nothing. The
volume of trade between Britain and Greece between 1923 and 1937
shrank to one-third of what it had been when Britain abandoned
Greece politically in 1922. Germany became Greece's best customer, and Greece, which before the First World War had been
securely in the sphere of British commercial and financial influence,
found herself drawn even more inextricably into the net of German
commercial and financial influence over the Near East and South-
East Europe.

Forgiveness is asked for obtruding these sordid facts upon a tale of
heroism; but British readers will do well to appreciate that the names
of Byron, Church, Hastings, Canning, Gladstone, and many another
philhellene whose memory is cherished gratefully in Hellas cannot
contend indefinitely with the hard facts of material interest. The
stomach rules, as Aesop pointed out long ago.

And yet even as that axiom is set down it is disproved by the action
of the Hellenes of October 28th 1940 and April 6th 1941.
Material interests were swept away by that defiance uttered to Italy
in 1940 and reiterated to Germany in 1941. Hellas chose freedom.

By the length of thy stride,
By the sweep of thy blade,
By thy countenance stern,
I know thee, proud maid.

The bones of the Hellenes
Have hallowed the tale:
As of old thou art standing:
Hail, Liberty, hail!

Withdrawn into darkness,
Shy, bitter, in pain,
The call wast thou waiting
To come forth again.

Long, long wast thou waiting,
Late, late came the call:

CHAPTER TWENTY

In the tomb of oppression
Fear held us in thrall.

Yet secretly wouldst thou
Frequent foreign lands,
Blood-stained, to beg aid from
More powerful hands.

Alone, didst thou wander,
Alone, didst return;
That doors open hardly
The needy must learn.

But now we have risen!
Hark, hark to the cry
Of thy Hellenes determined
To conquer or die.[1]

The effect upon the course of war of Greece's defiance and defeat of Italy was intensified and sharpened by her defiance and delay of Germany. Apart from the further upset of Hitler's time-table for his Russian adventure, those few weeks of bloody fighting on the mainland and in Crete spoilt any hope he had of saving the situation in the Near East imperilled by his accomplice's utter failure to play his part in the strategic plan. The parachute troops and aircraft which might have been used for the descent on Cyprus and Syria had suffered too heavily in Crete. The chance to save Rashid Ali's revolt in Iraq from aborting had vanished, and it was too late even to press Rommel's counter-offensive in Libya to a fruitful conclusion. In spite of the triumphant *blitzkrieg* in Yugoslavia and Greece, the situation in the Eastern Mediterranean was less favourable than it had been when Hitler and Mussolini made the world their oyster on October 4th, 1940. Italy's weakness had been exposed. Britain's strength was growing. France's prostrate form showed faint signs of returning life. Spain could congratulate herself upon her abstention from premature action. The deliberate starvation of Greece and the massacres in Yugoslavia ordered by a doomed madman whom the gods wished to destroy, and his insensate country with him, were little enough with which Hitler could console himself. The occupation of Greece and the manufacture of a Ruritanian kingdom out of a part of Yugoslavia, though they might give as much brief enter-

[1] Translation of the Greek National Anthem by Compton Mackenzie.

tainment as a Venetian masquerade, were not very solid comfort for the Doge Julius Caesar Mussolini and his burnt-cork Emperor of Ethiopia.

And if the effect of Greece's action was salutary in 1940, the effect of that action can be linked with the Battle of the Mediterranean which has begun as these pages draw to their close. It is difficult to believe that a future of comparable promise would present itself on November 10th, 1942, if those Evzone regiments, helped by the women of the Pindus villages who will be celebrated in the tale of Hellenic freedom with the women of Suli and Parga, had not thwarted the thrust of the Iulia on November 10th, 1940.

News comes from Greece that all the efforts of the Carabinieri, which included firing on a great crowd of ten thousand, were powerless to stop the demonstration of Hellenic life at the tomb of the Unknown Soldier on October 28th, 1942. It may be that Fascism will never achieve its majority and that before the next anniversary of the March on Rome another march will have been made, soldiers of Hellas in the vanguard with a bullet-torn blue and white flag to fly from the highest of Rome's seven hills, soldiers of Hellas who set out on October 28th, 1940.

But grateful though such a dream picture may be to the self-indulgence of the writer, it does not represent the Greek attitude toward their already beaten foe. The Hellenes seek no triumph. When the last Italian quits the soil of Hellas it will be as a beaten foe that he will be remembered. Nothing of his does Greece ask for herself. The Dodecanese is his only by the dishonouring of his word and his bond, and any claim Greece may make to the Dodecanese will be justified on every ground. The Northern Epirus should present no problem once all Italian machinations have been rendered impossible. The future of Cyprus is commended to the conscience of Great Britain. It would be unnecessary even to mention the Bulgar seizure of Greek Macedonia and Thrace if the Bulgars did not possess some mysterious gift for mesmerizing a certain section of British opinion into the belief that they are an industrious rose-growing people with a legitimate grievance. Bulgaria has always been the destructive force in Balkan unity. The following statement by Mr Bogdan Filov to the National Assembly in Sofia on November 1st, 1941, must be read, bearing in mind that the Bulgars had by that date driven 70,000 Greek farmers from their land and

massacred another ten thousand of the inhabitants of Greek Macedonia and Thrace:

"The policy of peace and neutrality which the government of
Bulgaria has followed since the outbreak of the present war has
been dictated by the interests of the nation and corresponds with
the interests of the Axis powers. Bulgaria is a small nation, but,
even so, her action has without doubt wrecked the much-discussed
plan of a Balkan *bloc*. It was because of Bulgaria's firm attitude
that this *bloc* never materialized, and thus a scheme the object of
which was the formation of hundreds of divisions to fight against
the Germans, was foiled. This fact emphatically proves that Bulgaria followed this policy in order to maintain harmony among the
Axis powers. To-day we stand firmly at the side of the Axis."

Compare with such an Ishmaelite's declaration the Agreement for
a Balkan Union signed in London on January 15th, 1942, by Greece
and Yugoslavia. This provides for the closest political, military, and
economic collaboration between the two countries, and aims to ensure
the independence and peace of the Balkan States by affirming the
principal of the Balkans for the Balkan peoples. The signatories
declare that they would welcome the future adhesion to the Agreement of other Balkan States ruled by Governments freely and legally
constituted in order to set up permanent machinery for the constant
collaboration of the statesmen, general staffs, economists, experts, and
parliaments of the member States. The Union is to act in a uniform
manner on the international plane, to settle all disputes by arbitration,
to coordinate commercial activities and customs tariffs, to adopt a
common plan of defence, and to defend the European frontiers of the
States of the Union.

When the representatives of Hellas are heard at the Peace Conference they will play their part as nobly in the reconstruction of
Europe as the representatives of Hellas in war have played their part
to avert its destruction.

In 490 B.C. the ten thousand Athenian hoplites who marched out
to stand against the might of Persia at Marathon were joined before
the battle by one thousand hoplites of the little city of Plataea. The
Plataeans owed the Athenians a debt for helping them against Theban
aggression: they desired to pay it by standing beside them in an hour
of mortal peril. Athens never forgot that action of Plataea. She

conferred upon all Plataeans her own civic rights in gratitude to the only city-state which had stood beside her against the overwhelming might of Persia.

To his countrymen the writer says, 'Britannia, de te fabula.' We above every nation in the world owe such a debt to the Hellas of to-day as Athens once owed, and paid to the little city-state of Plataea.

APPENDIX

The New Greek Forces at War

AFTER the Axis had occupied Greece, the Greek Government, which had been established in London, following its decision to continue the fight, proceeded immediately to reorganize the Greek armed forces abroad.

I

The Greek Army

The new Greek Army in the Middle East consists of:

i. Units of the Army who escaped to Egypt after the German occupation of Crete.

ii. The new forces conscripted among Greeks living abroad.

iii. Men of military age who escaped to the Middle East since the occupation of Greece.

1. Only a comparatively small force managed to get away from Greece because, during the last phase of fighting on the mainland and in Crete the Greek Army was covering the evacuation of the British forces. However, various units composed of veterans of the Albanian front, and numerous experienced officers, did escape to Egypt. Later they were moved to Palestine to be regrouped, reinforced, and re-equipped.

2. The Government, in their determination to continue the common struggle with all the Greek forces available, has undertaken the conscription of every Greek between the ages of 20 and 36, living outside Greece, particularly those domiciled in Egypt. The conscription of Greeks living outside their own country has been a complete success. Thousands of enthusiastic young men have hastened to enlist in the new Greek regiments, and an adequate number of officers and commanders has been found to lead them. A Military Agreement with Great Britain, signed on March 9th, 1942, defines the particulars of the organization and employment of the

265

new Greek Army. The preamble to the agreement declares that the contracting powers are determined to continue the struggle until final victory is achieved, and that they agree that the complete liberation of Greece, and the restoration of its independence, are included in the general war aims. As the Prime Minister, Mr Tsouderos, pointed out, "The agreement is a mark of Britain's friendship for our country, of her confidence in the valour of our soldiers, sailors, and airmen, and of her readiness to help us, by every moral and material means, to regain our cherished freedom. The Greeks will never forget the British."

A special unit which has been formed in the United States, from Greeks living there, is to be incorporated in the American Army. On December 16th, 1942, the American Secretary for War, Mr Stimson, made on the occasion the following statement: "The Greek fighting unit to be incorporated in the United States Army will live up to the traditions of Greece and the United States. As the Italians and Germans have learned, a Greek soldier armed with a rifle and bayonet is a formidable foe. Since the war began, the valour and fortitude of the Greek soldier has been demonstrated on all fronts, in Northern Epirus, in Macedonia, Crete, and, lately, in the Battle of Libya. It has been plainly demonstrated that the spirit of the heroes who won immortality at Thermopylae has survived the passage of the centuries. The Greek battalion now being formed in the United States may eventually participate in military operations in Africa and Europe for the liberation of the conquered countries from the abominable Nazi and Fascist yoke."

3. Many hundreds of young Greeks, especially junior officers, have succeeded in escaping from occupied Greece in order to join the Greek forces and continue the fight against the invaders. Risking their lives in small sailing-boats, they managed to reach the Middle East, where they were sent to special camps in Palestine to complete their training and fill the ranks of the new Greek Army. Many of them, caught during their escape, have been shot by the enemy; others have lost their lives in crossing the Mediterranean.

In the summer of 1942, several hundred junior officers in Palestine formed, at their own request, a special battalion of picked men known as the "Sacred Band". "This title", said Mr A. Michalopoulos, Greek Minister of Information, at a lecture given at the Chatham House, London, on February 11th, 1943, "commemorates the famous Theban detachment of that name, which in the fourth century B.C. pledged itself to conquer or to die: never to surrender. It fully redeemed that pledge. This is the watchword of Greece's Commando Battalion in the Middle East. Its unique and distinctive feature is that it is composed entirely of officers serving as troopers, an arrangement which has partially solved one of our difficulties arising out of the fact that the number of officers steadily escaping from Greece is out of all proportion to that of ordinary soldiers. The officers chosen for service in the Commando Battalion must have the following qualifications: they must be volunteers, they must be under thirty years of age—except in the case of certain specialists,—they must have fought in Albania and have at least been mentioned in despatches, and they must pass an intelligence test. You will understand that in this way we have succeeded in forming a small but highly efficient body of men ready to act with daring and personal initiative in operations of a dangerous and delicate nature, and they have repeatedly been proved in action. Among these men are several naval officers who are expert navigators—a qualification which is most valuable in desert warfare, which as you all know so greatly resembles naval warfare—great fleets of tanks and isolated units fighting battles against equally isolated enemy groups in the boundless ocean of sand. Greek Commando navigators have proved so successful that they have been detailed to guide British Commando and tank forces in their operations."

The reorganized Greek land forces took part in the Battle of Egypt during September 1942 and in the great Allied offensive of October, which resulted in such a brilliant victory for the Eighth Army.

Mr Kanellopoulos, the Greek Vice-Premier and Minister of Defence, who visited the Greek Units at the front, was impressed by the excellent combination of enthusiasm, physical fitness, and sound training among these men.

All those who have witnessed the Greek units in action said they can understand why the Greeks despised the Italian Army in Albania, and resisted the Germans in Macedonia and Crete.

On September 18th, 1942, the British General under whose command the Greek forces were attached declared that he was happy to have such warriors under him, and added, "I have under my command many fine units, and I do not hesitate to say that the Greek forces are among the best in the Western Desert Front".

The Greek Brigade played a distinguished part in the victorious operations which began with the offensive of October 23rd.

In a letter to the Greek commander the British General commanding the 50th Division said: "I want to emphasize the excellent way by which your men carried on every mission entrusted to them. I had absolute confidence in them, and trust that they would execute every military operation with no regard to the sacrifices. I found the staff work excellent, and the discipline of the officers and men splendid."

In his report of December 1942, the same British General relates the activities of the Greek Brigade from September 8th to the end of November, and draws attention to their successful attack against the Italian Brescia Division, and their contribution to the smashing of the Axis forces.

General Sir Harold Alexander, C.-in-C. of the Eighth Army, said in a telegram to His Majesty the King of the Hellenes, on November 10th, 1942: "In this great victory the Greek Brigade has played a splendid part and fought magnificently".

The participation of the Greek forces in the Battle of Egypt and Libya has been several times mentioned in the official British communiqués.   Many men won British and Greek decorations for gallantry.

II

The Royal Hellenic Navy

The Greek Navy has never ceased its efforts in the fight against the Axis since Greece entered the war.   After the collapse of the Allied resistance in Greece and Crete, the Greek Navy, although it had lost one-third of its striking force as a result of German air action, managed to escape to Alexandria to continue the struggle.   Not one of the ships afloat surrendered to the enemy.   The remaining Greek fleet consisted of 1 cruiser, 7 destroyers, 3 torpedo-boats, 5 submarines, and a number of auxiliary vessels.   As soon as they had been repaired they were put into active service, with the British fleet, in the Mediterranean, the Red Sea, and the Indian Ocean.   During the campaign of 1941–42 they took part in several naval actions, apart from routine convoys and patrols.

In 1942 four new destroyers and one corvette were handed over to the Greek Navy by the British.   Hundreds of seamen have been conscripted, among the Greeks living abroad, to man these vessels.   At present 25 Greek warships manned by 5500 men are carrying on the fight for victory and liberation.   Mentioned below are a few of the recent exploits of Greek warships.

On October 5th, 1942, the submarine *Nereus*, patrolling near the island of Rhodes, torpedoed and sank a transport ship of 1500 tons.   Five hundred Axis soldiers were drowned.   A short time later the same submarine sank a small enemy motor vessel of 80 tons.

On December 5th, 1942, the submarine *Papanikolis* sank an enemy supply ship of 6500 tons.   At the end of December the Greek destroyer *Queen Olga* participated with five British warships in a successful action in the central Mediterranean, which resulted in the destruction of several enemy ships and one submarine.

Heroic was the fighting end of the submarine *Triton*. The commander of the German warship which destroyed the Greek submarine, said: "I ordered an attack with depth charges. Then, would you believe it, while we were actually covering that submarine with depth charges, those fellows fired a torpedo at us."

He went on to tell how the *Triton* remained submerged for 6½ hours and then surfaced and tried to man her guns under the withering fire of waiting enemy ships. Not until she had been rammed was she captured.

III

The Royal Hellenic Air Force

At the beginning of the war with Italy the R.H.A.F. had hardly one hundred fighter planes. During the five months of the Albanian campaign they fought an infinitely superior enemy force, but at the end of the resistance only two Greek machines were left. In spite of this, nearly 800 pilots and other ranks managed to escape to Crete and from there to the Middle East, where they formed, with the assistance of the R.A.F., the nucleus of a re-organized Greek Air Force. Hundreds of young airmen have since been trained by British officers in special camps in the Middle East. They formed their own squadrons which from the beginning took part in the Battle of Egypt. Side by side with the R.A.F. they played their part in the great Allied victory. Air Chief Marshal Sir Arthur Tedder, in a telegram to the King of the Hellenes on November 10th, 1942, paid tribute to the gallantry of the Greek airmen: "You will, I know," he says, "be glad to hear your fighters have taken a gallant part in the present battle. We are proud to have them beside us."

IV

The Greek Mercantile Marine

Before the Italian aggression, Greece's merchant fleet held the ninth place in the world from the point of view of gross tonnage, the third among the Mediterranean nations (France and Italy being the two first), and the fourth place in the world from the point of view of ocean-going tramp shipping and also with regard to the proportion of gross tonnage to the population of the country. Of the total of 1,800,000 tons which the Greek Mercantile Marine possessed before the outbreak of this war, one million tons is still afloat, all ocean-going cargo ships. It is now all chartered to the British Government, but controlled by the Greek Shipping Committee in London. Greek seamen have been conscripted to serve in the Greek merchant fleet. A Greek Maritime Court was established in England in 1942.

The 800,00 tons of shipping lost to the Greek Mercantile Marine was sunk by enemy action, none of it being captured. Nearly all was sunk on the great ocean routes where, long before Greece entered the war, it was already serving the Allied cause. At the time of the German attack the German dive-bombers—for the Italians did little at sea and in the air except attack, sometimes with the Greek colours on their wings, undefended provincial towns and villages—found in Greek territorial waters nothing but a comparatively small number of ships assigned to coastal service or transformed into hospital ships, which were all sunk, including fishing-boats, pleasure yachts, and barges.

INDEX

INDEX

THE END

PRINTED IN GREAT BRITAIN
BY R. & R. CLARK, LIMITED
EDINBURGH

E4